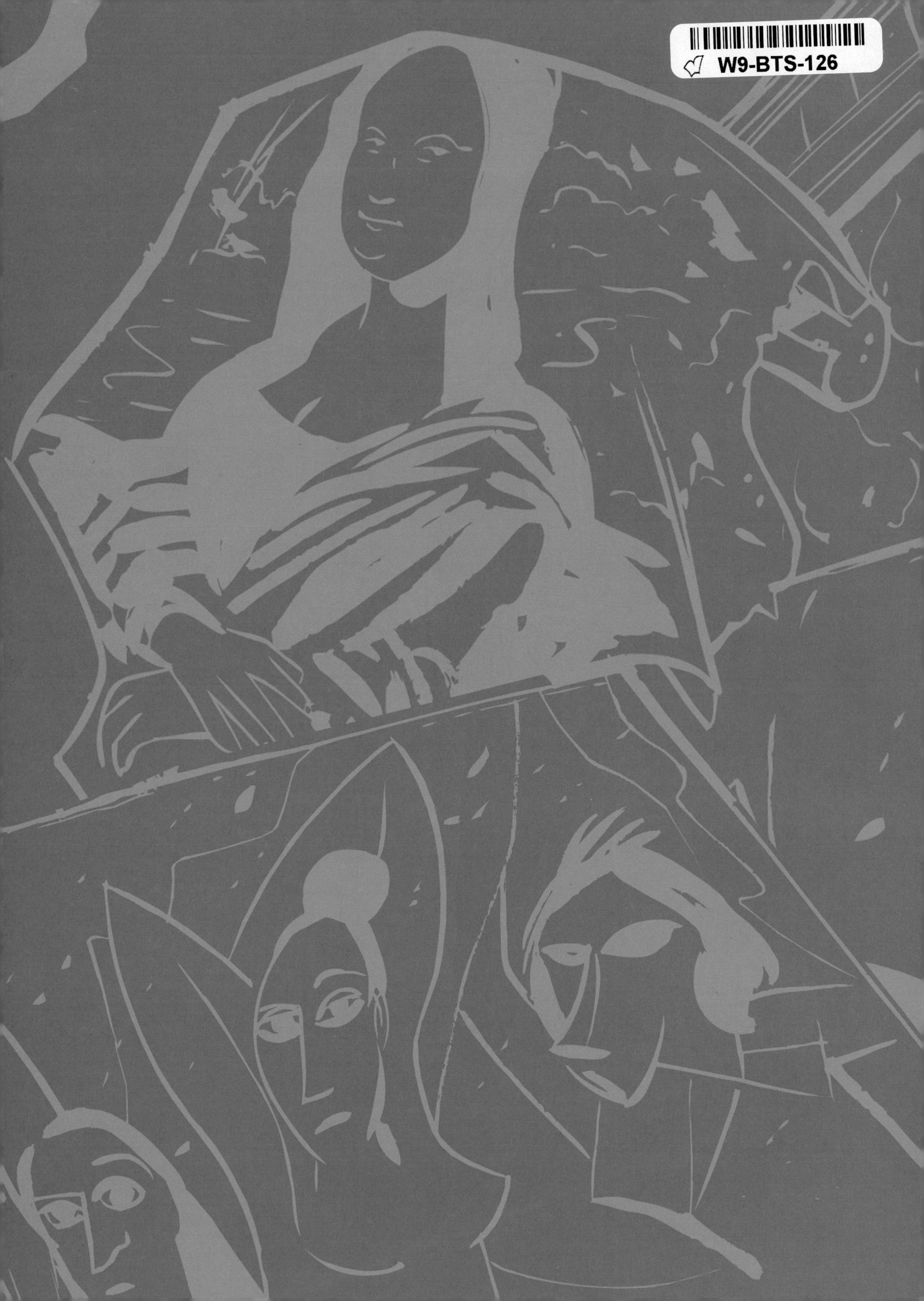

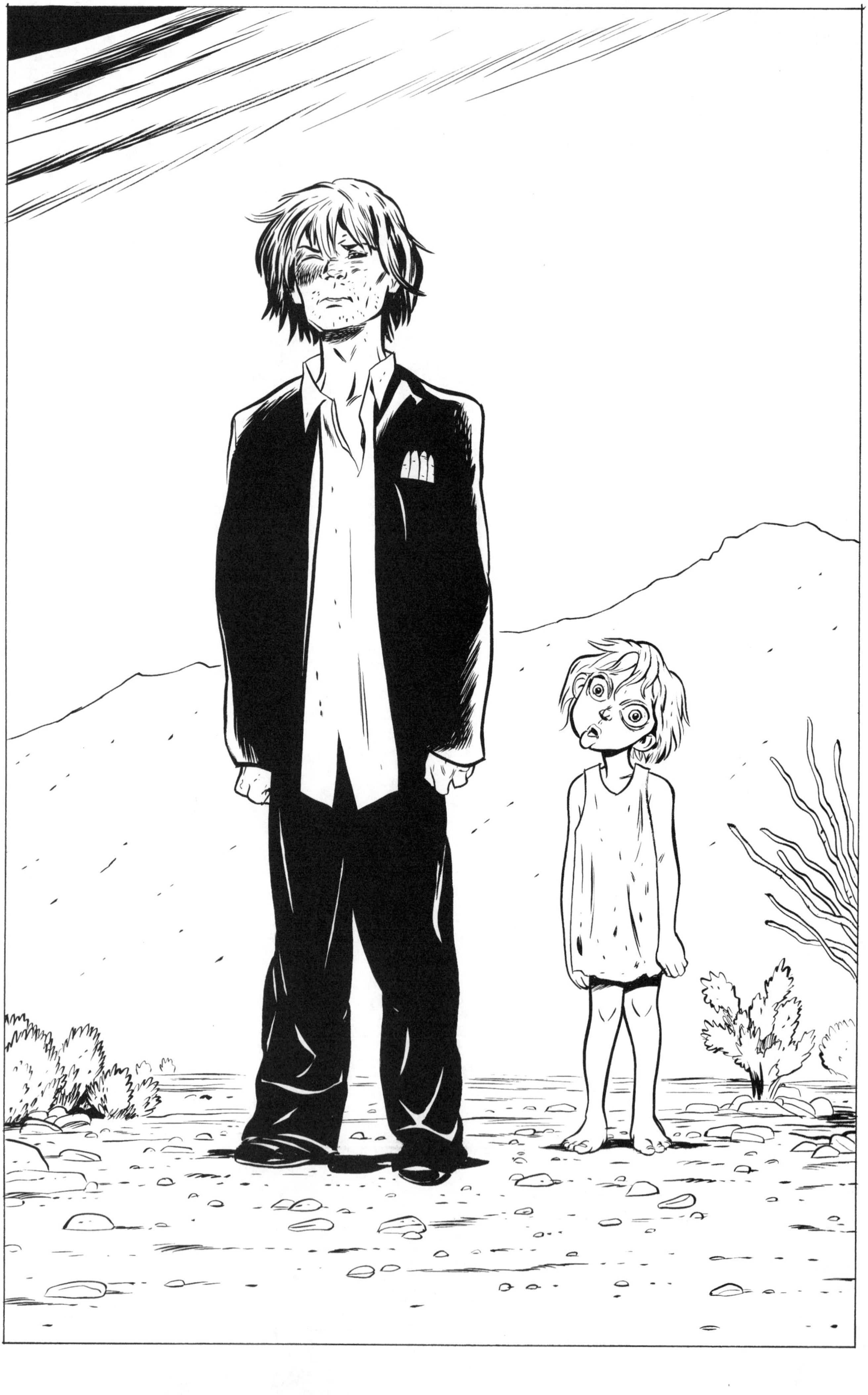

# RASL

## BY

RASL Volume 3: Romance at the Speed of Light

The chapters in this book were originally published in the comic book RASL
RASL™ is © 2011 by Jeff Smith.

For Cartoon Books:
Cover Art by Jeff Smith
Cover Color & Logo/Design by Steve Hamaker
Published by Vijaya Iyer
Production Manager: Kathleen Glosan
PrePress/Design: Tom Gaadt

For information write:
Cartoon Books
P.O. Box 16973
Columbus, OH  43216

4/12  B+T  9,00

Softcover ISBN-10:   1-888963-33-6
Softcover ISBN-13:   978-1-888963-33-5

10 9 8 7 6 5 4 3 2 1

Printed in the U.S.A

"Our virtues and our failures are inseparable, like force and matter.
When they separate, man is no more."

-Nikola Tesla

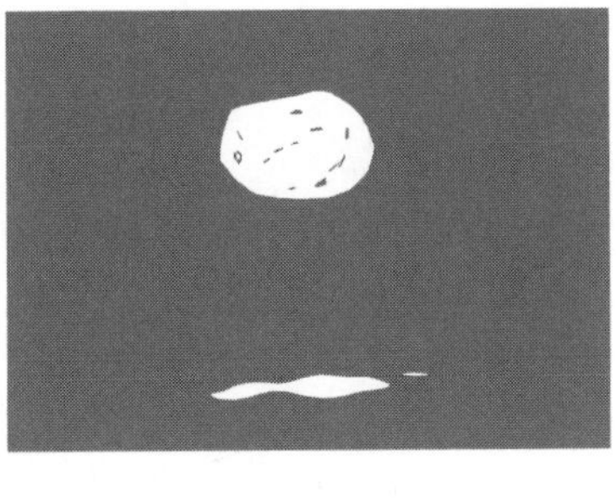

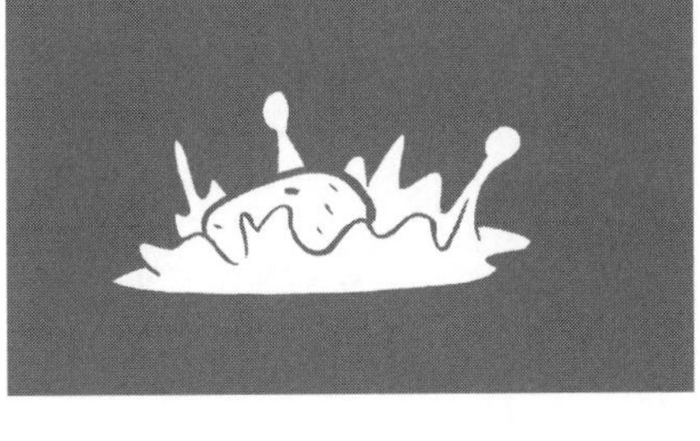

# 8.
# ROMANCE AT THE SPEED OF LIGHT

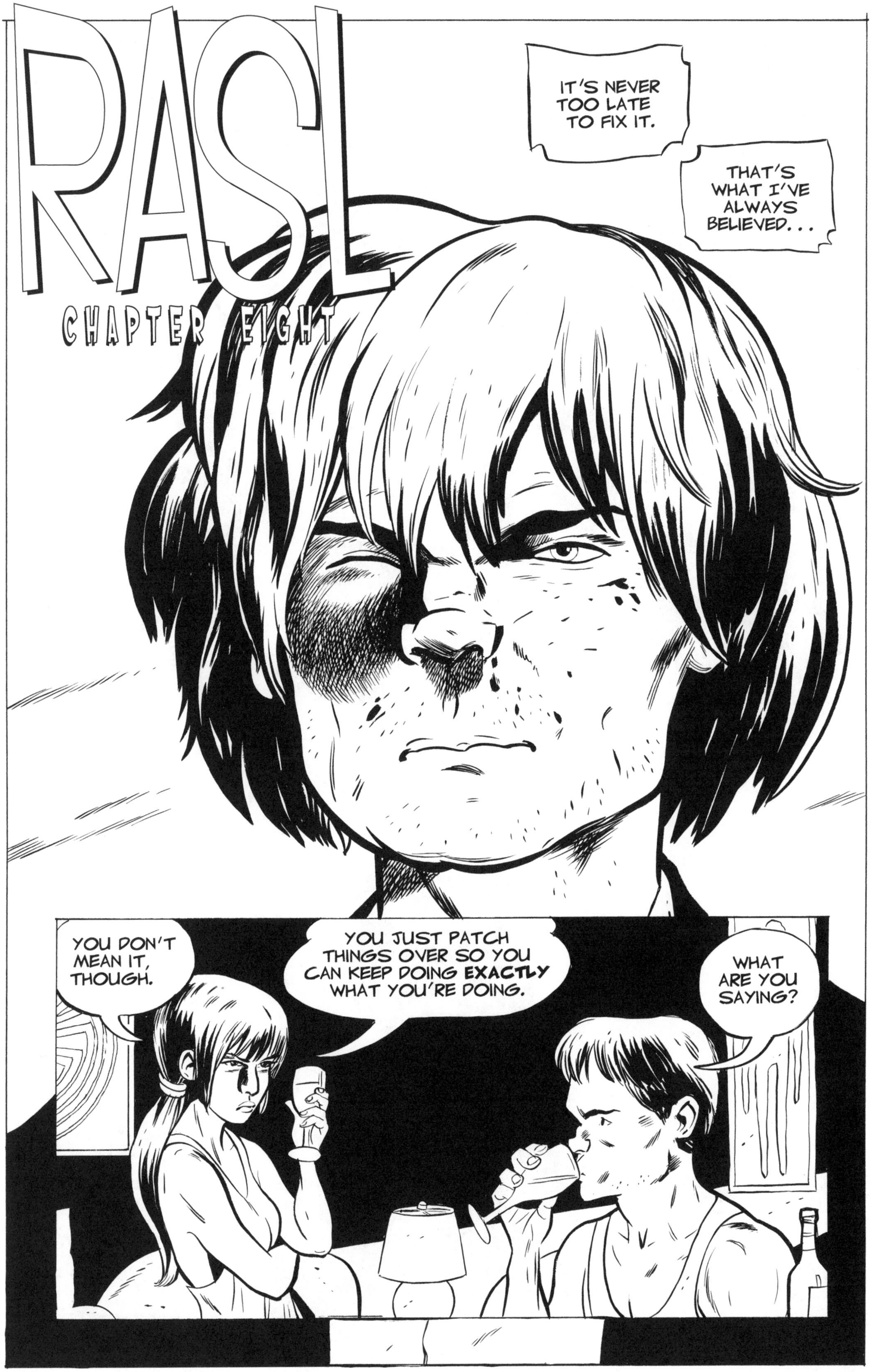
RASL
CHAPTER EIGHT
IT'S NEVER TOO LATE TO FIX IT.
THAT'S WHAT I'VE ALWAYS BELIEVED...
YOU DON'T MEAN IT, THOUGH.
YOU JUST PATCH THINGS OVER SO YOU CAN KEEP DOING **EXACTLY** WHAT YOU'RE DOING.
WHAT ARE YOU SAYING?

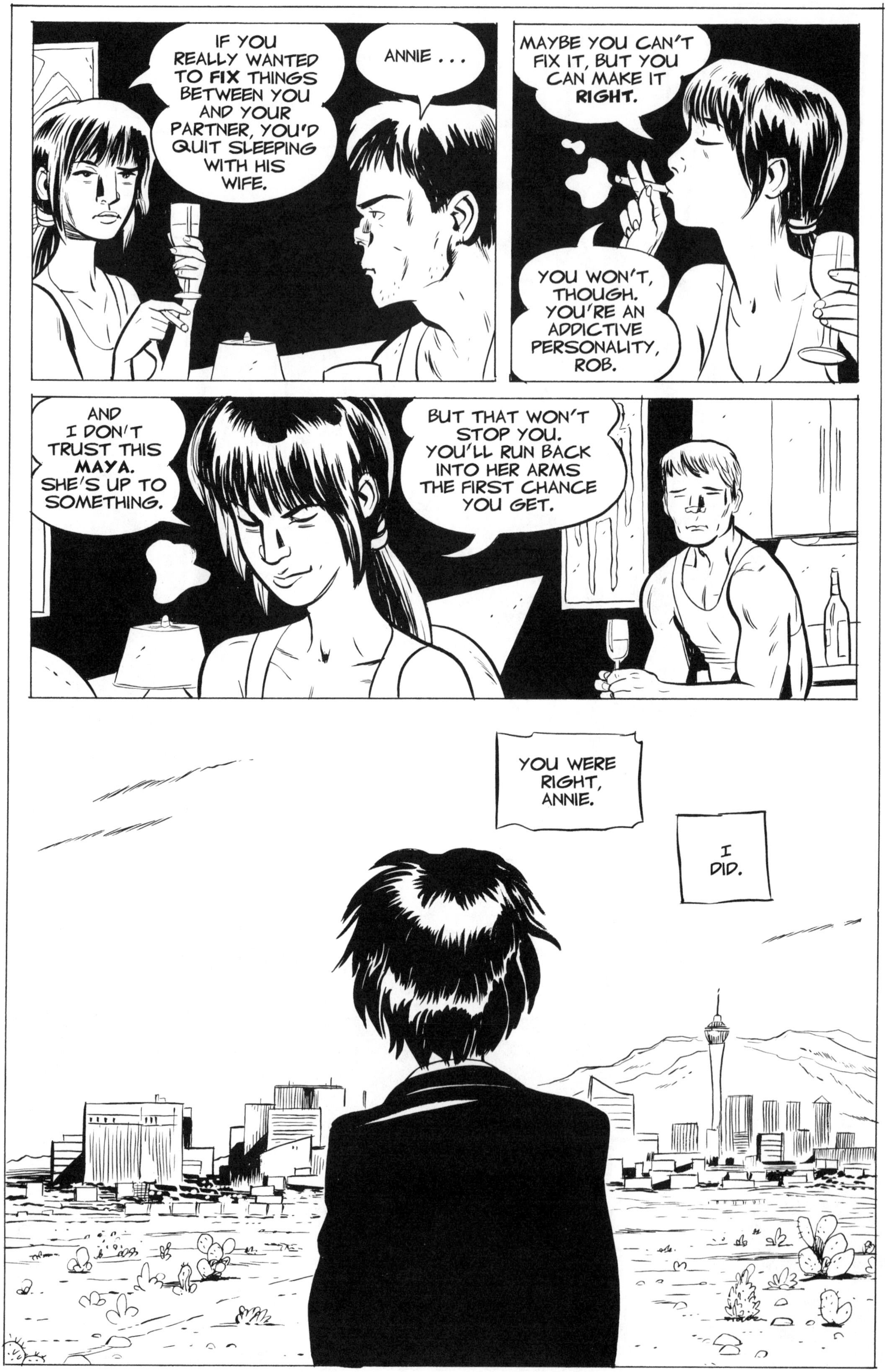
IF YOU REALLY WANTED TO FIX THINGS BETWEEN YOU AND YOUR PARTNER, YOU'D QUIT SLEEPING WITH HIS WIFE.
ANNIE . . .
MAYBE YOU CAN'T FIX IT, BUT YOU CAN MAKE IT RIGHT.
YOU WON'T, THOUGH. YOU'RE AN ADDICTIVE PERSONALITY, ROB.
AND I DON'T TRUST THIS MAYA. SHE'S UP TO SOMETHING.
BUT THAT WON'T STOP YOU. YOU'LL RUN BACK INTO HER ARMS THE FIRST CHANCE YOU GET.
YOU WERE RIGHT, ANNIE.
I DID.

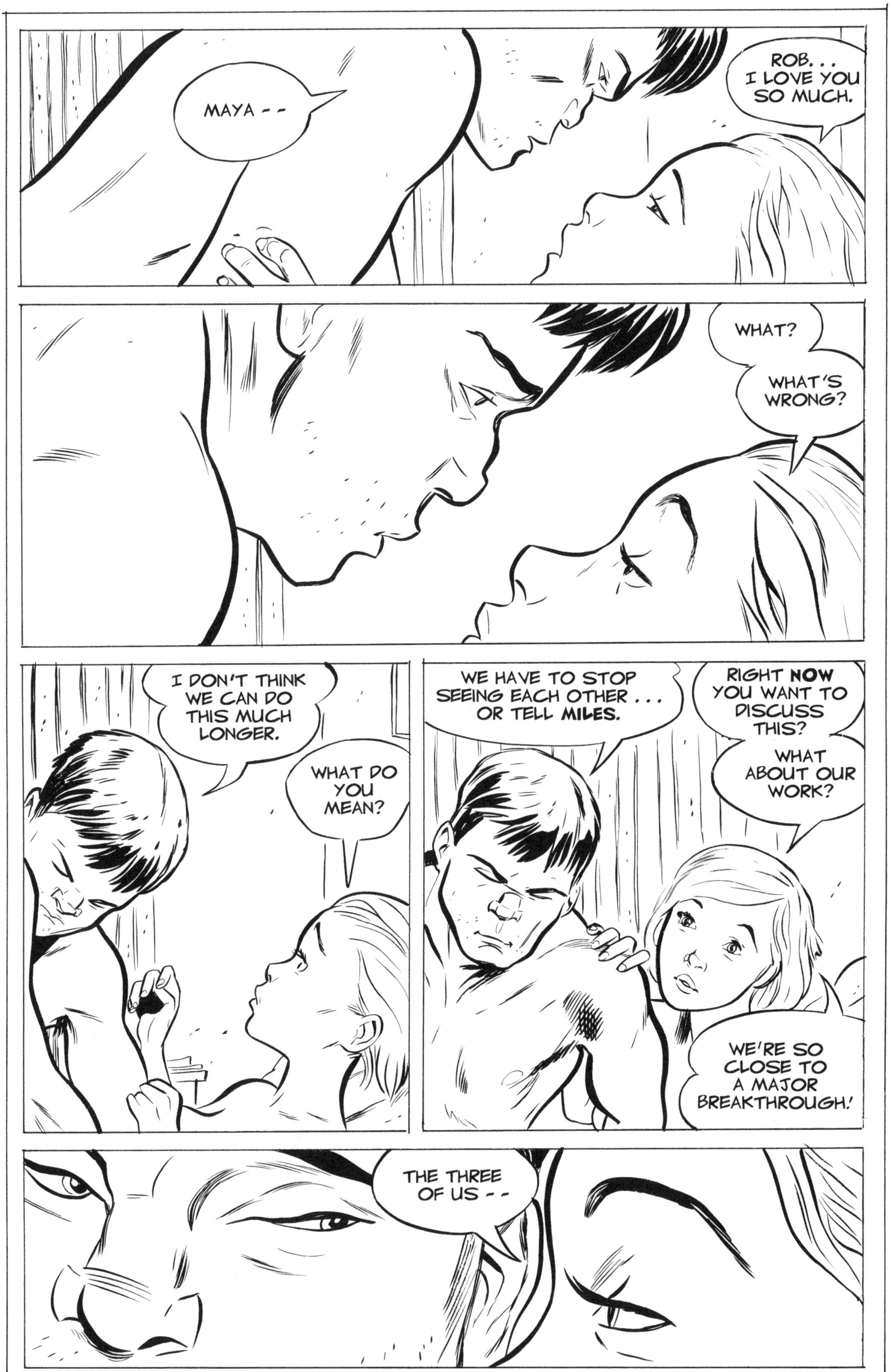
MAYA --
ROB... I LOVE YOU SO MUCH.
WHAT?
WHAT'S WRONG?
I DON'T THINK WE CAN DO THIS MUCH LONGER.
WHAT DO YOU MEAN?
WE HAVE TO STOP SEEING EACH OTHER ... OR TELL MILES.
RIGHT NOW YOU WANT TO DISCUSS THIS?
WHAT ABOUT OUR WORK?
WE'RE SO CLOSE TO A MAJOR BREAKTHROUGH!
THE THREE OF US --

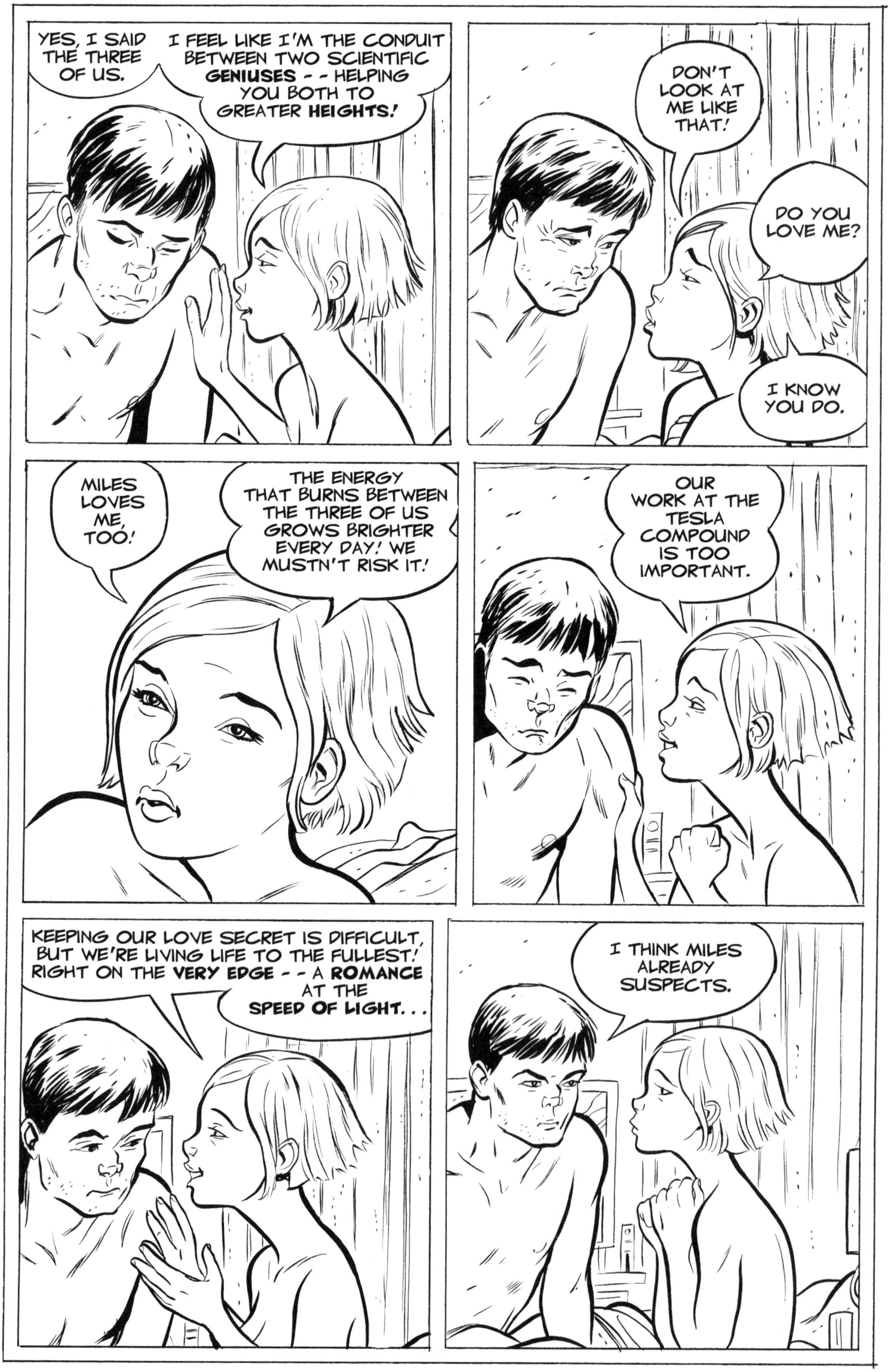
YES, I SAID THE THREE OF US.
I FEEL LIKE I'M THE CONDUIT BETWEEN TWO SCIENTIFIC GENIUSES - - HELPING YOU BOTH TO GREATER HEIGHTS!
DON'T LOOK AT ME LIKE THAT!
DO YOU LOVE ME?
I KNOW YOU DO.
MILES LOVES ME, TOO!
THE ENERGY THAT BURNS BETWEEN THE THREE OF US GROWS BRIGHTER EVERY DAY! WE MUSTN'T RISK IT!
OUR WORK AT THE TESLA COMPOUND IS TOO IMPORTANT.
KEEPING OUR LOVE SECRET IS DIFFICULT, BUT WE'RE LIVING LIFE TO THE FULLEST! RIGHT ON THE VERY EDGE - - A ROMANCE AT THE SPEED OF LIGHT...
I THINK MILES ALREADY SUSPECTS.

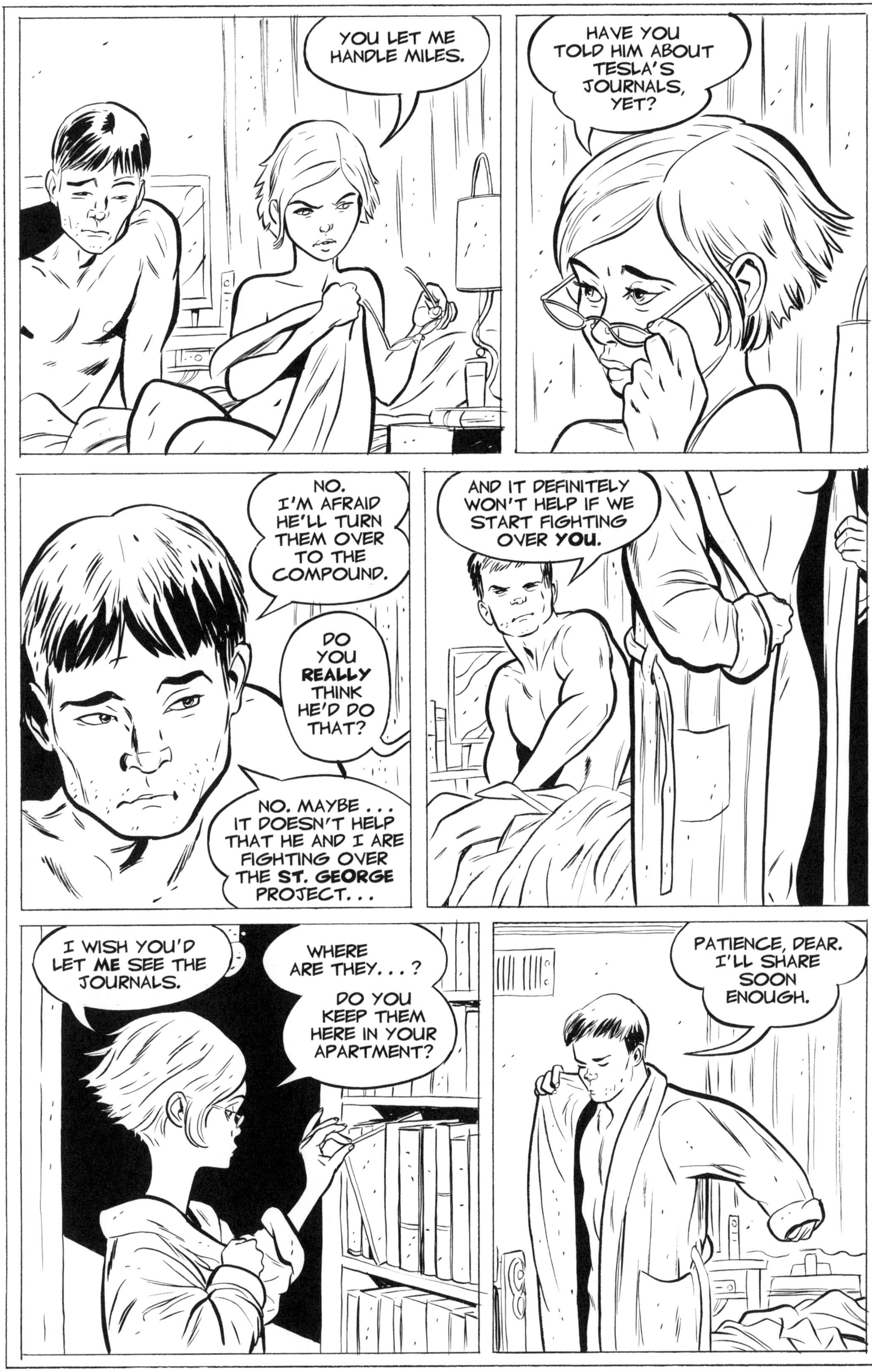
YOU LET ME HANDLE MILES.
HAVE YOU TOLD HIM ABOUT TESLA'S JOURNALS, YET?
NO. I'M AFRAID HE'LL TURN THEM OVER TO THE COMPOUND.
DO YOU REALLY THINK HE'D DO THAT?
NO. MAYBE . . . IT DOESN'T HELP THAT HE AND I ARE FIGHTING OVER THE ST. GEORGE PROJECT. . .
AND IT DEFINITELY WON'T HELP IF WE START FIGHTING OVER YOU.
I WISH YOU'D LET ME SEE THE JOURNALS.
WHERE ARE THEY. . . ?
DO YOU KEEP THEM HERE IN YOUR APARTMENT?
PATIENCE, DEAR. I'LL SHARE SOON ENOUGH.

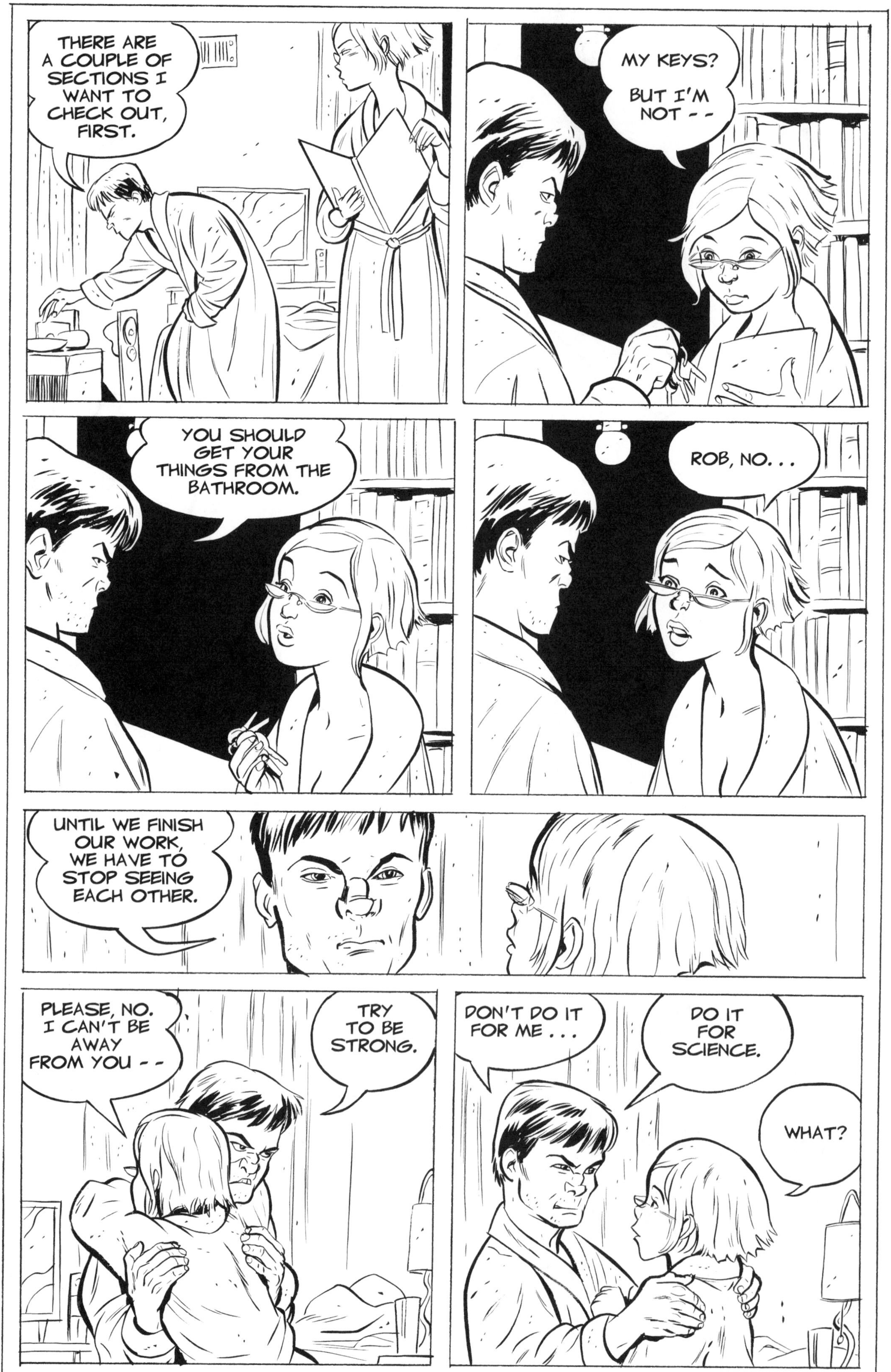
THERE ARE A COUPLE OF SECTIONS I WANT TO CHECK OUT, FIRST.
MY KEYS?
BUT I'M NOT - -
YOU SHOULD GET YOUR THINGS FROM THE BATHROOM.
ROB, NO. . .
UNTIL WE FINISH OUR WORK, WE HAVE TO STOP SEEING EACH OTHER.
PLEASE, NO. I CAN'T BE AWAY FROM YOU - -
TRY TO BE STRONG.
DON'T DO IT FOR ME . . .
DO IT FOR SCIENCE.
WHAT?

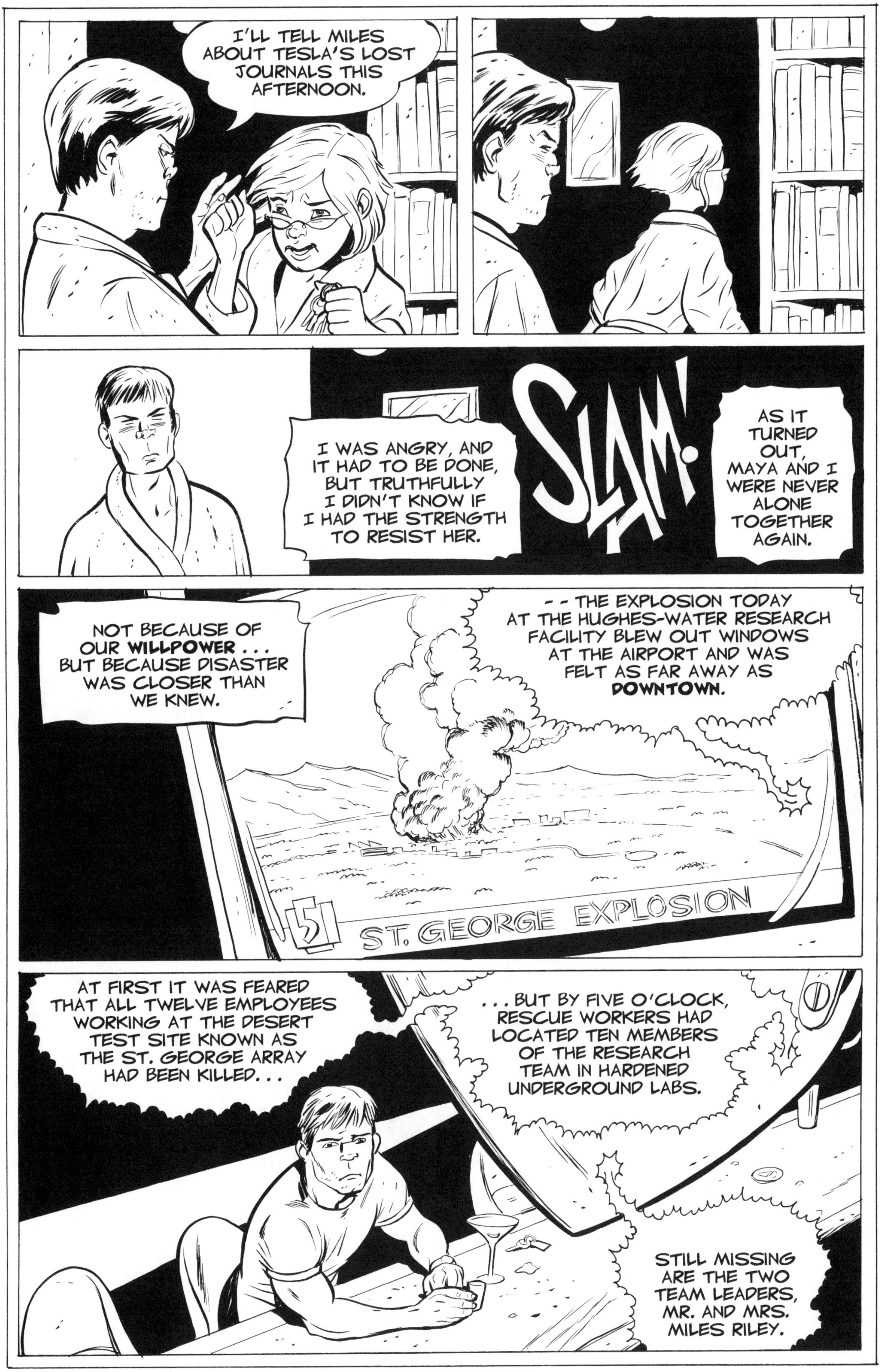
I'LL TELL MILES ABOUT TESLA'S LOST JOURNALS THIS AFTERNOON.
I WAS ANGRY, AND IT HAD TO BE DONE, BUT TRUTHFULLY I DIDN'T KNOW IF I HAD THE STRENGTH TO RESIST HER.
SLAM!
AS IT TURNED OUT, MAYA AND I WERE NEVER ALONE TOGETHER AGAIN.
NOT BECAUSE OF OUR **WILLPOWER** . . . BUT BECAUSE DISASTER WAS CLOSER THAN WE KNEW.
-- THE EXPLOSION TODAY AT THE HUGHES-WATER RESEARCH FACILITY BLEW OUT WINDOWS AT THE AIRPORT AND WAS FELT AS FAR AWAY AS **DOWNTOWN.**
5
ST. GEORGE EXPLOSION
AT FIRST IT WAS FEARED THAT ALL TWELVE EMPLOYEES WORKING AT THE DESERT TEST SITE KNOWN AS THE ST. GEORGE ARRAY HAD BEEN KILLED. . .
. . . BUT BY FIVE O'CLOCK, RESCUE WORKERS HAD LOCATED TEN MEMBERS OF THE RESEARCH TEAM IN HARDENED UNDERGROUND LABS.
STILL MISSING ARE THE TWO TEAM LEADERS, MR. AND MRS. MILES RILEY.

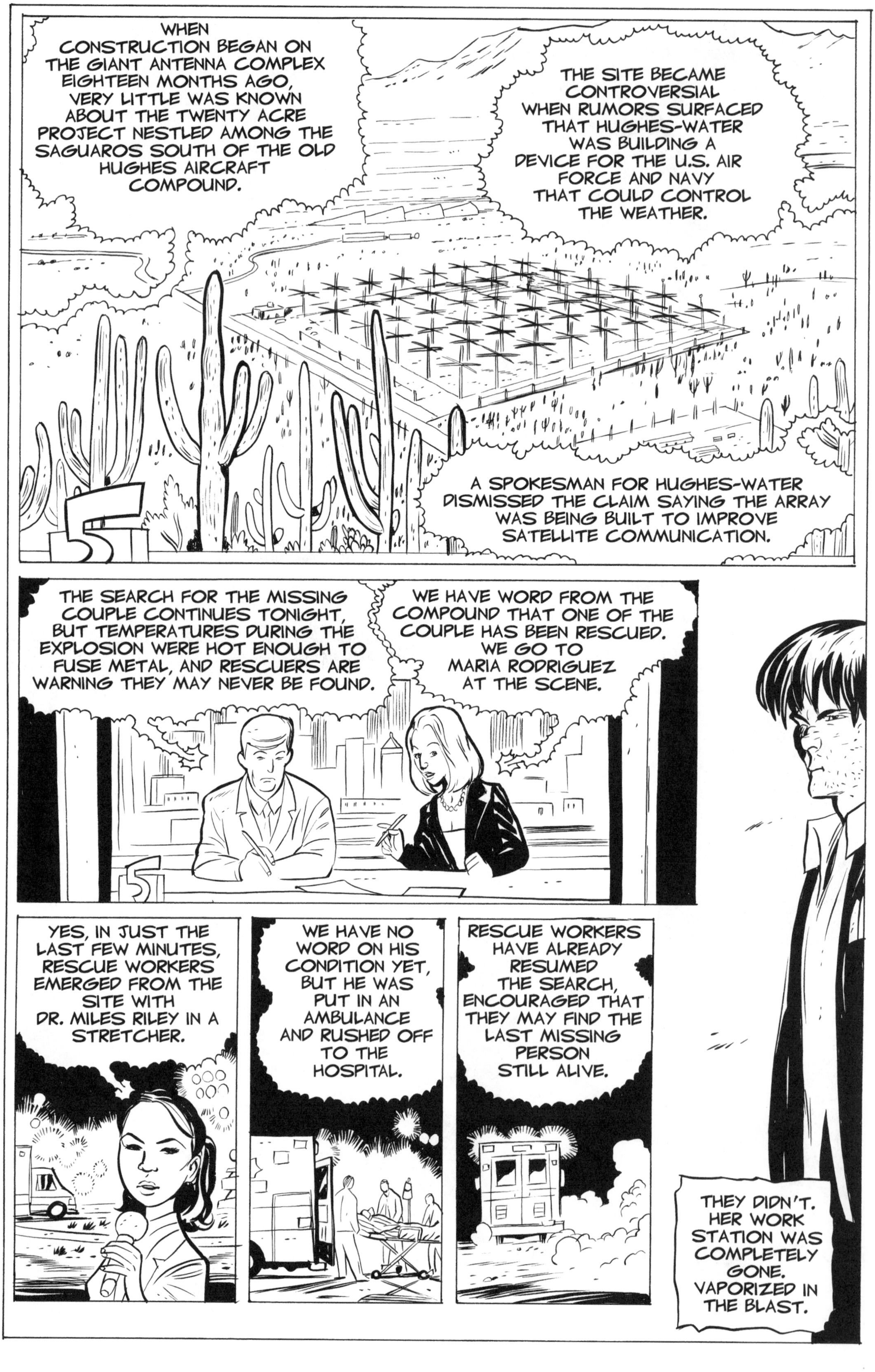
WHEN CONSTRUCTION BEGAN ON THE GIANT ANTENNA COMPLEX EIGHTEEN MONTHS AGO, VERY LITTLE WAS KNOWN ABOUT THE TWENTY ACRE PROJECT NESTLED AMONG THE SAGUAROS SOUTH OF THE OLD HUGHES AIRCRAFT COMPOUND.
THE SITE BECAME CONTROVERSIAL WHEN RUMORS SURFACED THAT HUGHES-WATER WAS BUILDING A DEVICE FOR THE U.S. AIR FORCE AND NAVY THAT COULD CONTROL THE WEATHER.
A SPOKESMAN FOR HUGHES-WATER DISMISSED THE CLAIM SAYING THE ARRAY WAS BEING BUILT TO IMPROVE SATELLITE COMMUNICATION.
THE SEARCH FOR THE MISSING COUPLE CONTINUES TONIGHT, BUT TEMPERATURES DURING THE EXPLOSION WERE HOT ENOUGH TO FUSE METAL, AND RESCUERS ARE WARNING THEY MAY NEVER BE FOUND.
WE HAVE WORD FROM THE COMPOUND THAT ONE OF THE COUPLE HAS BEEN RESCUED. WE GO TO MARIA RODRIGUEZ AT THE SCENE.
YES, IN JUST THE LAST FEW MINUTES, RESCUE WORKERS EMERGED FROM THE SITE WITH DR. MILES RILEY IN A STRETCHER.
WE HAVE NO WORD ON HIS CONDITION YET, BUT HE WAS PUT IN AN AMBULANCE AND RUSHED OFF TO THE HOSPITAL.
RESCUE WORKERS HAVE ALREADY RESUMED THE SEARCH, ENCOURAGED THAT THEY MAY FIND THE LAST MISSING PERSON STILL ALIVE.
THEY DIDN'T. HER WORK STATION WAS COMPLETELY GONE. VAPORIZED IN THE BLAST.

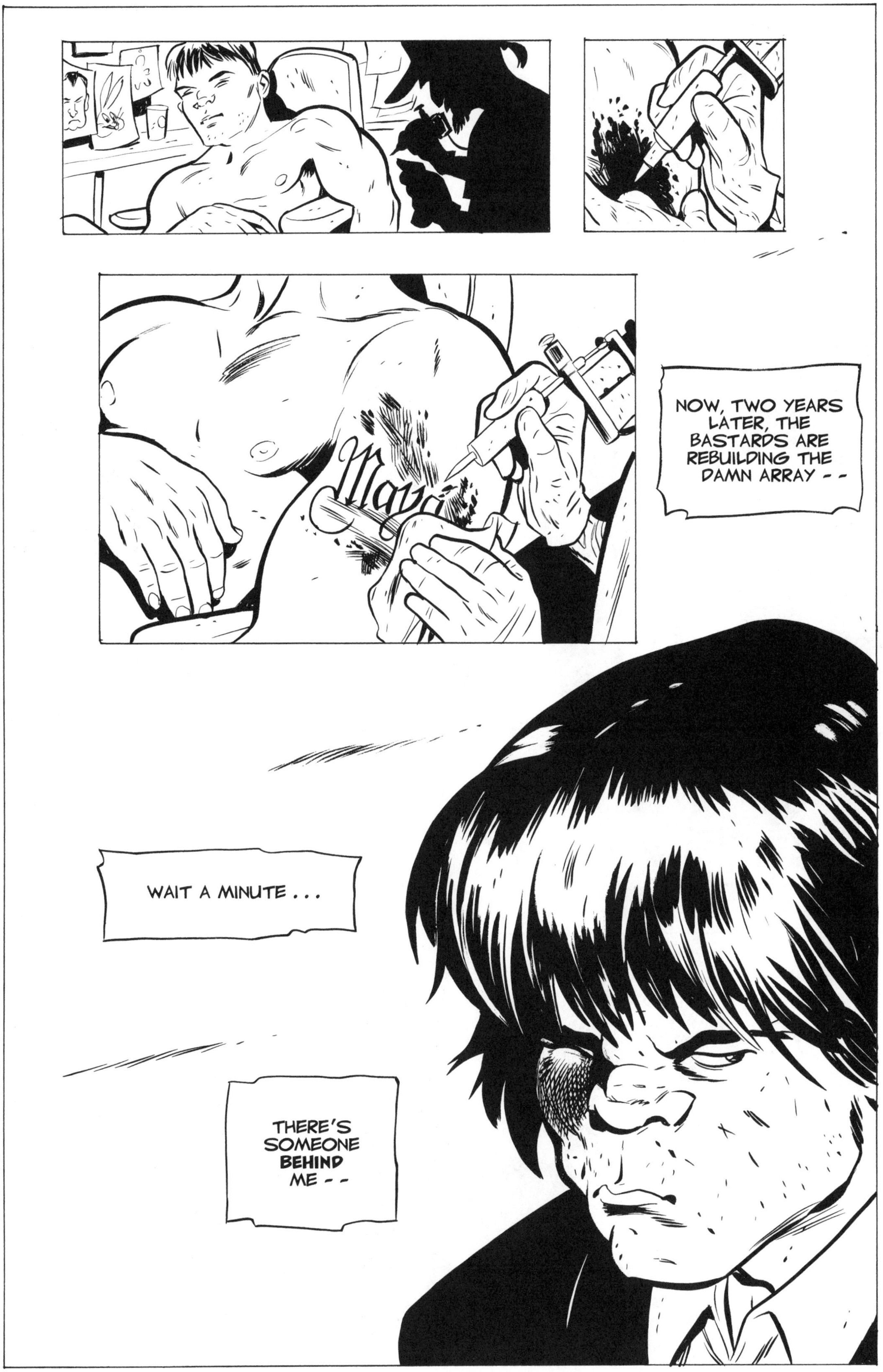
NOW, TWO YEARS LATER, THE BASTARDS ARE REBUILDING THE DAMN ARRAY --
WAIT A MINUTE . . .
THERE'S SOMEONE **BEHIND** ME --

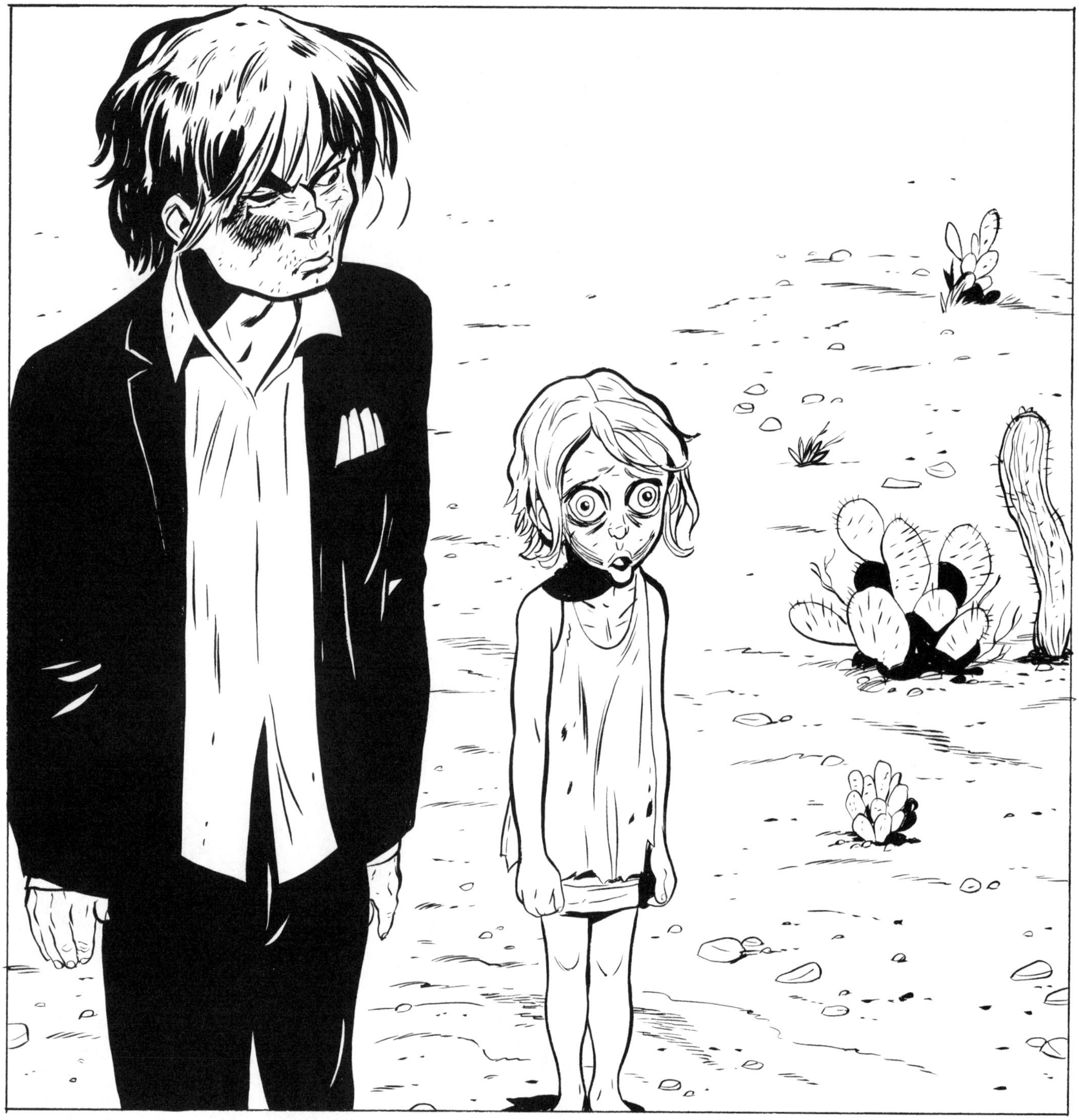

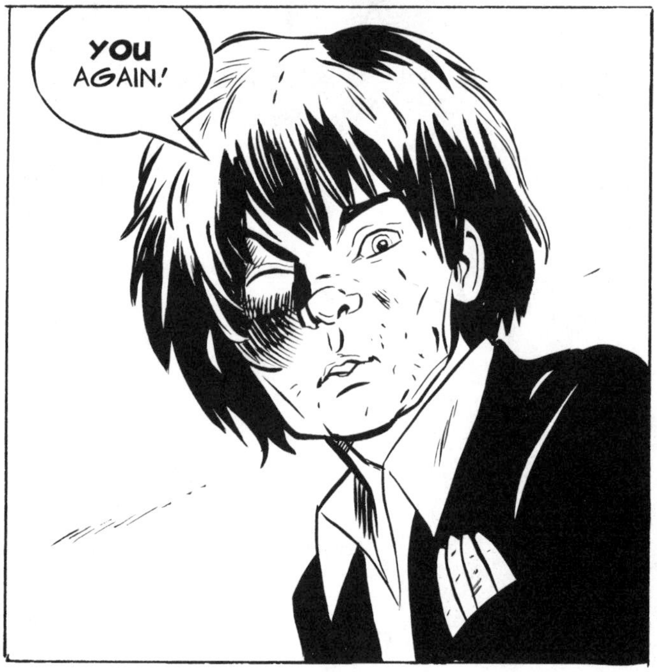
YOU AGAIN.'

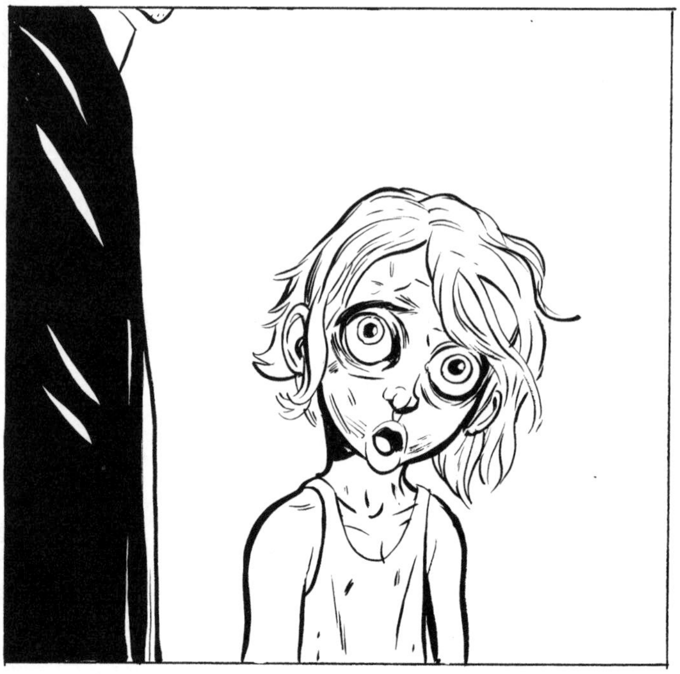

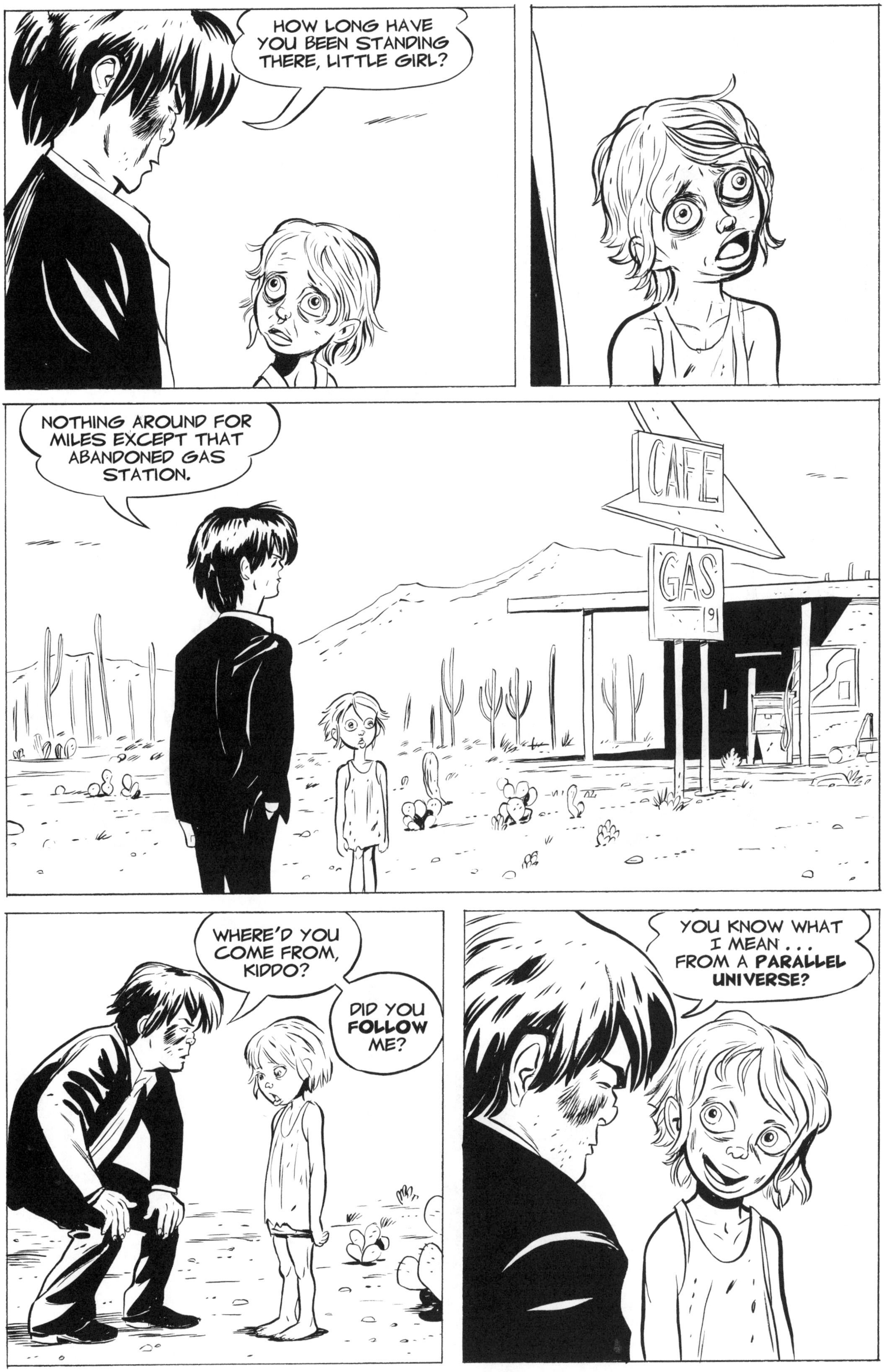
HOW LONG HAVE YOU BEEN STANDING THERE, LITTLE GIRL?
NOTHING AROUND FOR MILES EXCEPT THAT ABANDONED GAS STATION.
CAFE
GAS
WHERE'D YOU COME FROM, KIDDO?
DID YOU **FOLLOW** ME?
YOU KNOW WHAT I MEAN . . . FROM A **PARALLEL UNIVERSE?**

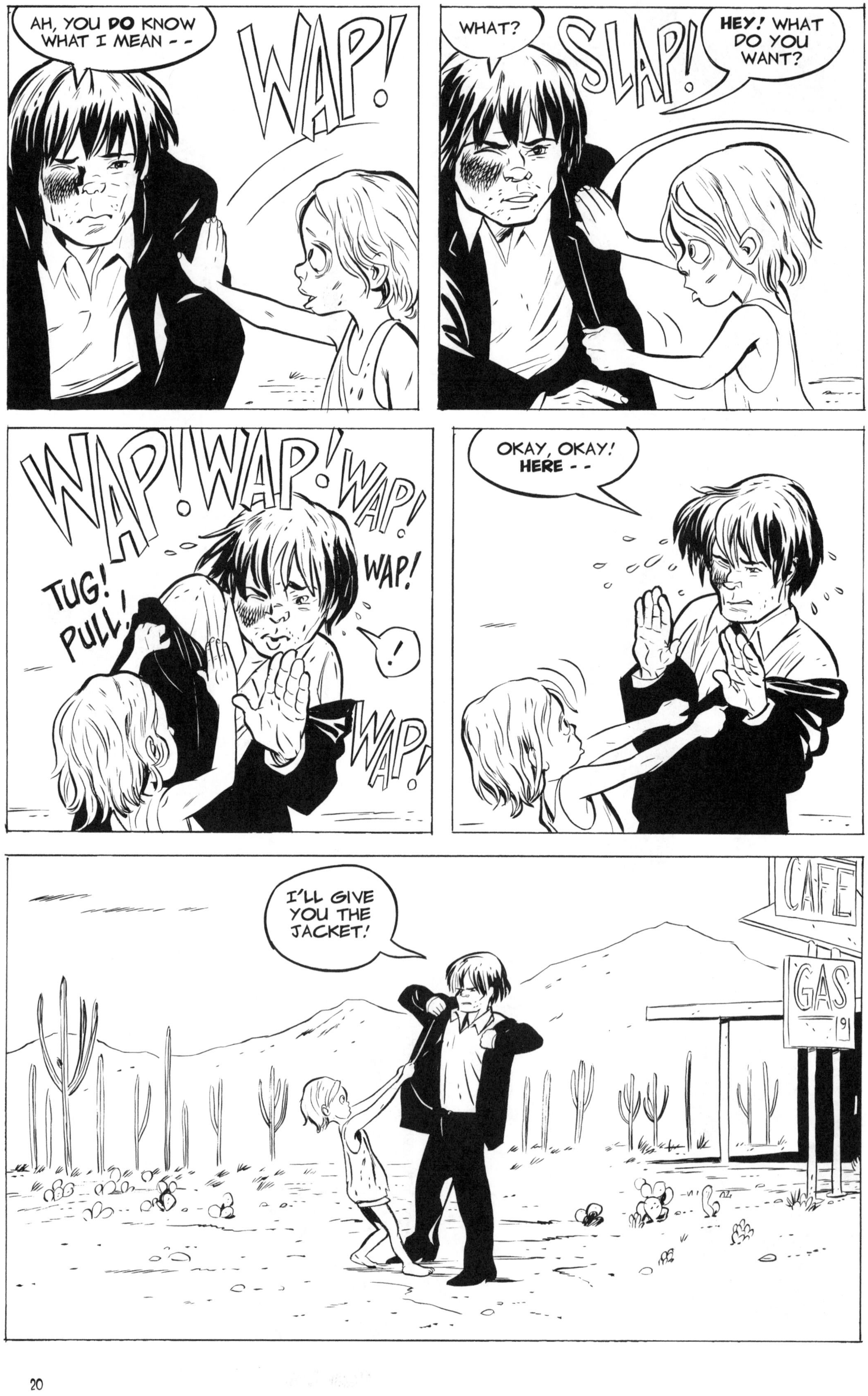
AH, YOU **DO** KNOW WHAT I MEAN - -
WAP!
WHAT?
SLAP!
**HEY!** WHAT DO YOU WANT?
WAP! WAP! WAP!
WAP!
TUG! PULL!
!
WAP!
OKAY, OKAY! **HERE** - -
I'LL GIVE YOU THE JACKET!
CAFE
GAS
9

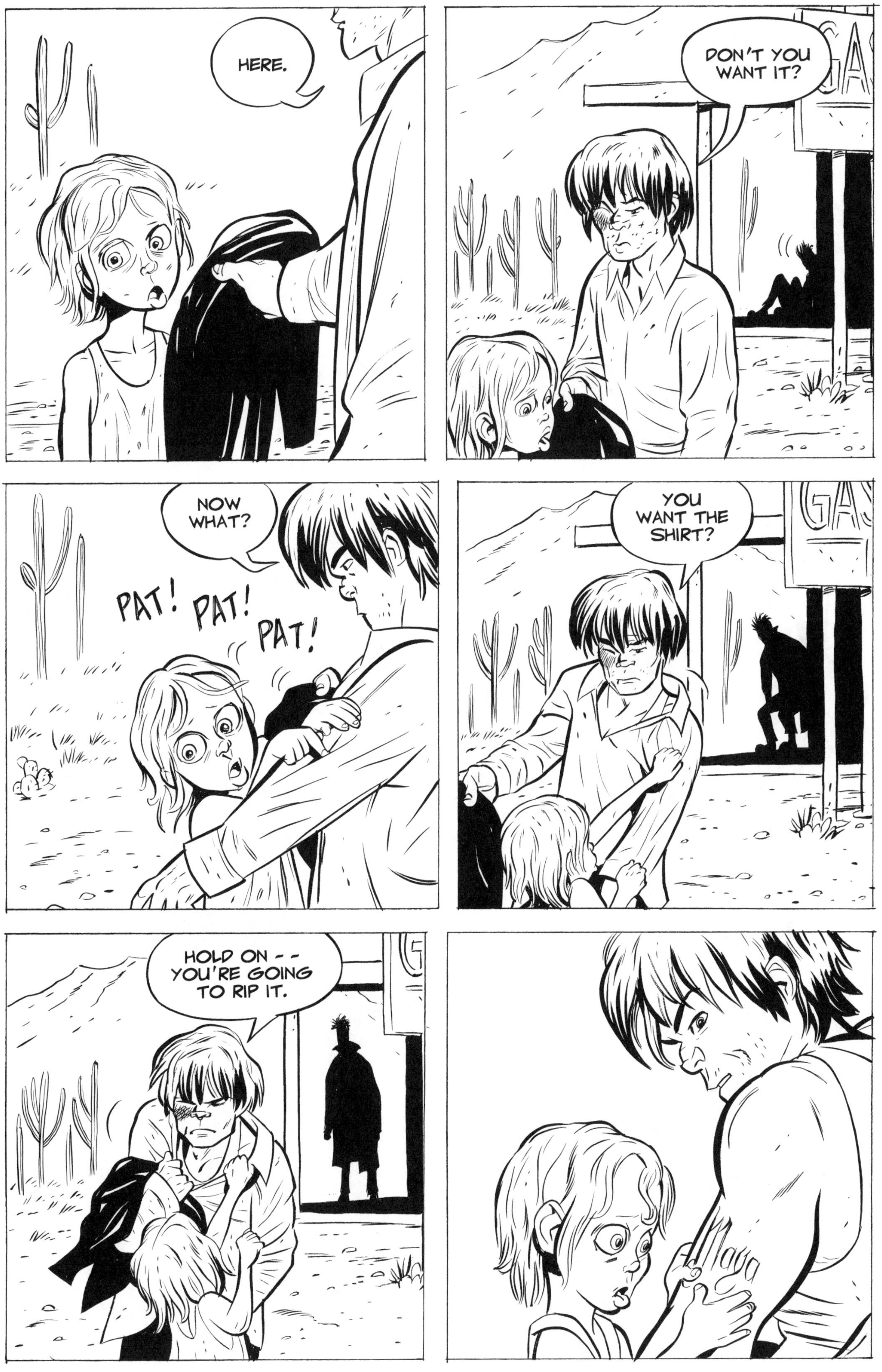
HERE.
DON'T YOU WANT IT?
NOW WHAT?
PAT! PAT! PAT!
YOU WANT THE SHIRT?
HOLD ON -- YOU'RE GOING TO RIP IT.

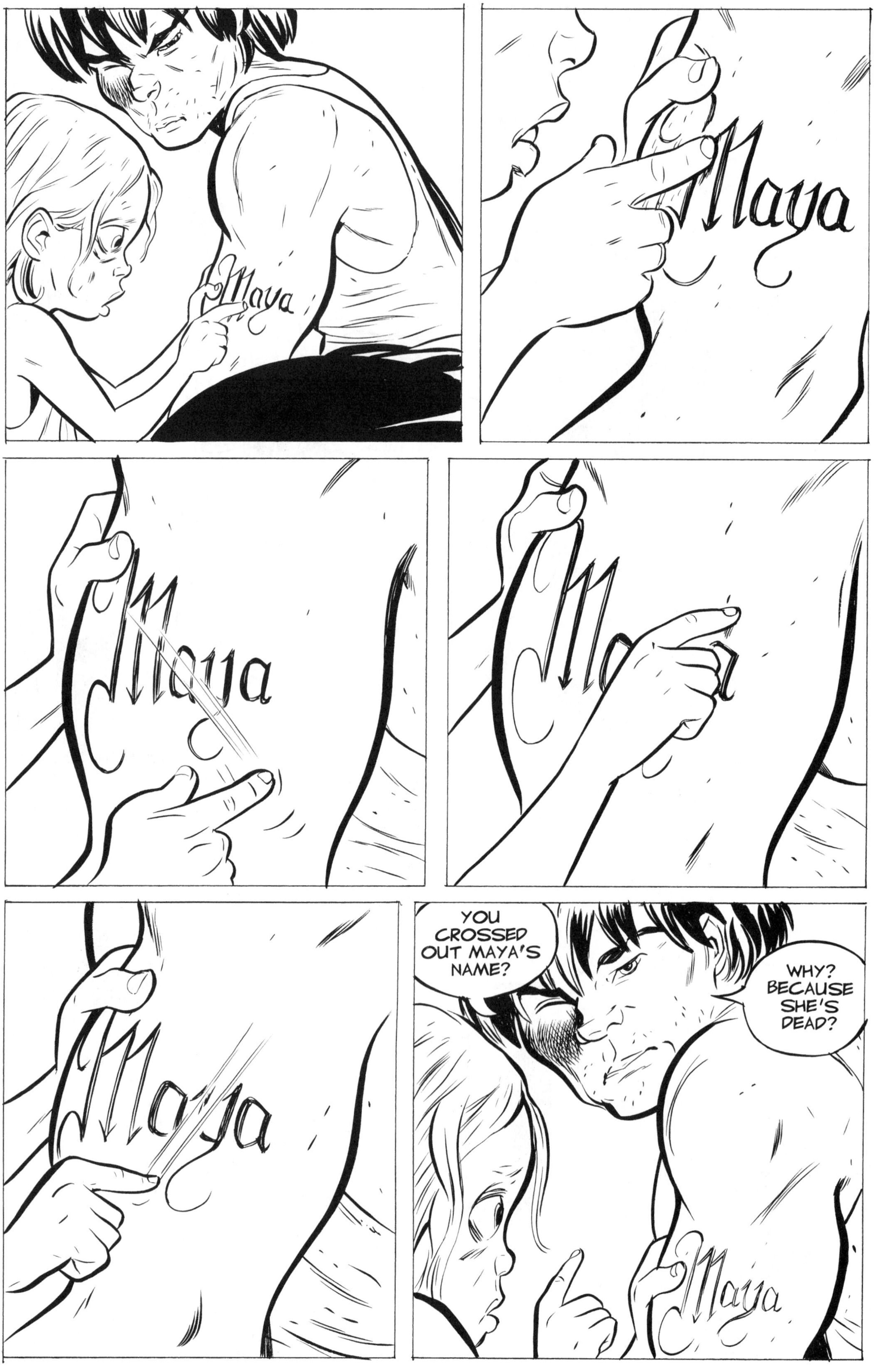
Maya
Maya
Maya
Maya
Maya
YOU CROSSED OUT MAYA'S NAME?
WHY? BECAUSE SHE'S DEAD?
Maya

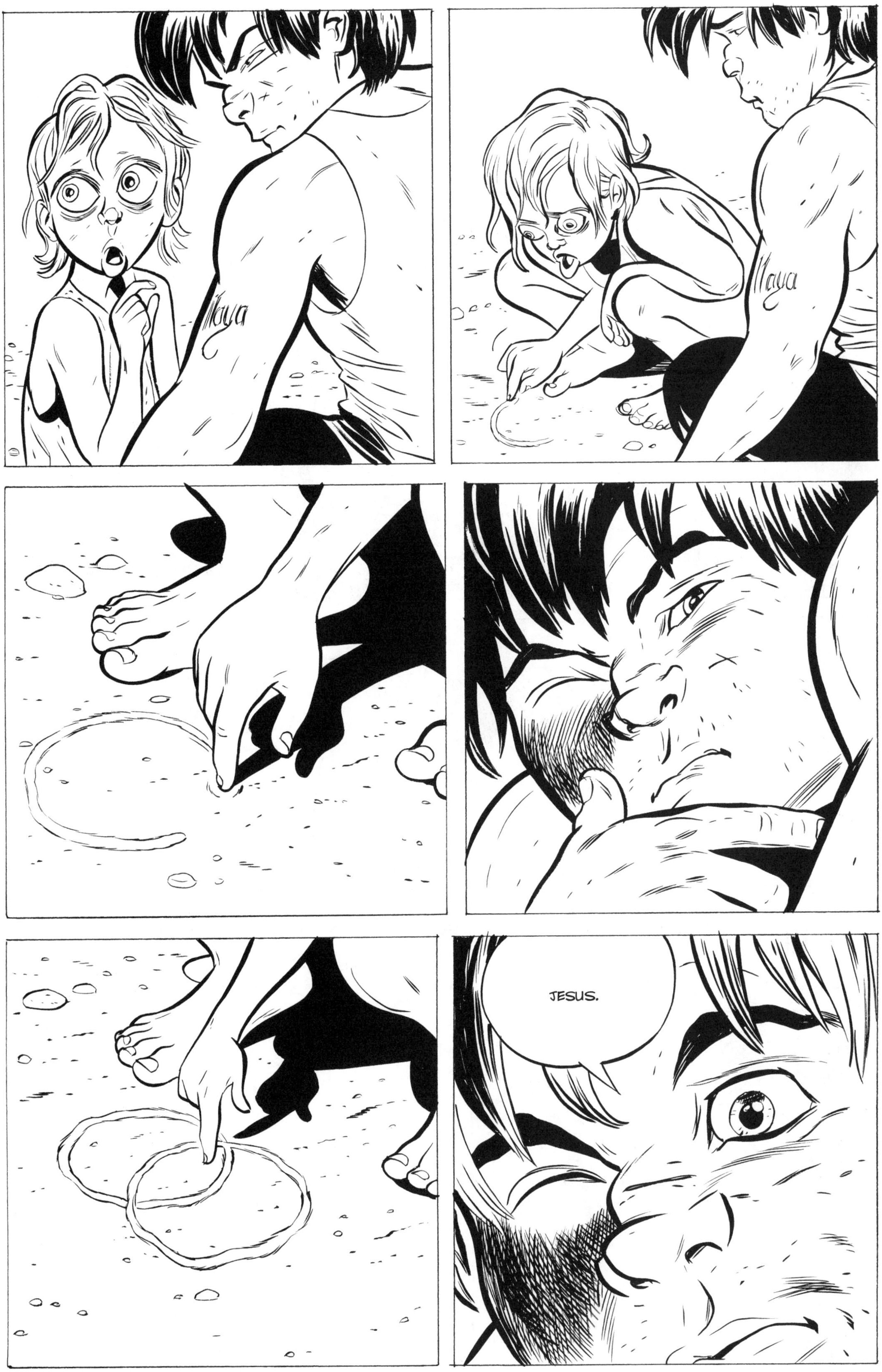
Maya
Maya
JESUS.

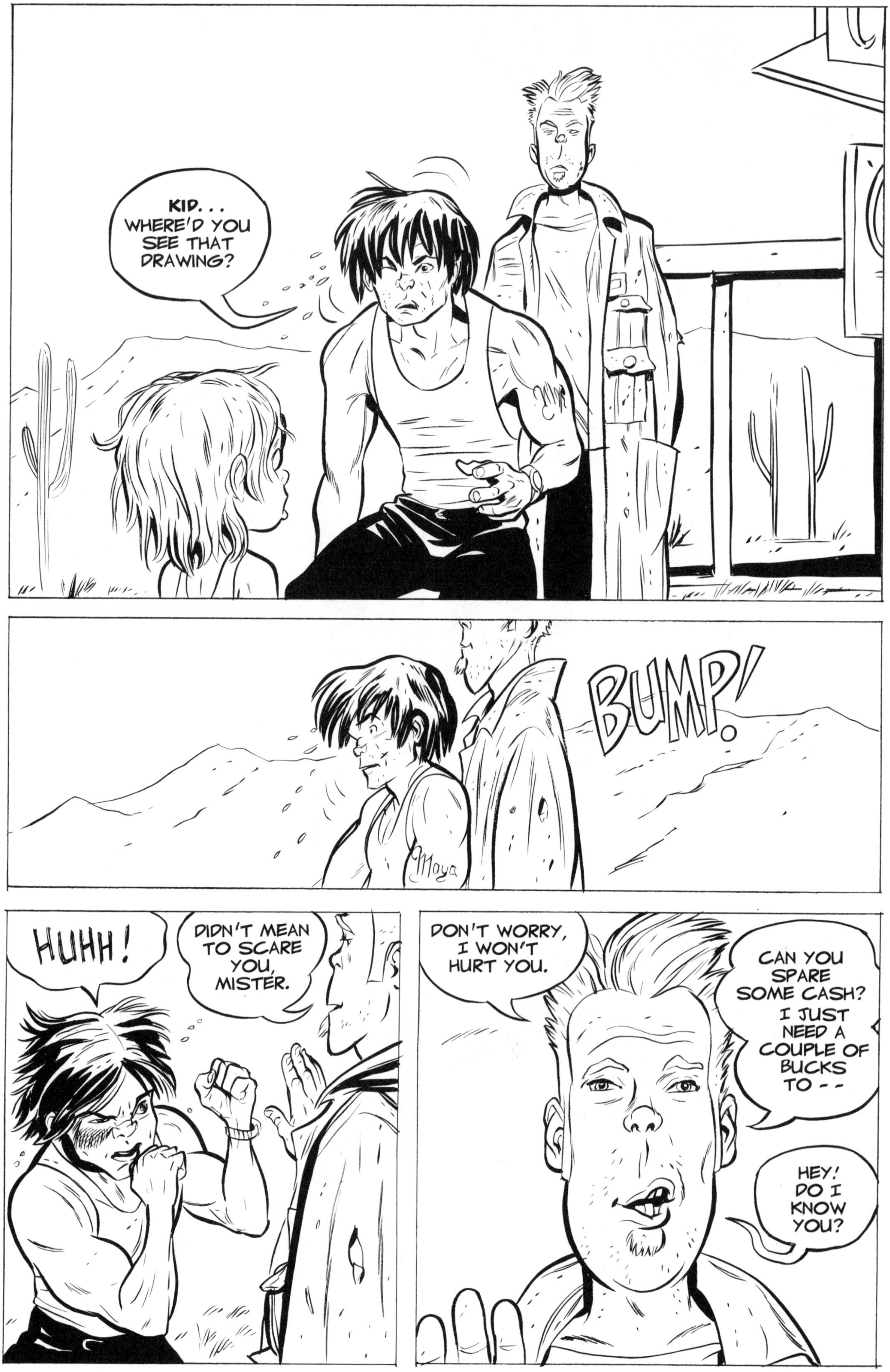
KID... WHERE'D YOU SEE THAT DRAWING?
BUMP!
Maya
HUHH!
DIDN'T MEAN TO SCARE YOU, MISTER.
DON'T WORRY, I WON'T HURT YOU.
CAN YOU SPARE SOME CASH? I JUST NEED A COUPLE OF BUCKS TO --
HEY! DO I KNOW YOU?

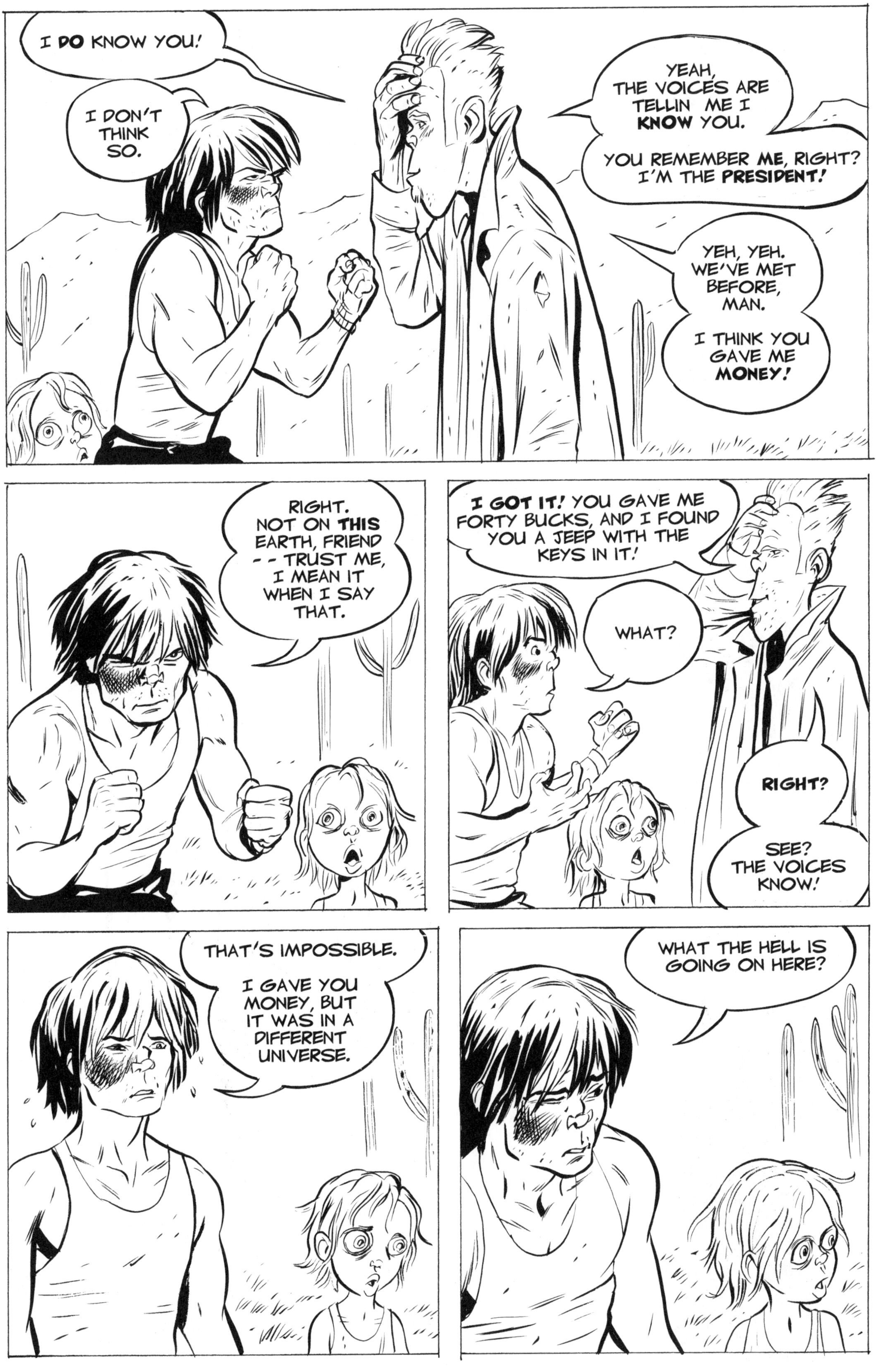
I DO KNOW YOU!
I DON'T THINK SO.
YEAH, THE VOICES ARE TELLIN ME I KNOW YOU.
YOU REMEMBER ME, RIGHT? I'M THE PRESIDENT!
YEH, YEH. WE'VE MET BEFORE, MAN.
I THINK YOU GAVE ME MONEY!
RIGHT. NOT ON THIS EARTH, FRIEND -- TRUST ME, I MEAN IT WHEN I SAY THAT.
I GOT IT! YOU GAVE ME FORTY BUCKS, AND I FOUND YOU A JEEP WITH THE KEYS IN IT!
WHAT?
RIGHT?
SEE? THE VOICES KNOW!
THAT'S IMPOSSIBLE.
I GAVE YOU MONEY, BUT IT WAS IN A DIFFERENT UNIVERSE.
WHAT THE HELL IS GOING ON HERE?

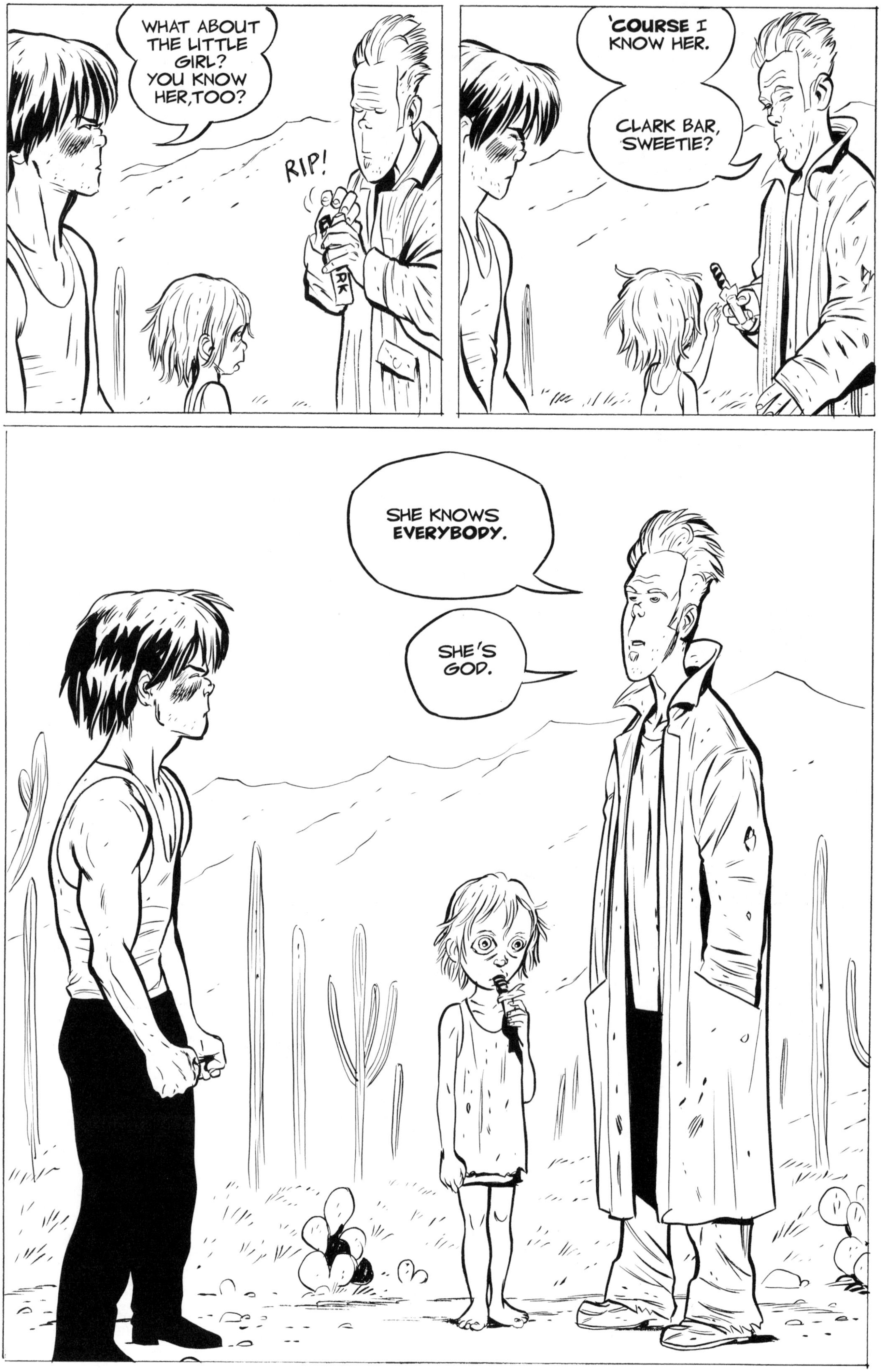
WHAT ABOUT THE LITTLE GIRL? YOU KNOW HER,TOO?
RIP!
'COURSE I KNOW HER.
CLARK BAR, SWEETIE?
SHE KNOWS EVERYBODY.
SHE'S GOD.

# 9.
# THE WARNING

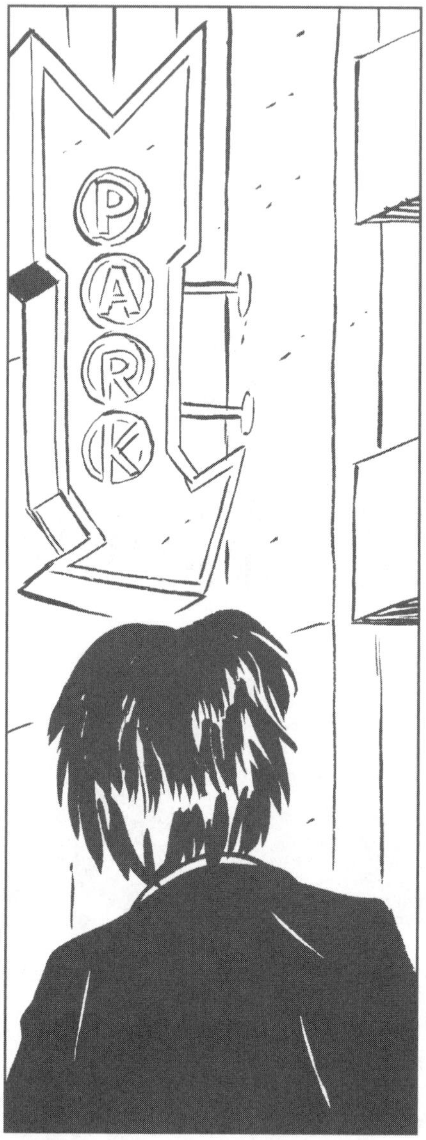
PARK

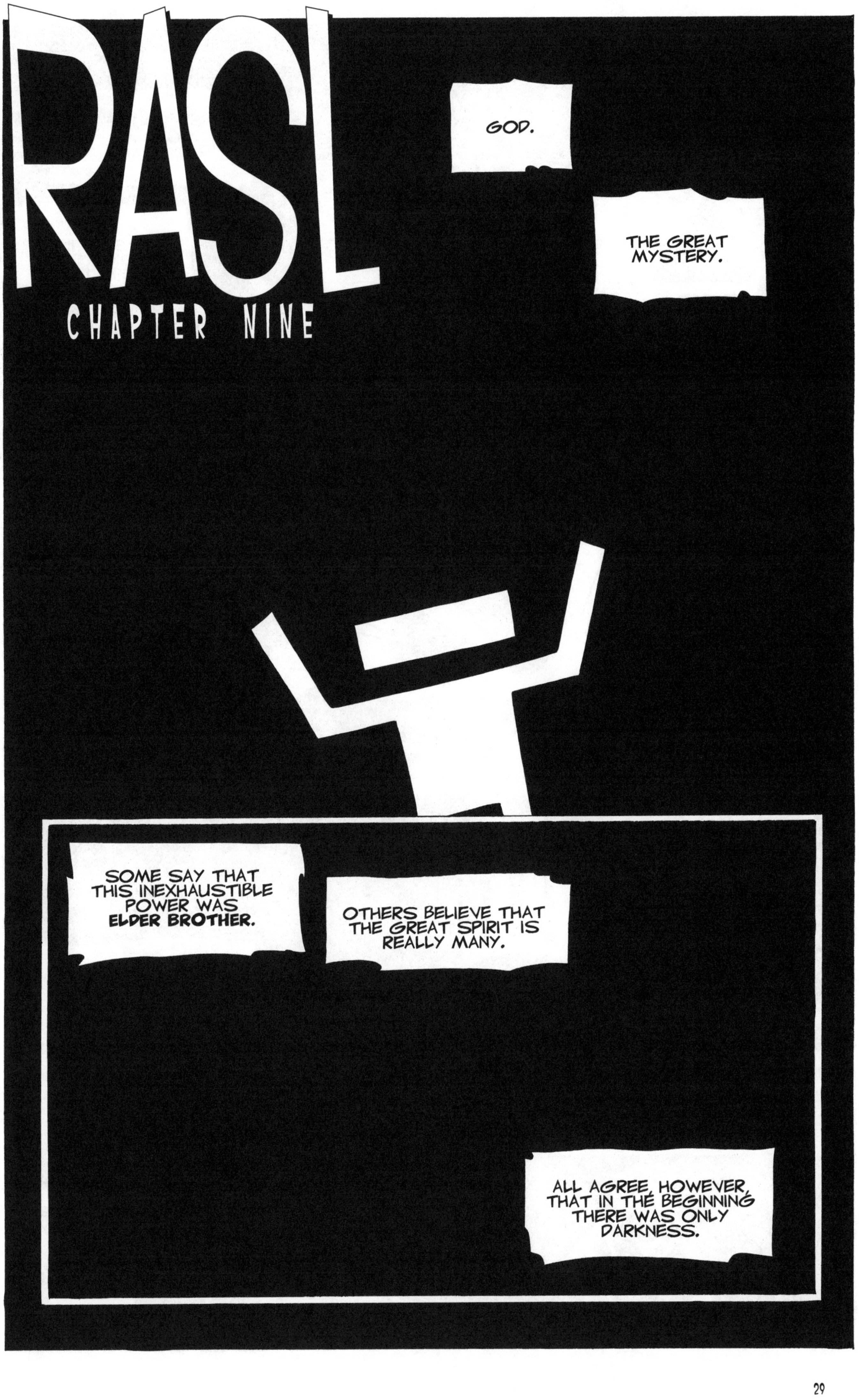
RASL
CHAPTER NINE
GOD.
THE GREAT MYSTERY.
SOME SAY THAT THIS INEXHAUSTIBLE POWER WAS **ELDER BROTHER.**
OTHERS BELIEVE THAT THE GREAT SPIRIT IS REALLY MANY.
ALL AGREE, HOWEVER, THAT IN THE BEGINNING THERE WAS ONLY DARKNESS.

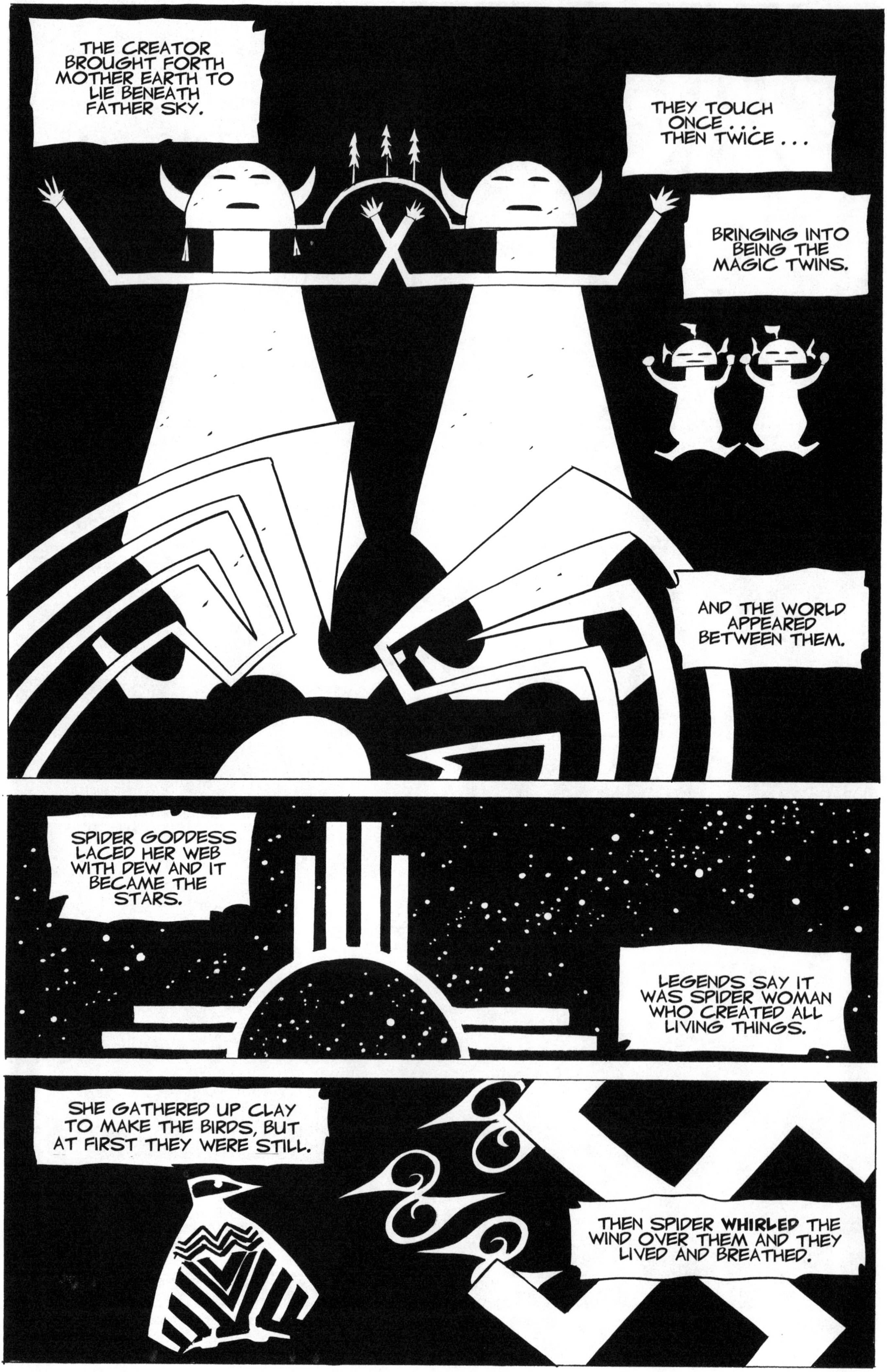
THE CREATOR BROUGHT FORTH MOTHER EARTH TO LIE BENEATH FATHER SKY.
THEY TOUCH ONCE . . . THEN TWICE . . .
BRINGING INTO BEING THE MAGIC TWINS.
AND THE WORLD APPEARED BETWEEN THEM.
SPIDER GODDESS LACED HER WEB WITH DEW AND IT BECAME THE STARS.
LEGENDS SAY IT WAS SPIDER WOMAN WHO CREATED ALL LIVING THINGS.
SHE GATHERED UP CLAY TO MAKE THE BIRDS, BUT AT FIRST THEY WERE STILL.
THEN SPIDER **WHIRLED** THE WIND OVER THEM AND THEY LIVED AND BREATHED.

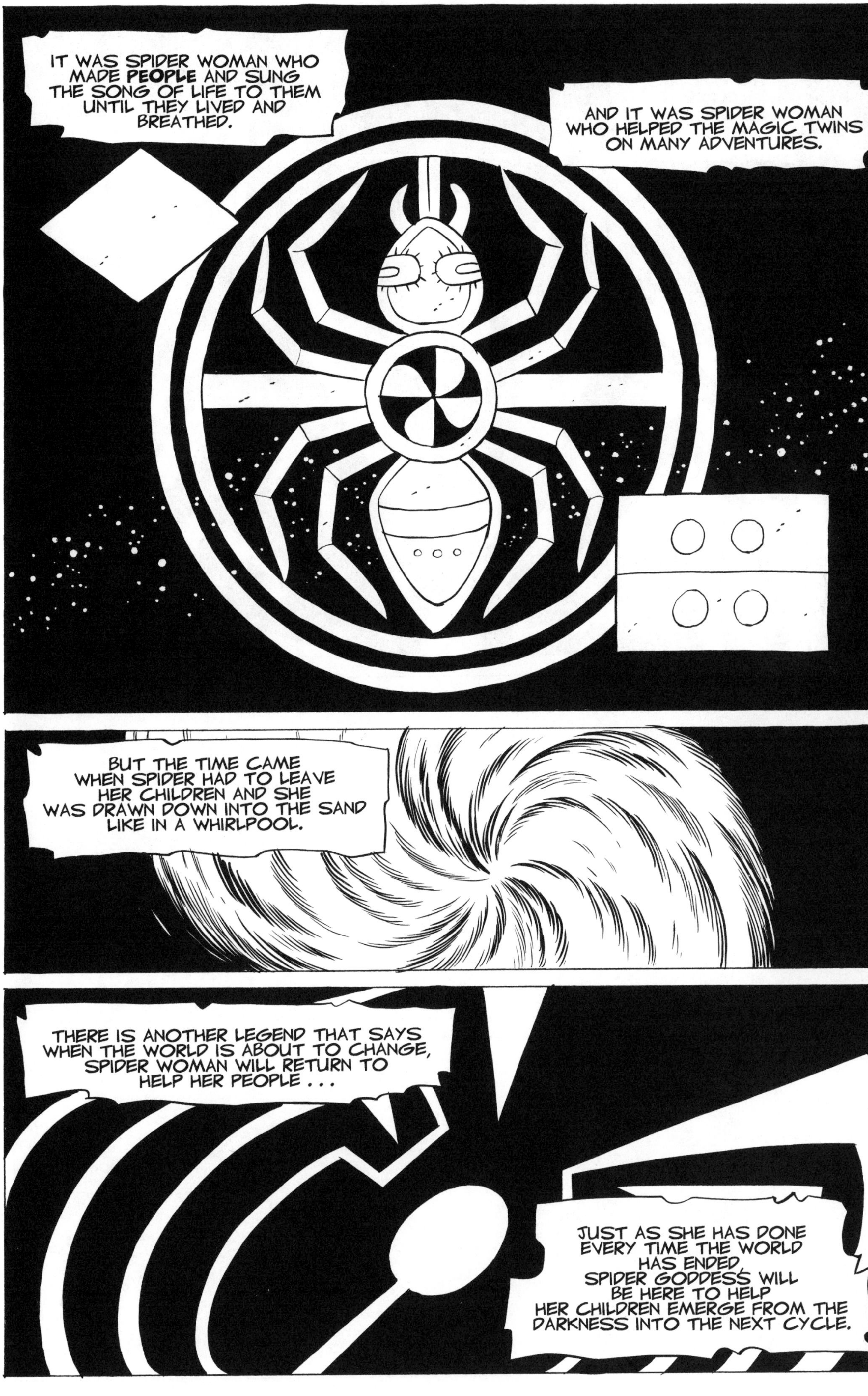
IT WAS SPIDER WOMAN WHO MADE PEOPLE AND SUNG THE SONG OF LIFE TO THEM UNTIL THEY LIVED AND BREATHED.
AND IT WAS SPIDER WOMAN WHO HELPED THE MAGIC TWINS ON MANY ADVENTURES.
BUT THE TIME CAME WHEN SPIDER HAD TO LEAVE HER CHILDREN AND SHE WAS DRAWN DOWN INTO THE SAND LIKE IN A WHIRLPOOL.
THERE IS ANOTHER LEGEND THAT SAYS WHEN THE WORLD IS ABOUT TO CHANGE, SPIDER WOMAN WILL RETURN TO HELP HER PEOPLE . . .
JUST AS SHE HAS DONE EVERY TIME THE WORLD HAS ENDED, SPIDER GODDESS WILL BE HERE TO HELP HER CHILDREN EMERGE FROM THE DARKNESS INTO THE NEXT CYCLE.

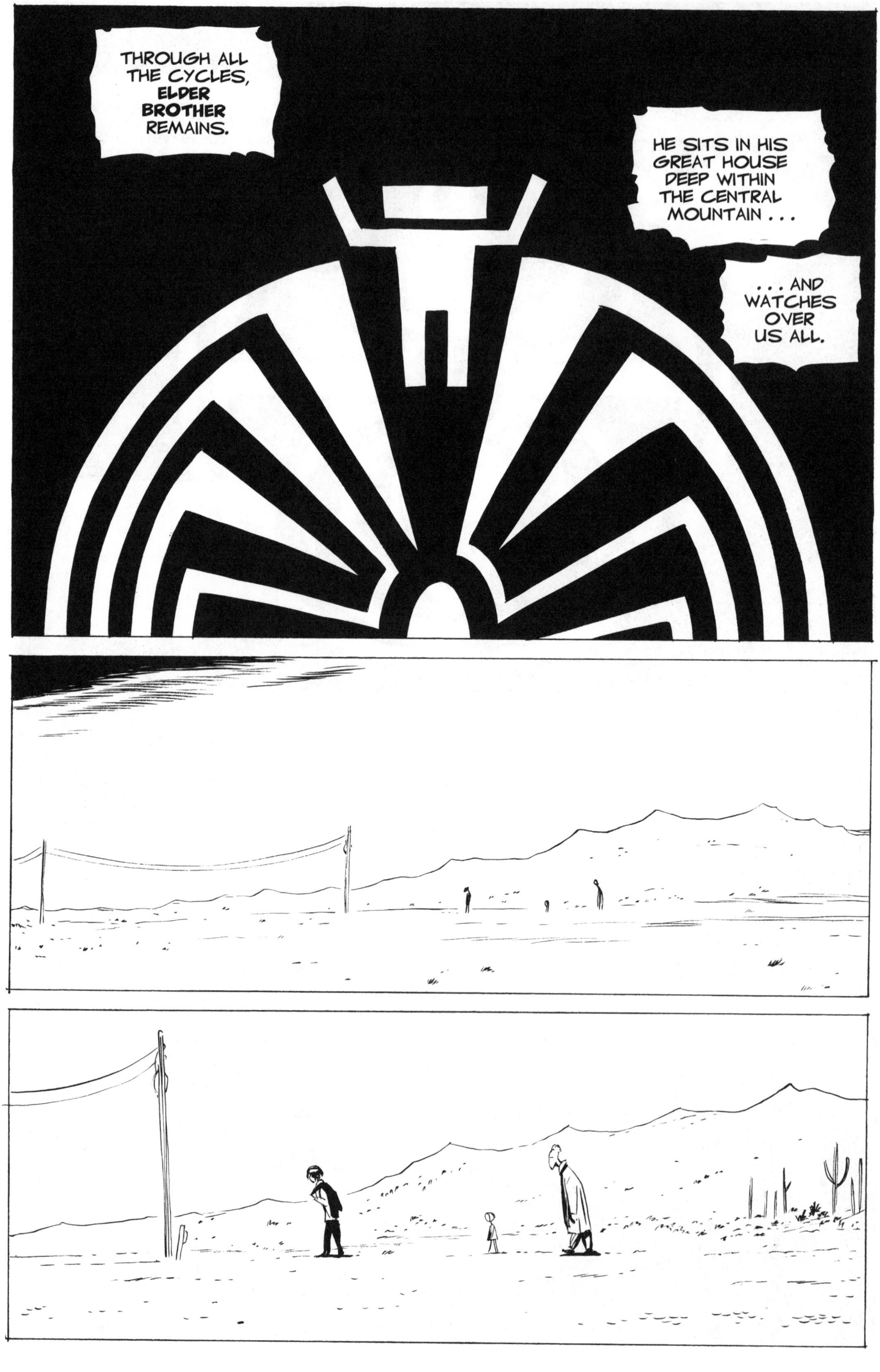
THROUGH ALL THE CYCLES, ELDER BROTHER REMAINS.
HE SITS IN HIS GREAT HOUSE DEEP WITHIN THE CENTRAL MOUNTAIN . . .
. . . AND WATCHES OVER US ALL.

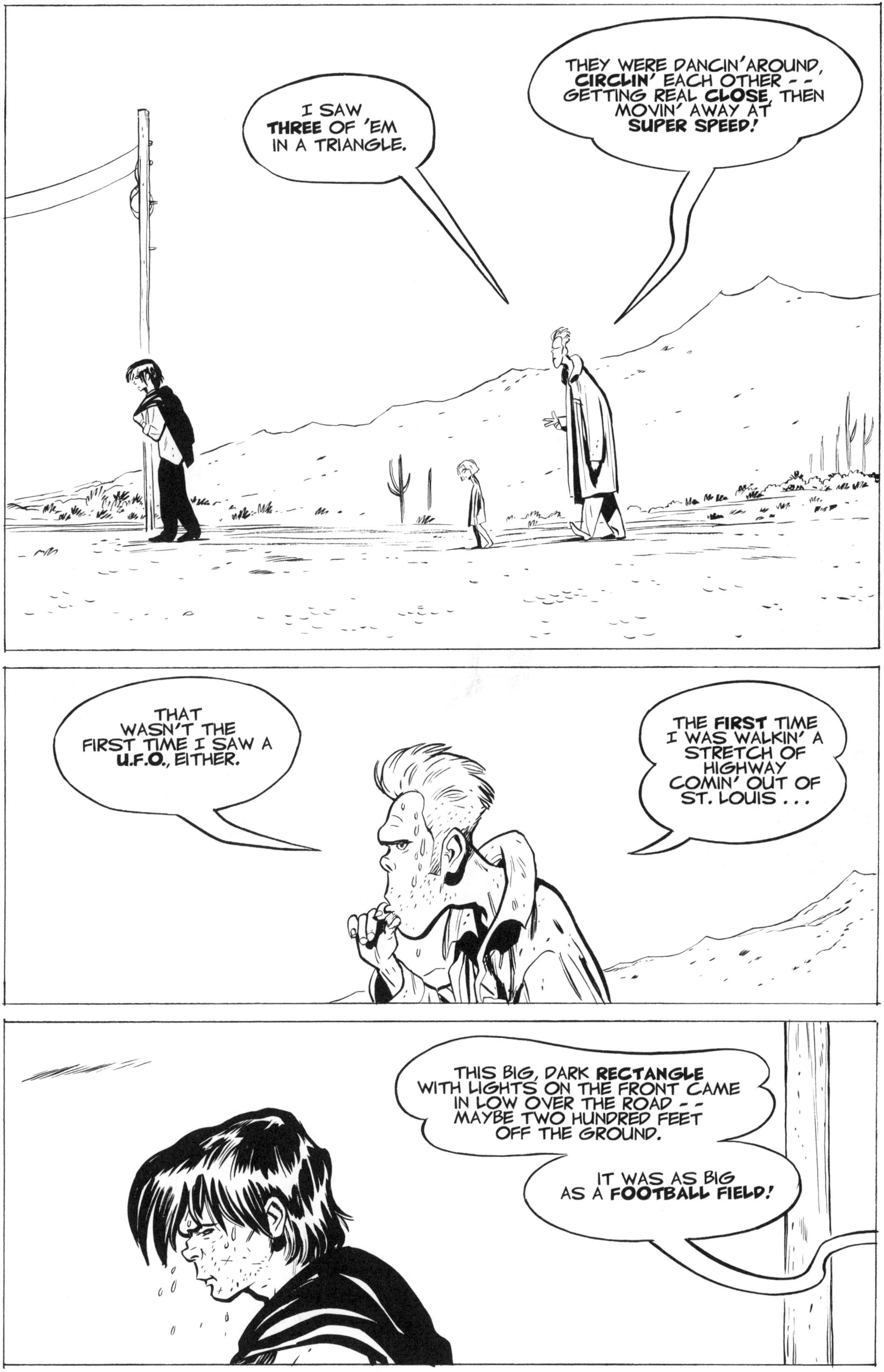
I SAW THREE OF 'EM IN A TRIANGLE.
THEY WERE DANCIN' AROUND, CIRCLIN' EACH OTHER - - GETTING REAL CLOSE, THEN MOVIN' AWAY AT SUPER SPEED!
THAT WASN'T THE FIRST TIME I SAW A U.F.O., EITHER.
THE FIRST TIME I WAS WALKIN' A STRETCH OF HIGHWAY COMIN' OUT OF ST. LOUIS . . .
THIS BIG, DARK RECTANGLE WITH LIGHTS ON THE FRONT CAME IN LOW OVER THE ROAD - - MAYBE TWO HUNDRED FEET OFF THE GROUND.
IT WAS AS BIG AS A FOOTBALL FIELD!

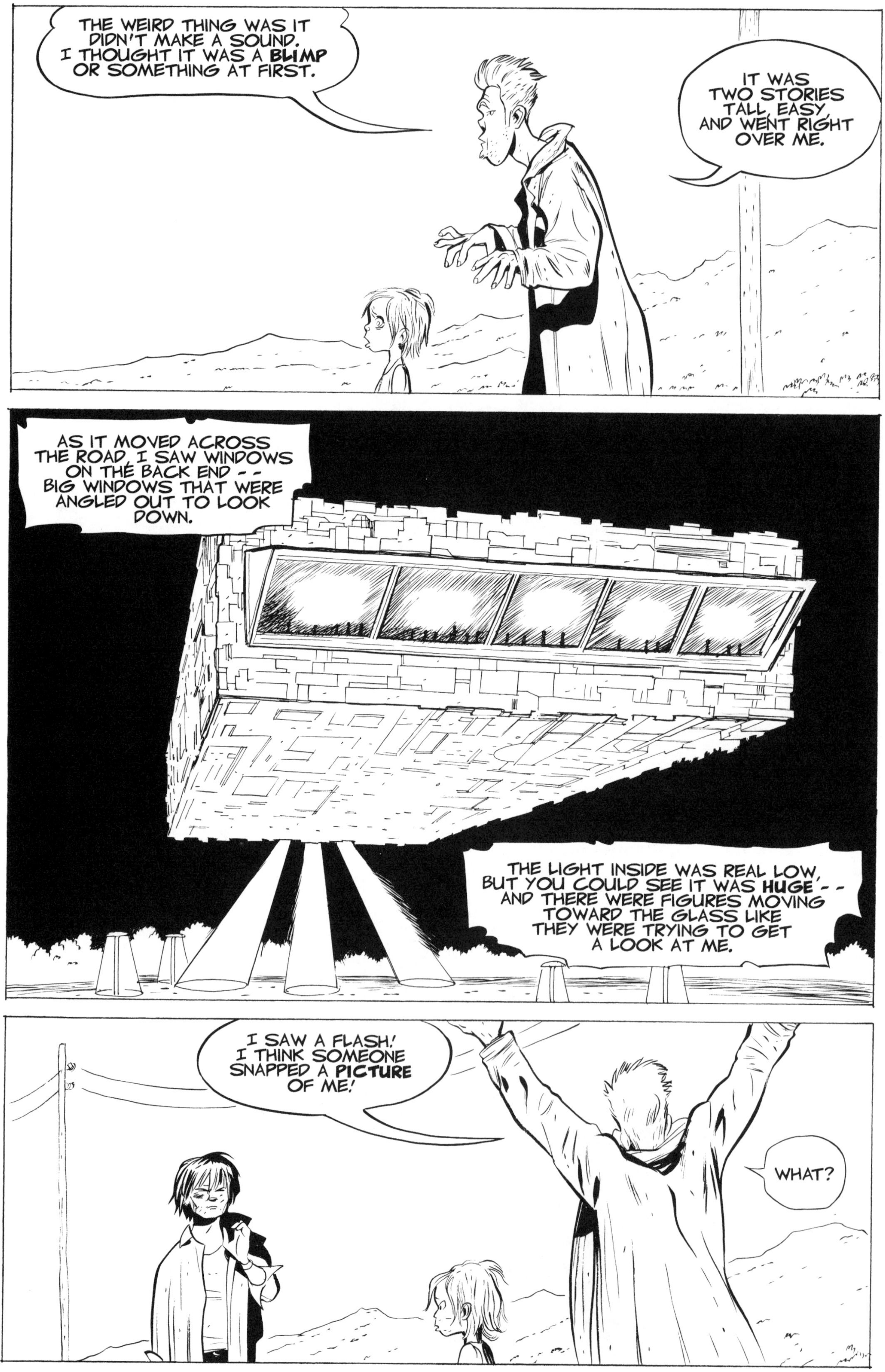
THE WEIRD THING WAS IT DIDN'T MAKE A SOUND. I THOUGHT IT WAS A BLIMP OR SOMETHING AT FIRST.
IT WAS TWO STORIES TALL, EASY, AND WENT RIGHT OVER ME.
AS IT MOVED ACROSS THE ROAD, I SAW WINDOWS ON THE BACK END -- BIG WINDOWS THAT WERE ANGLED OUT TO LOOK DOWN.
THE LIGHT INSIDE WAS REAL LOW, BUT YOU COULD SEE IT WAS HUGE -- AND THERE WERE FIGURES MOVING TOWARD THE GLASS LIKE THEY WERE TRYING TO GET A LOOK AT ME.
I SAW A FLASH! I THINK SOMEONE SNAPPED A PICTURE OF ME!
WHAT?

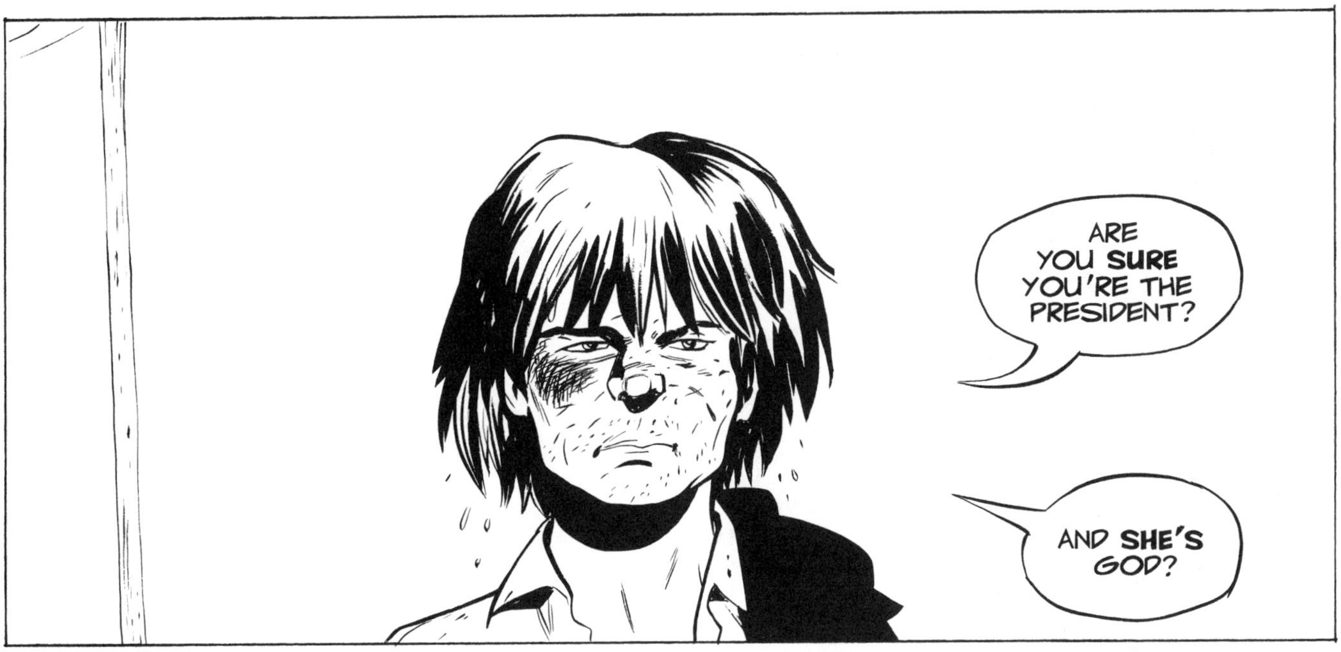
ARE YOU **SURE** YOU'RE THE PRESIDENT?
AND **SHE'S** GOD?

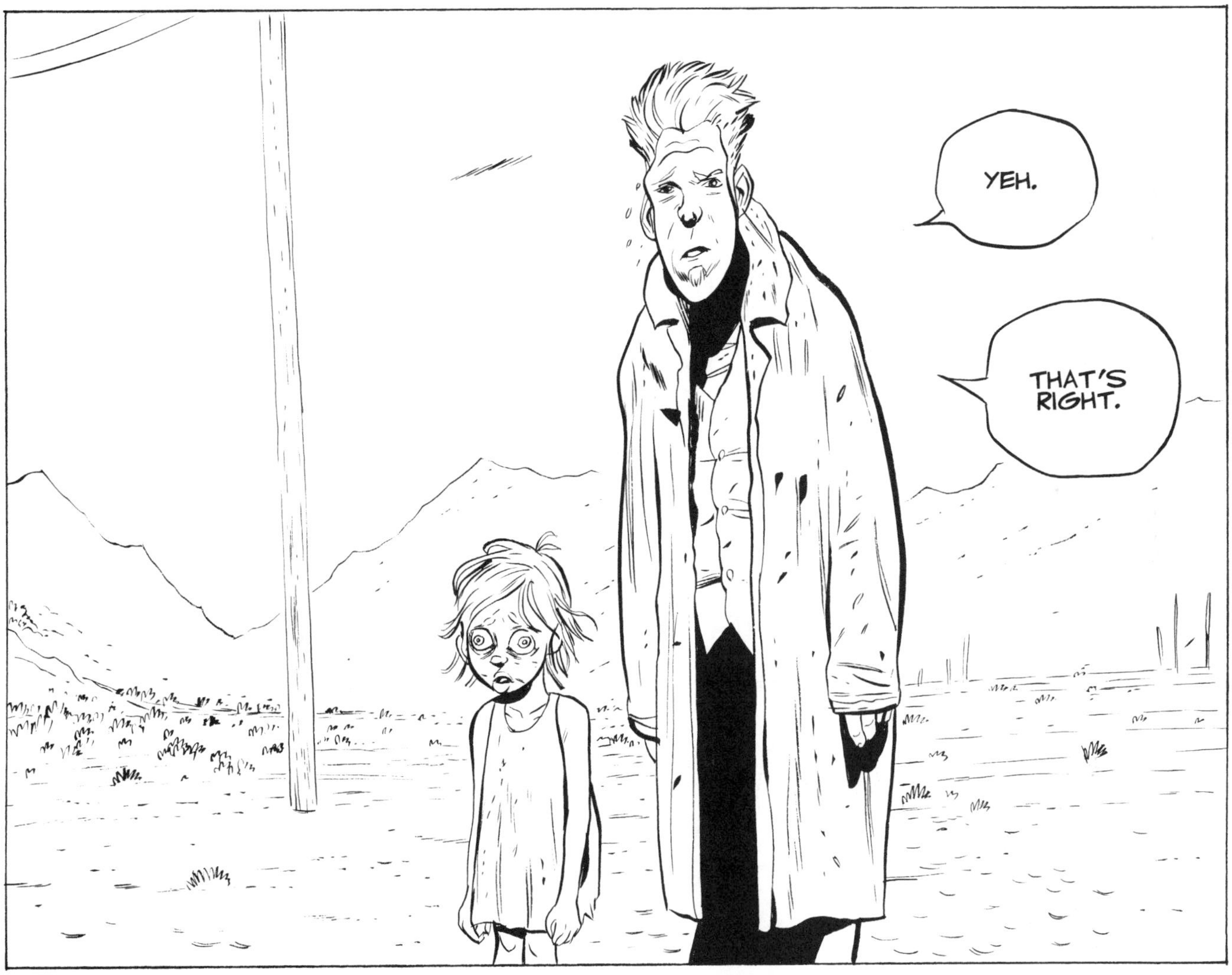
YEH.
THAT'S RIGHT.

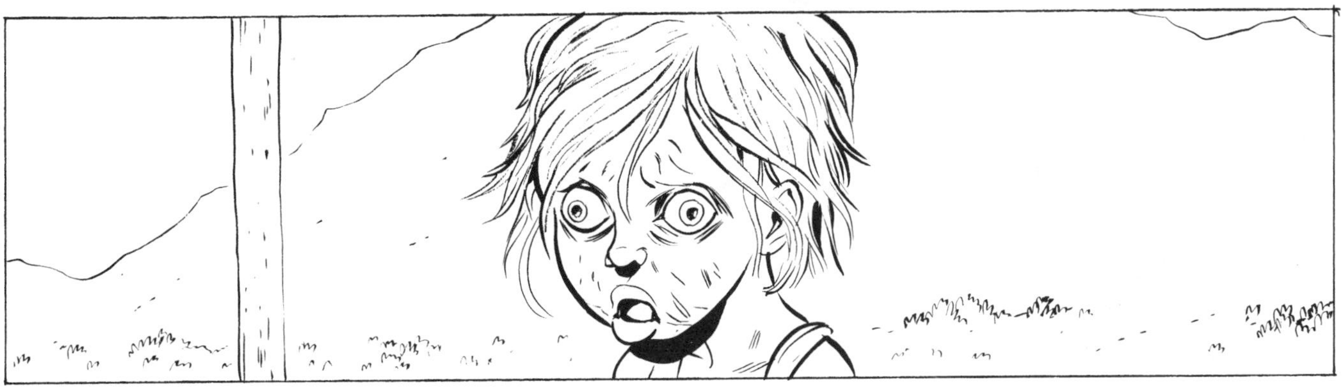

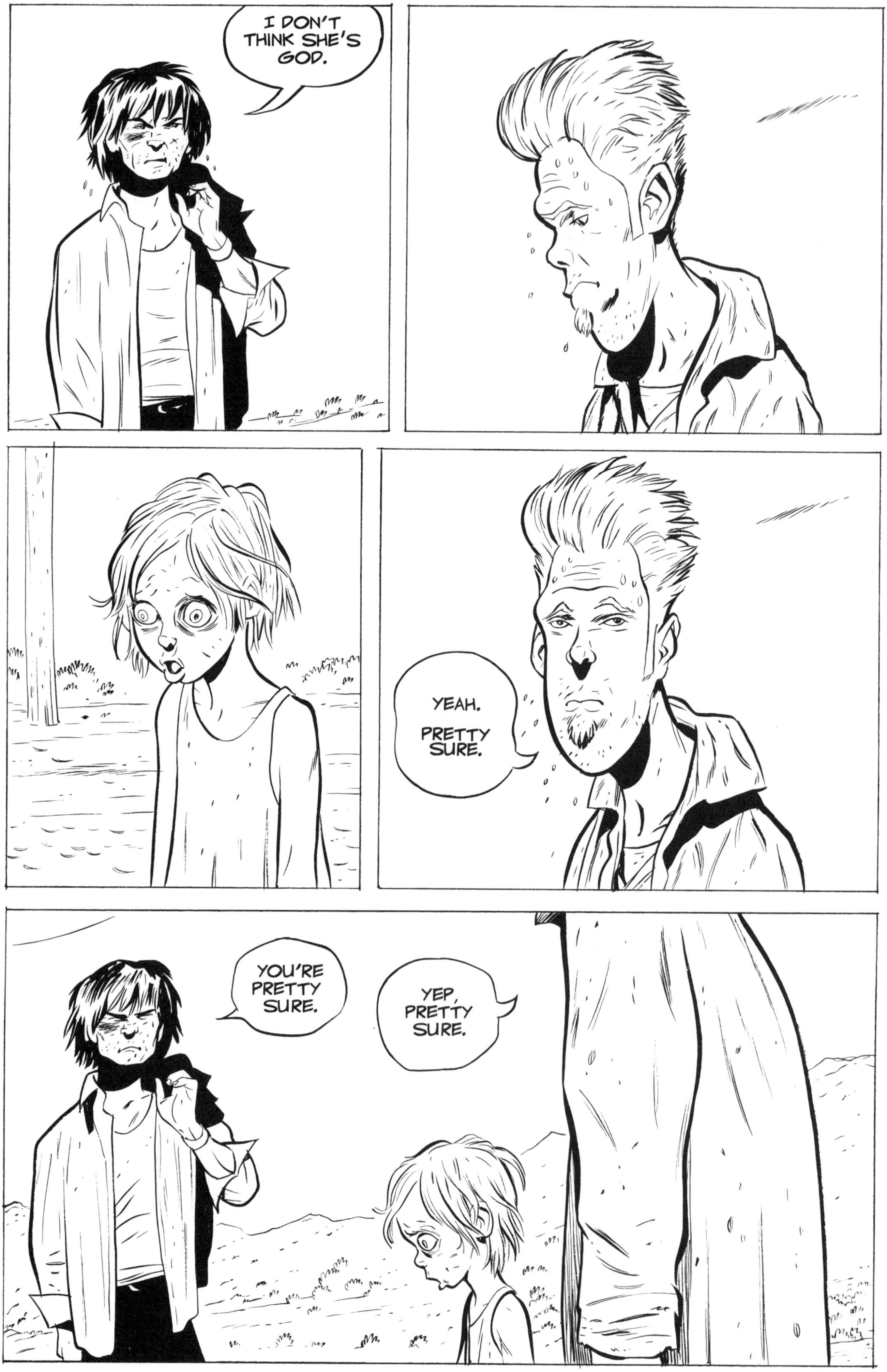
I DON'T THINK SHE'S GOD.
YEAH.
PRETTY SURE.
YOU'RE PRETTY SURE.
YEP, PRETTY SURE.

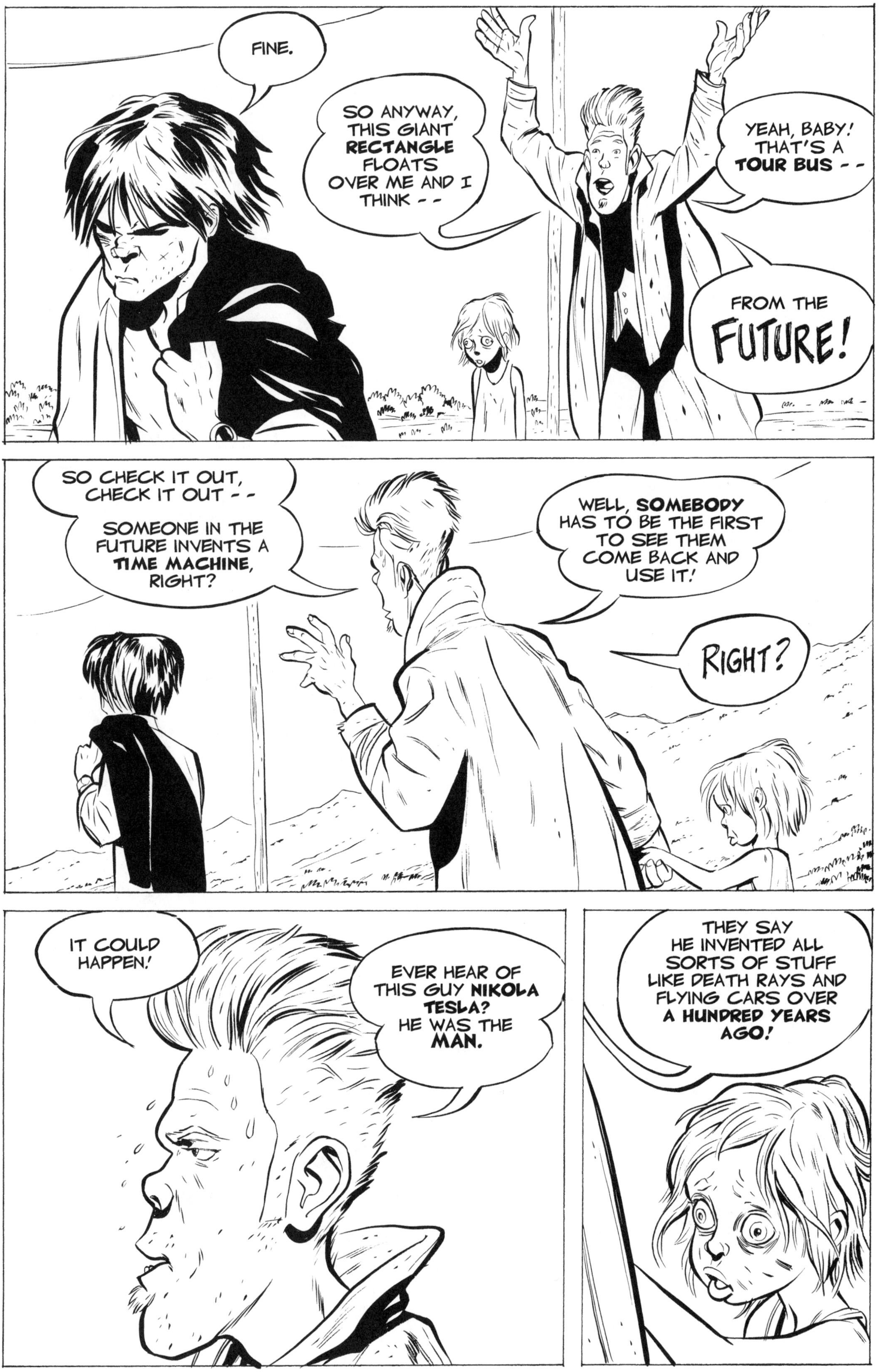
FINE.
SO ANYWAY, THIS GIANT RECTANGLE FLOATS OVER ME AND I THINK - -
YEAH, BABY! THAT'S A TOUR BUS - -
FROM THE FUTURE!
SO CHECK IT OUT, CHECK IT OUT - -
SOMEONE IN THE FUTURE INVENTS A TIME MACHINE, RIGHT?
WELL, SOMEBODY HAS TO BE THE FIRST TO SEE THEM COME BACK AND USE IT!
RIGHT?
IT COULD HAPPEN!
EVER HEAR OF THIS GUY NIKOLA TESLA? HE WAS THE MAN.
THEY SAY HE INVENTED ALL SORTS OF STUFF LIKE DEATH RAYS AND FLYING CARS OVER A HUNDRED YEARS AGO!

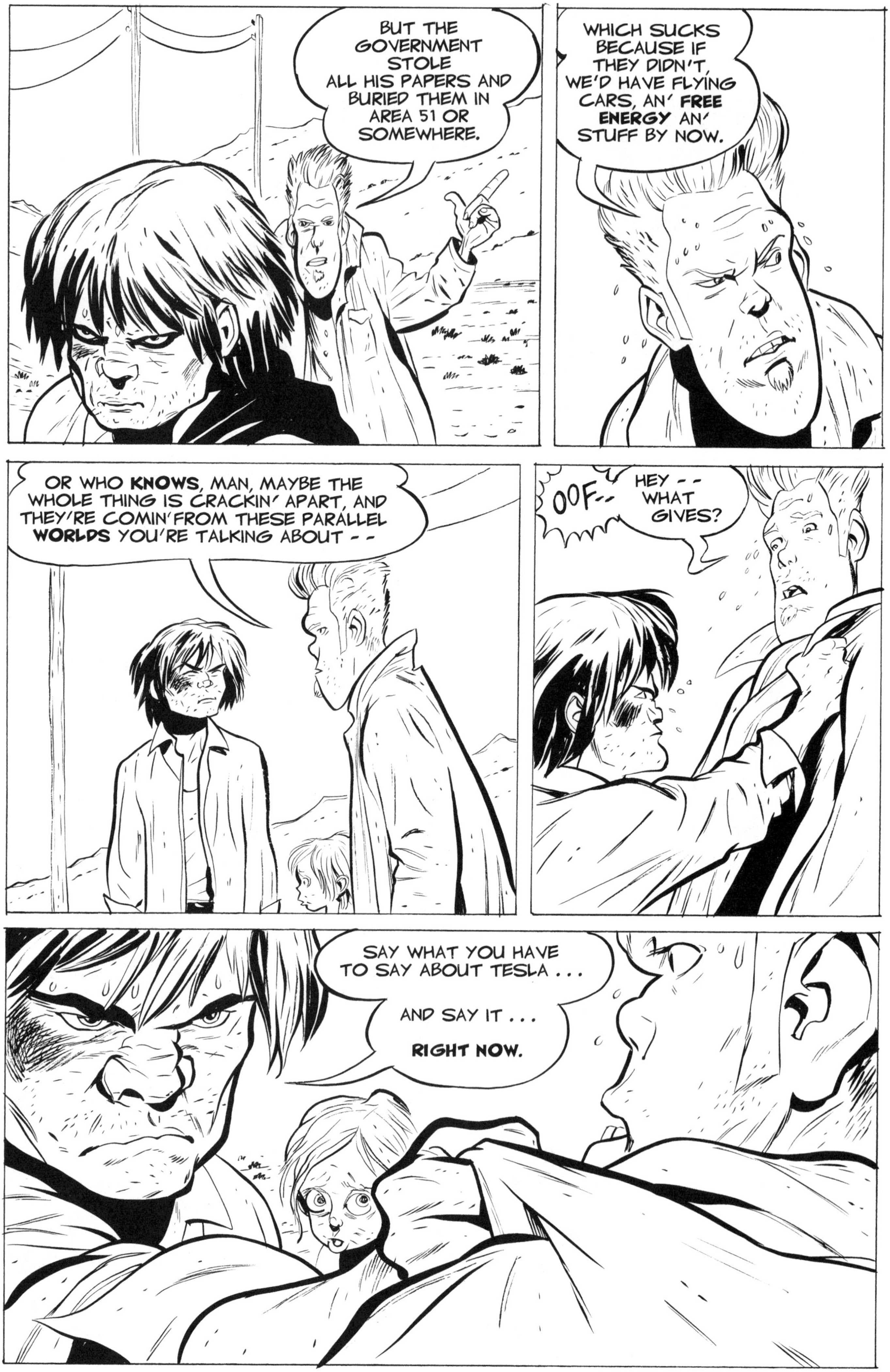
BUT THE GOVERNMENT STOLE ALL HIS PAPERS AND BURIED THEM IN AREA 51 OR SOMEWHERE.
WHICH SUCKS BECAUSE IF THEY DIDN'T, WE'D HAVE FLYING CARS, AN' FREE ENERGY AN' STUFF BY NOW.
OR WHO KNOWS, MAN, MAYBE THE WHOLE THING IS CRACKIN' APART, AND THEY'RE COMIN' FROM THESE PARALLEL WORLDS YOU'RE TALKING ABOUT - -
OOF - -
HEY - - WHAT GIVES?
SAY WHAT YOU HAVE TO SAY ABOUT TESLA . . .
AND SAY IT . . .
RIGHT NOW.

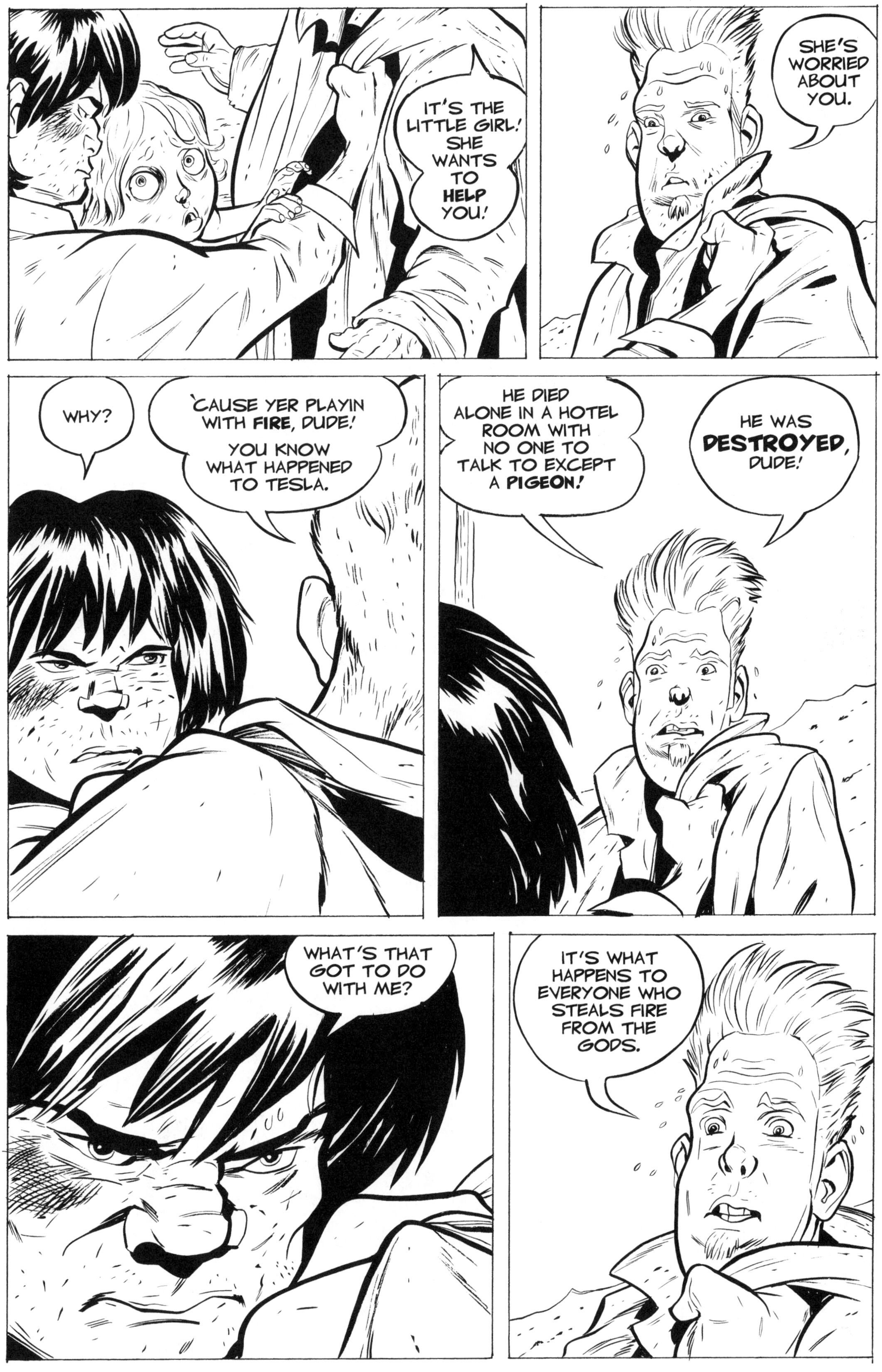
IT'S THE LITTLE GIRL! SHE WANTS TO **HELP** YOU!
SHE'S WORRIED ABOUT YOU.
WHY?
'CAUSE YER PLAYIN WITH **FIRE**, DUDE!
YOU KNOW WHAT HAPPENED TO TESLA.
HE DIED ALONE IN A HOTEL ROOM WITH NO ONE TO TALK TO EXCEPT A **PIGEON**!
HE WAS **DESTROYED**, DUDE!
WHAT'S THAT GOT TO DO WITH ME?
IT'S WHAT HAPPENS TO EVERYONE WHO STEALS FIRE FROM THE GODS.

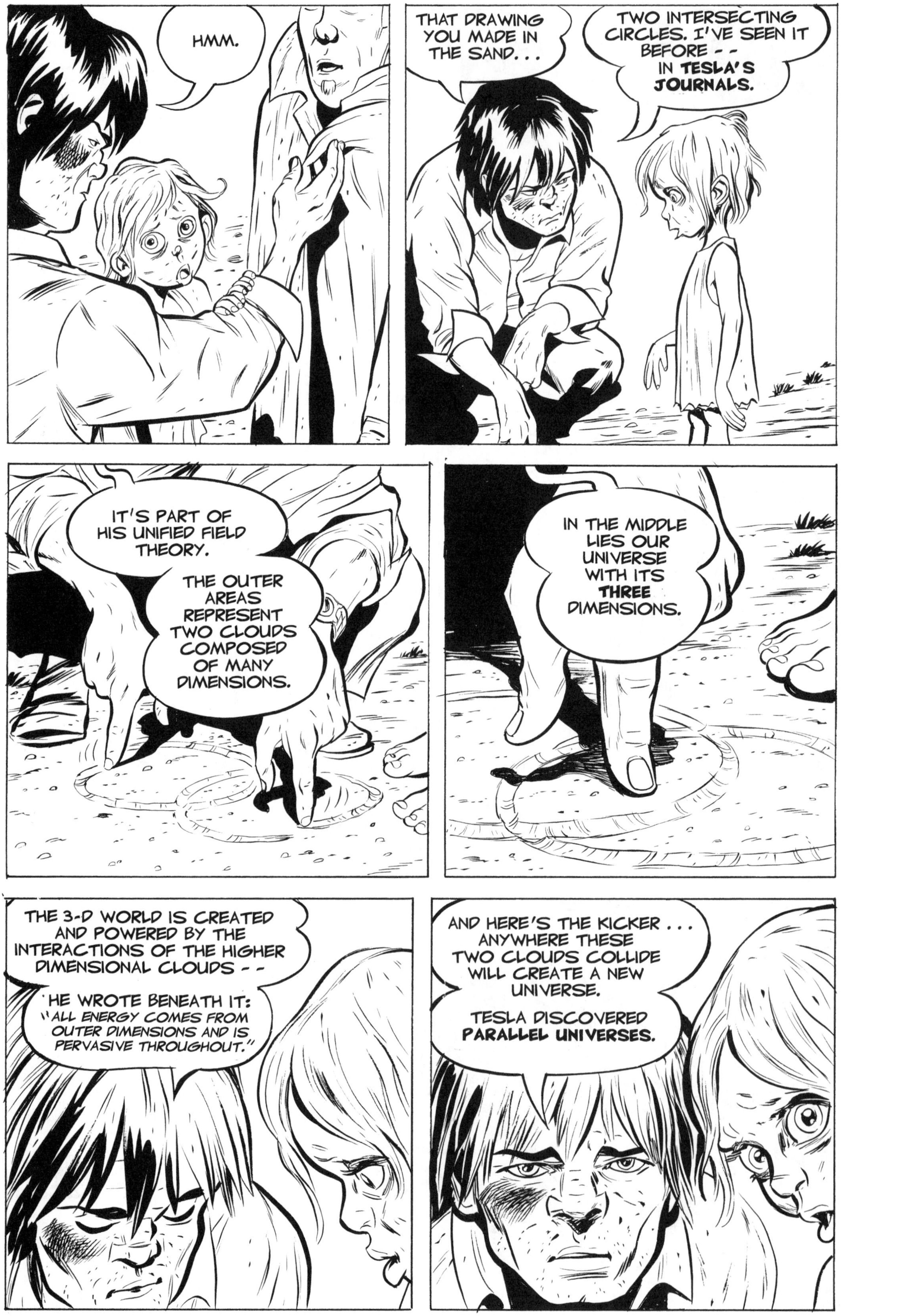
HMM.
THAT DRAWING YOU MADE IN THE SAND...
TWO INTERSECTING CIRCLES. I'VE SEEN IT BEFORE -- IN TESLA'S JOURNALS.
IT'S PART OF HIS UNIFIED FIELD THEORY.
THE OUTER AREAS REPRESENT TWO CLOUDS COMPOSED OF MANY DIMENSIONS.
IN THE MIDDLE LIES OUR UNIVERSE WITH ITS THREE DIMENSIONS.
THE 3-D WORLD IS CREATED AND POWERED BY THE INTERACTIONS OF THE HIGHER DIMENSIONAL CLOUDS --
HE WROTE BENEATH IT: "ALL ENERGY COMES FROM OUTER DIMENSIONS AND IS PERVASIVE THROUGHOUT."
AND HERE'S THE KICKER... ANYWHERE THESE TWO CLOUDS COLLIDE WILL CREATE A NEW UNIVERSE.
TESLA DISCOVERED PARALLEL UNIVERSES.

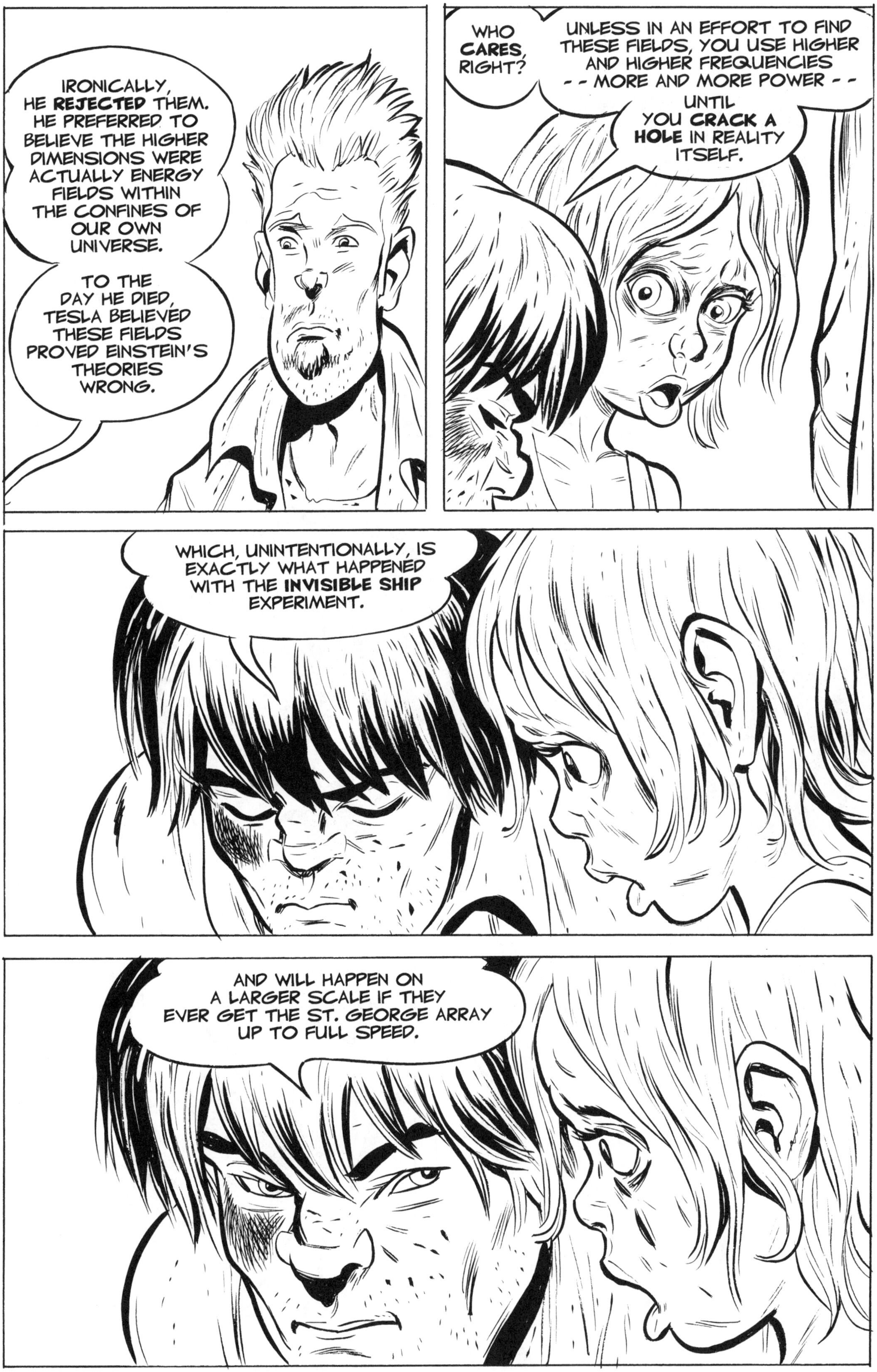
IRONICALLY, HE REJECTED THEM. HE PREFERRED TO BELIEVE THE HIGHER DIMENSIONS WERE ACTUALLY ENERGY FIELDS WITHIN THE CONFINES OF OUR OWN UNIVERSE.
TO THE DAY HE DIED, TESLA BELIEVED THESE FIELDS PROVED EINSTEIN'S THEORIES WRONG.
WHO CARES, RIGHT?
UNLESS IN AN EFFORT TO FIND THESE FIELDS, YOU USE HIGHER AND HIGHER FREQUENCIES - - MORE AND MORE POWER - -
UNTIL YOU CRACK A HOLE IN REALITY ITSELF.
WHICH, UNINTENTIONALLY, IS EXACTLY WHAT HAPPENED WITH THE INVISIBLE SHIP EXPERIMENT.
AND WILL HAPPEN ON A LARGER SCALE IF THEY EVER GET THE ST. GEORGE ARRAY UP TO FULL SPEED.

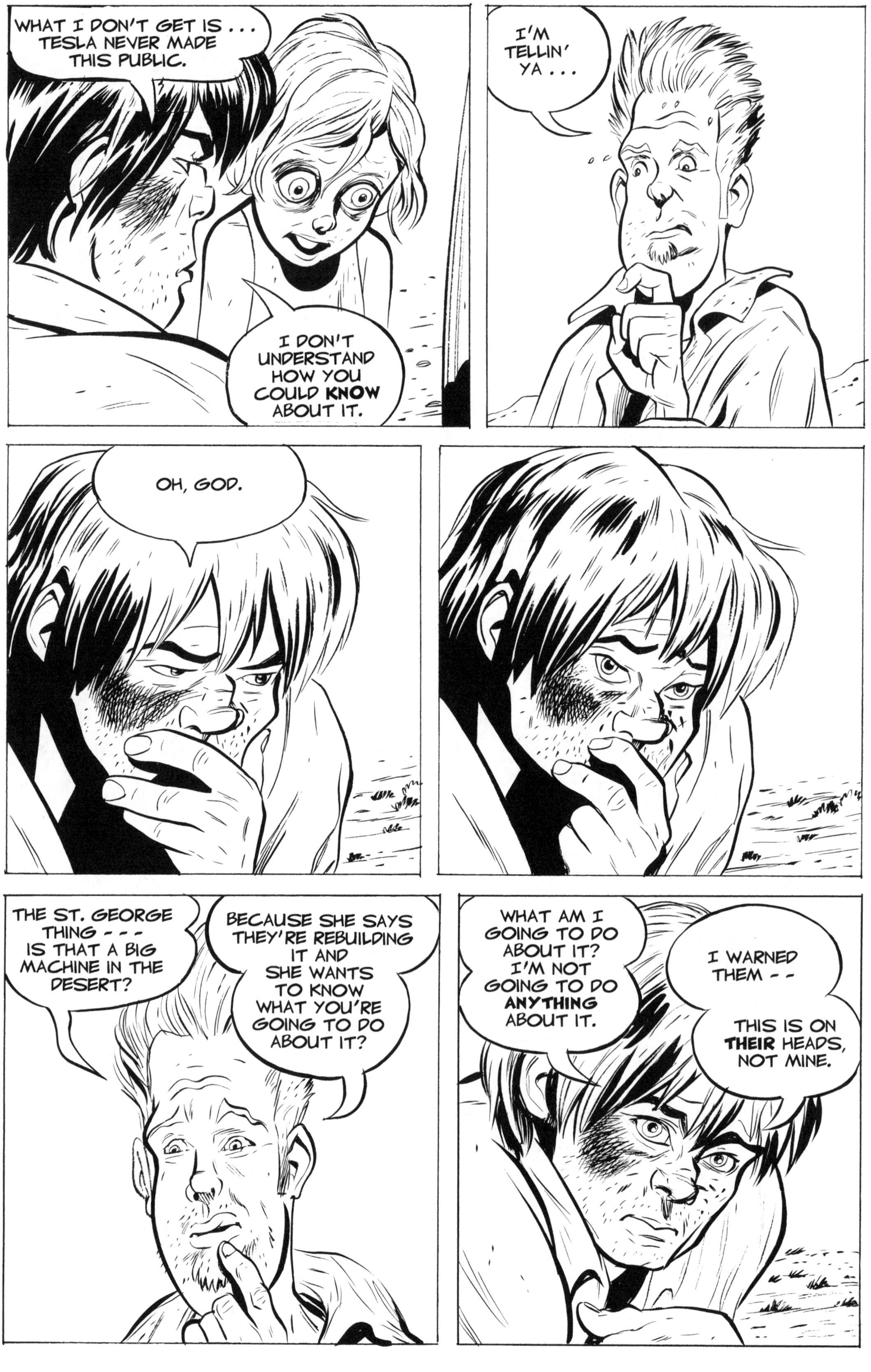
WHAT I DON'T GET IS . . . TESLA NEVER MADE THIS PUBLIC.
I DON'T UNDERSTAND HOW YOU COULD KNOW ABOUT IT.
I'M TELLIN' YA . . .
OH, GOD.
THE ST. GEORGE THING - - - IS THAT A BIG MACHINE IN THE DESERT?
BECAUSE SHE SAYS THEY'RE REBUILDING IT AND SHE WANTS TO KNOW WHAT YOU'RE GOING TO DO ABOUT IT?
WHAT AM I GOING TO DO ABOUT IT? I'M NOT GOING TO DO ANYTHING ABOUT IT.
I WARNED THEM - -
THIS IS ON THEIR HEADS, NOT MINE.

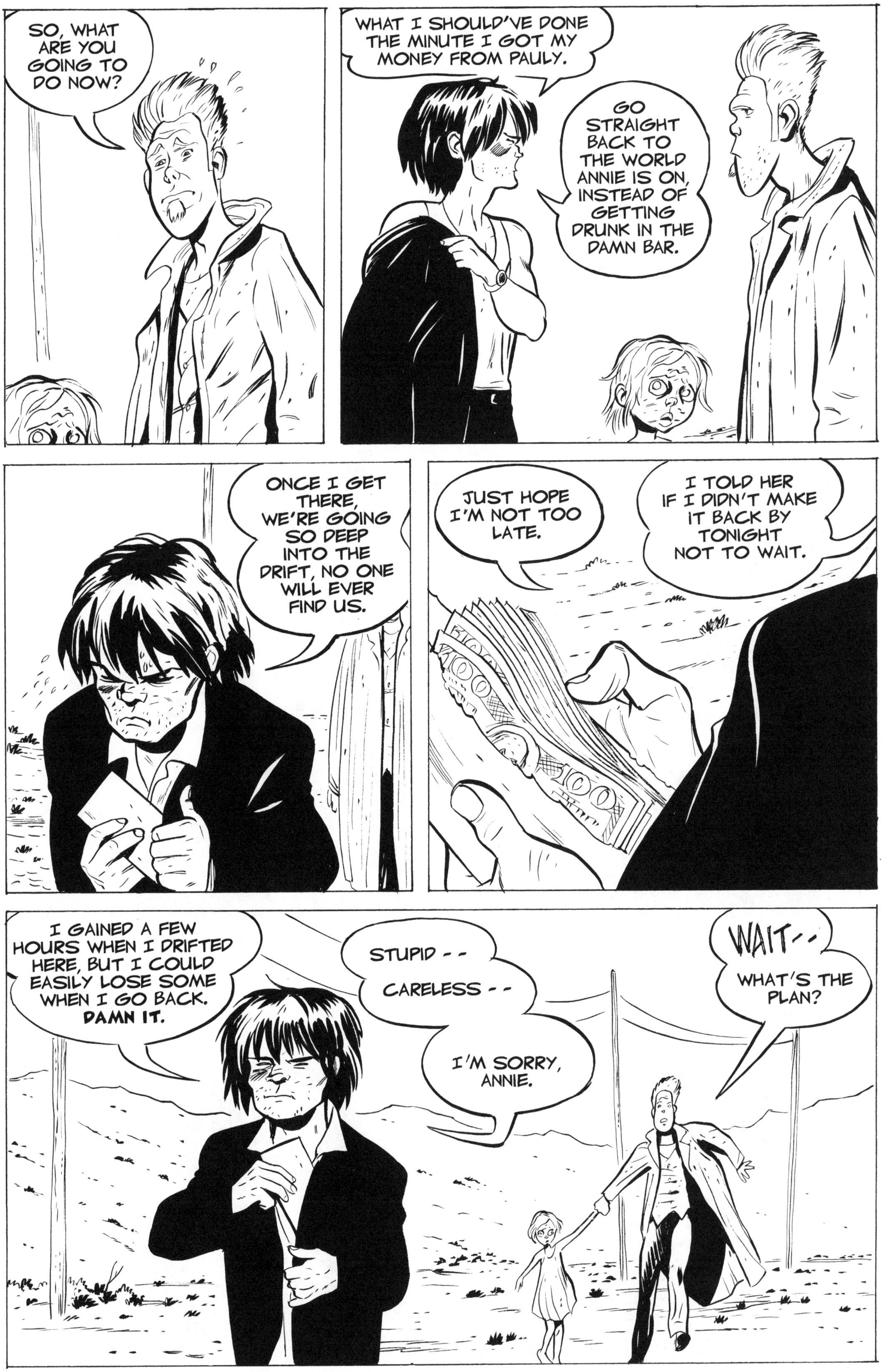

SO, WHAT ARE YOU GOING TO DO NOW?
WHAT I SHOULD'VE DONE THE MINUTE I GOT MY MONEY FROM PAULY.
GO STRAIGHT BACK TO THE WORLD ANNIE IS ON, INSTEAD OF GETTING DRUNK IN THE DAMN BAR.
ONCE I GET THERE, WE'RE GOING SO DEEP INTO THE DRIFT, NO ONE WILL EVER FIND US.
JUST HOPE I'M NOT TOO LATE.
I TOLD HER IF I DIDN'T MAKE IT BACK BY TONIGHT NOT TO WAIT.
I GAINED A FEW HOURS WHEN I DRIFTED HERE, BUT I COULD EASILY LOSE SOME WHEN I GO BACK. **DAMN IT.**
STUPID - -
CARELESS - -
I'M SORRY, ANNIE.
WAIT- -
WHAT'S THE PLAN?

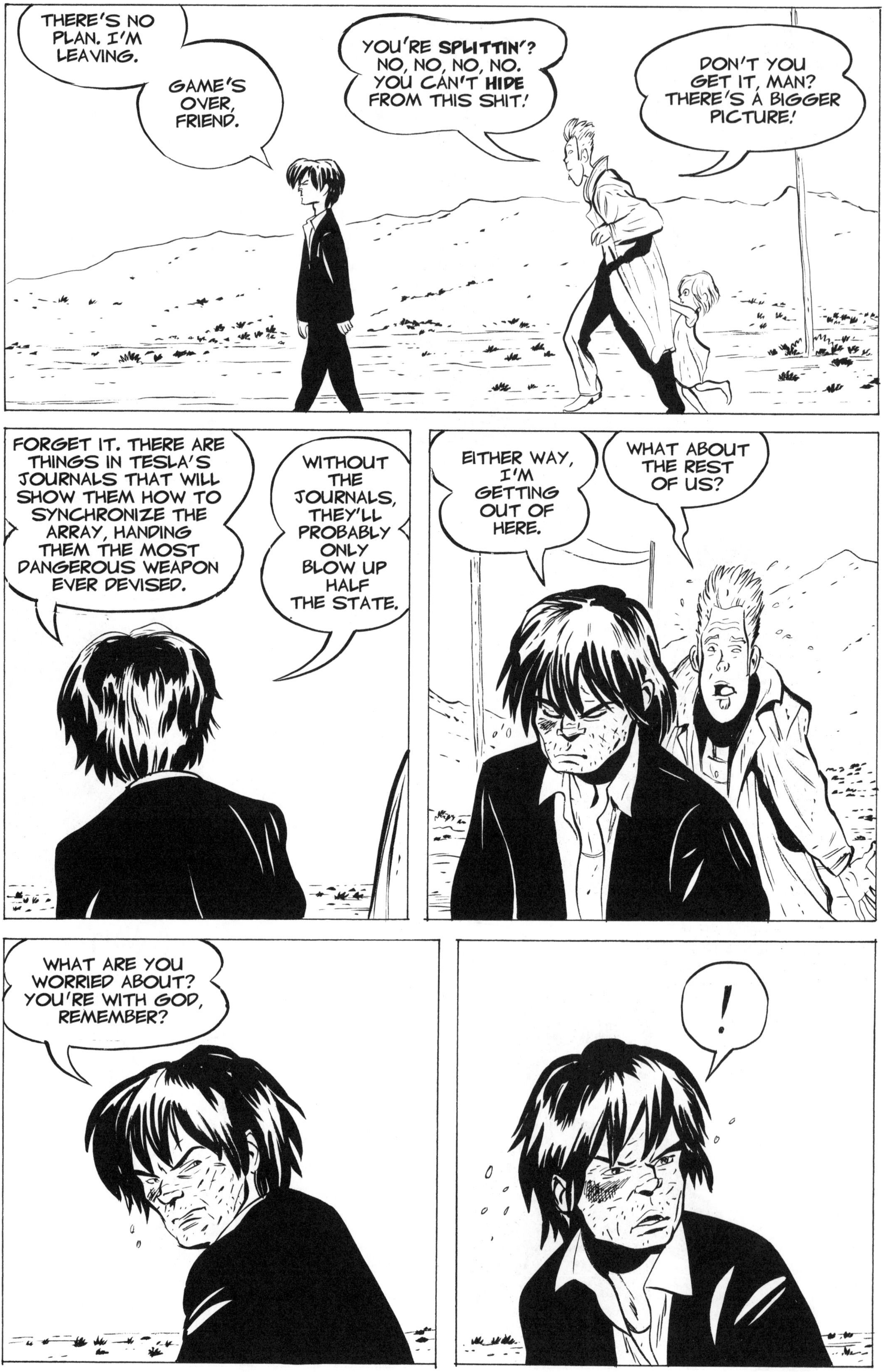
THERE'S NO PLAN. I'M LEAVING.
GAME'S OVER, FRIEND.
YOU'RE **SPLITTIN'**? NO, NO, NO, NO. YOU CAN'T **HIDE** FROM THIS SHIT!
DON'T YOU GET IT, MAN? THERE'S A BIGGER PICTURE!
FORGET IT. THERE ARE THINGS IN TESLA'S JOURNALS THAT WILL SHOW THEM HOW TO SYNCHRONIZE THE ARRAY, HANDING THEM THE MOST DANGEROUS WEAPON EVER DEVISED.
WITHOUT THE JOURNALS, THEY'LL PROBABLY ONLY BLOW UP HALF THE STATE.
EITHER WAY, I'M GETTING OUT OF HERE.
WHAT ABOUT THE REST OF US?
WHAT ARE YOU WORRIED ABOUT? YOU'RE WITH GOD, REMEMBER?
!

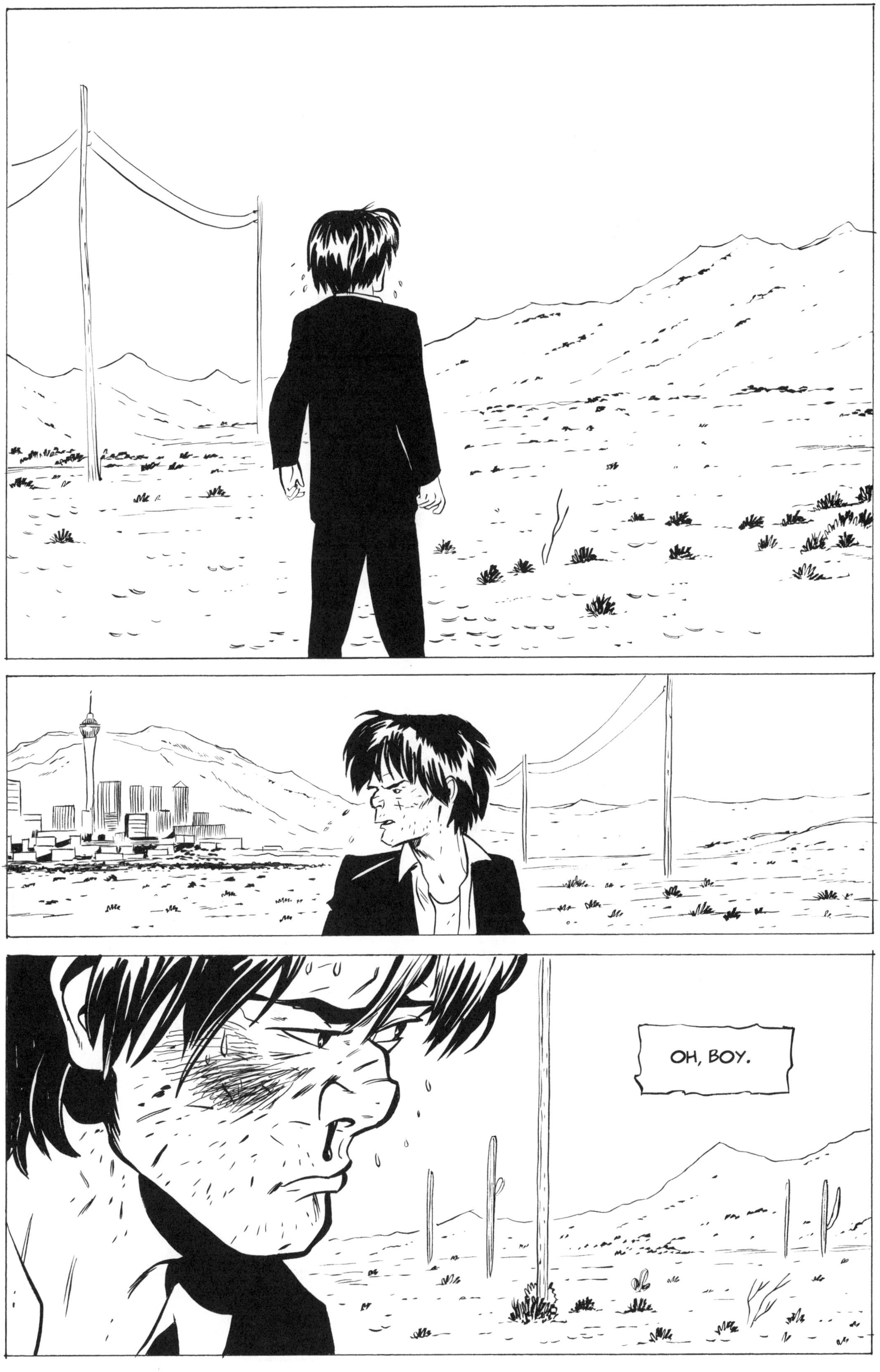
OH, BOY.

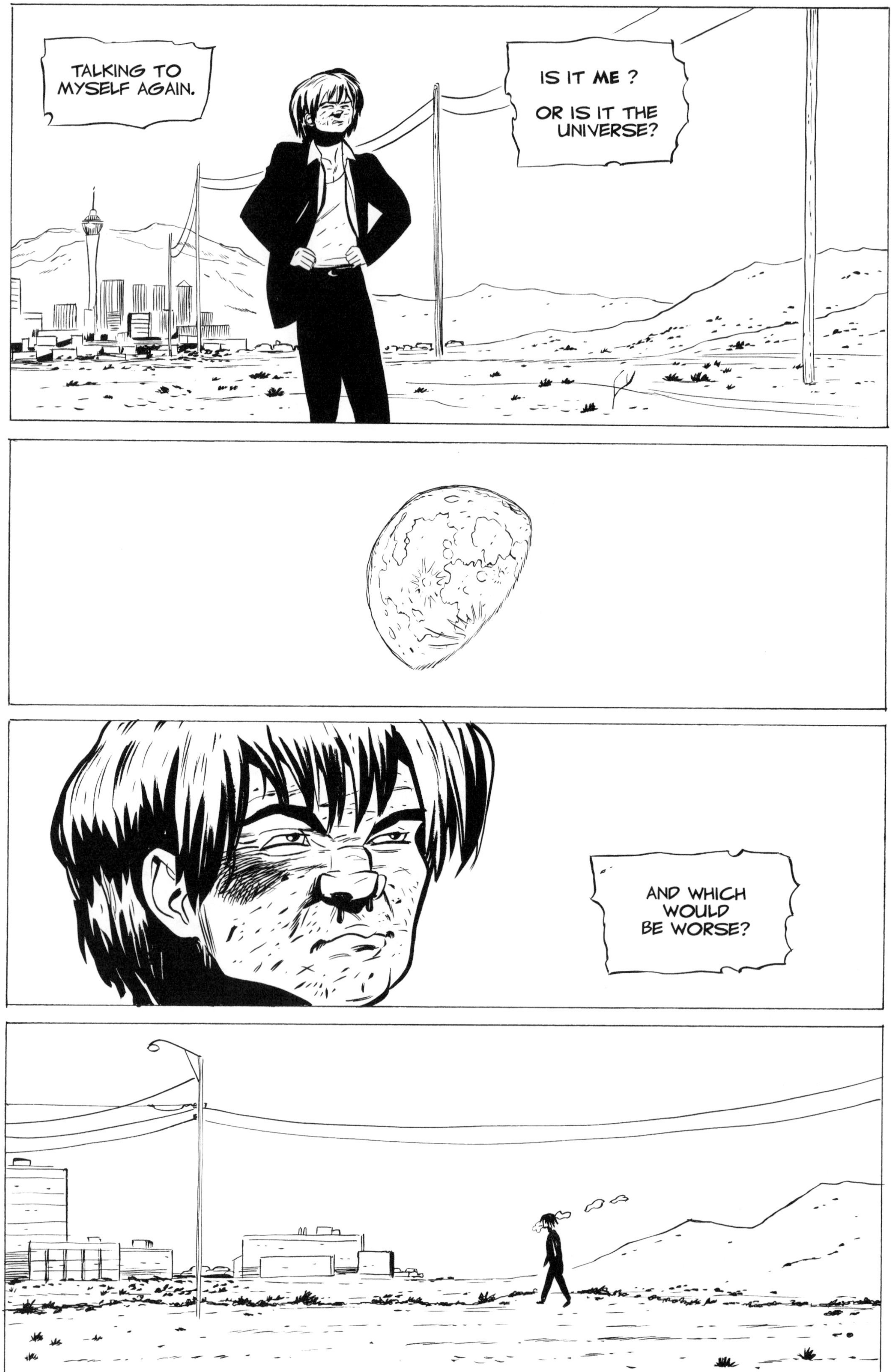
TALKING TO MYSELF AGAIN.
IS IT ME ?
OR IS IT THE UNIVERSE?
AND WHICH WOULD BE WORSE?

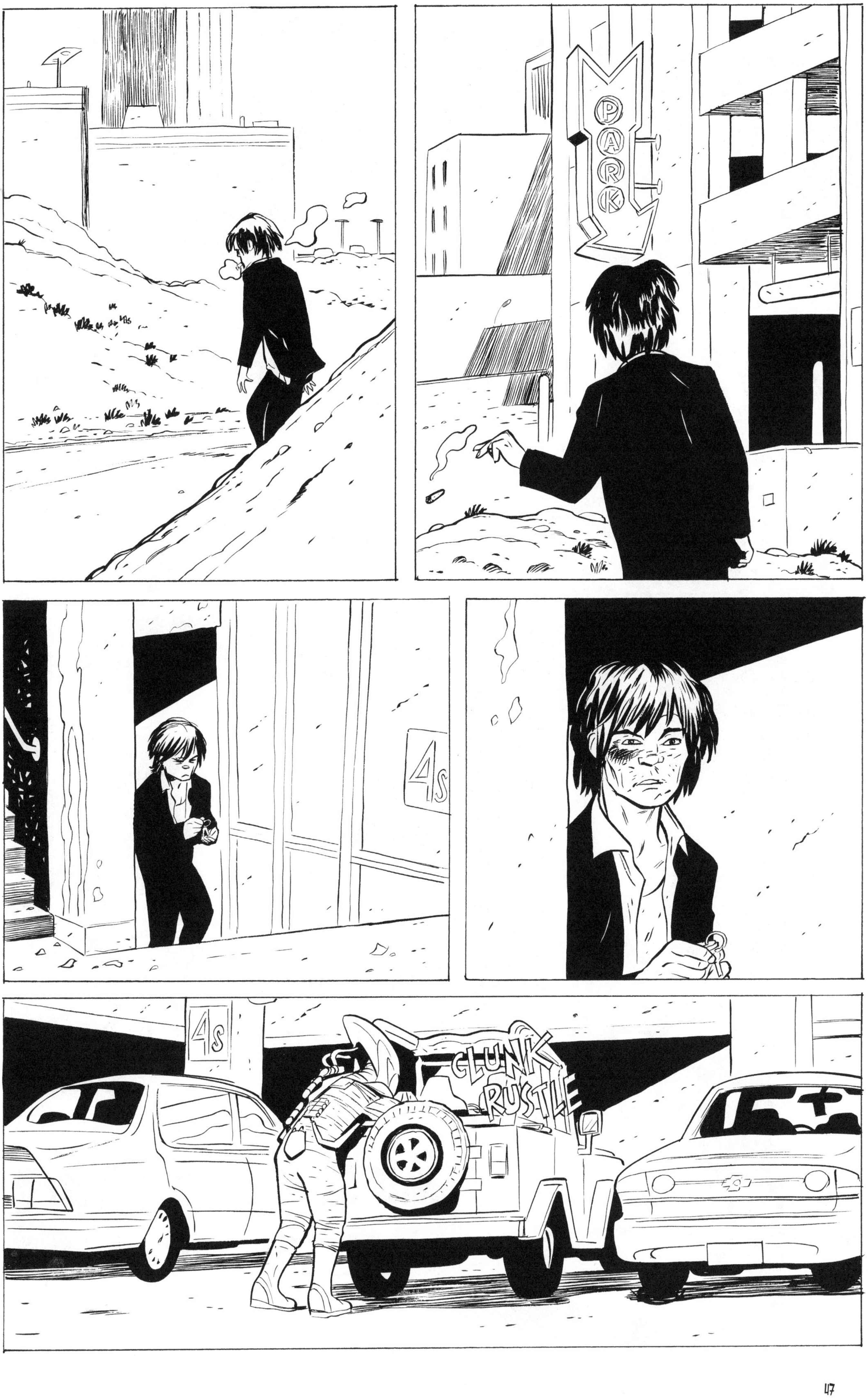
PARK
4s
4s
CLUNK
RUSTLE

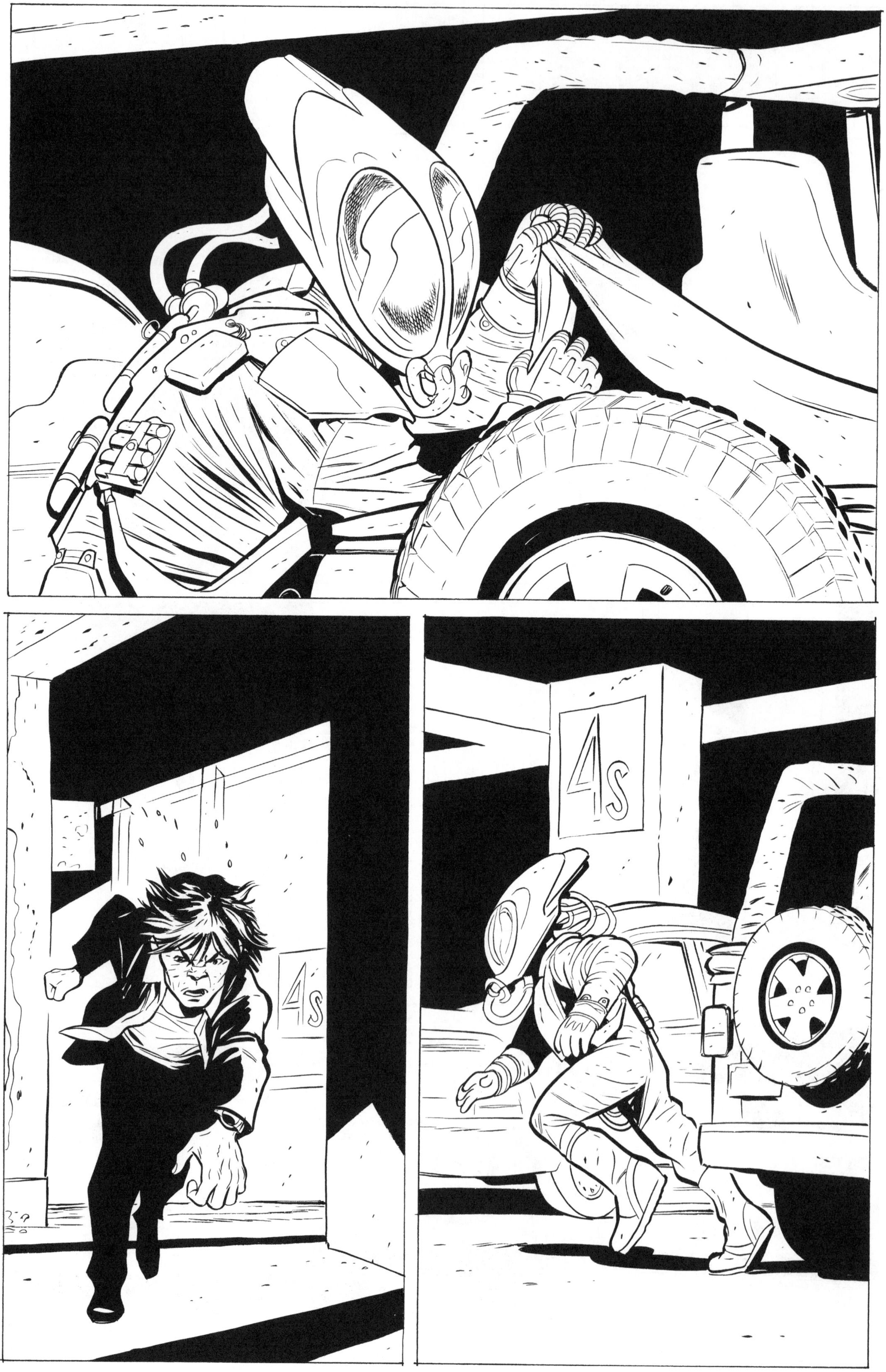
4s
4s

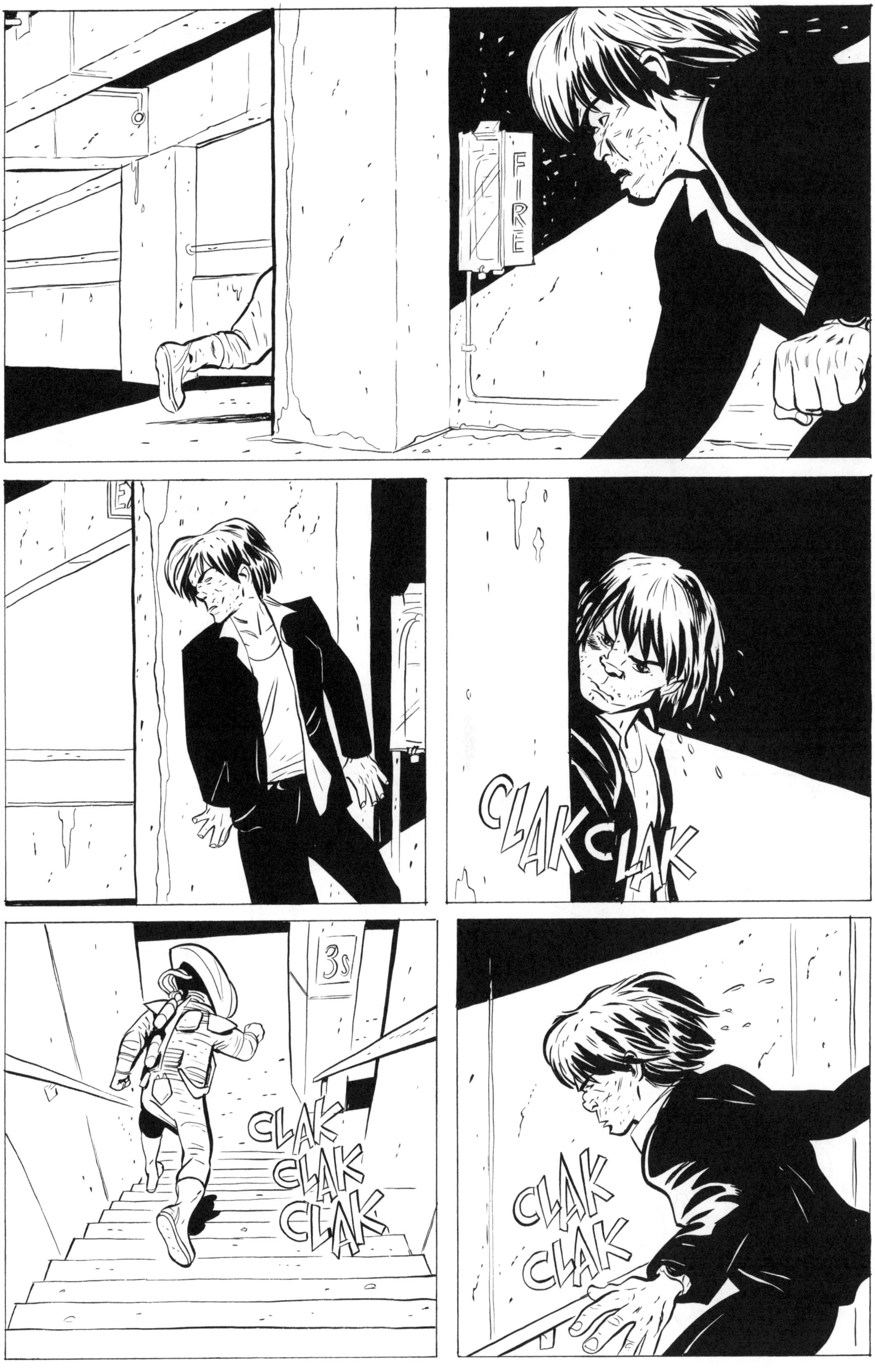
FIRE
CLAK CLAK
3s
CLAK
CLAK
CLAK
CLAK
CLAK

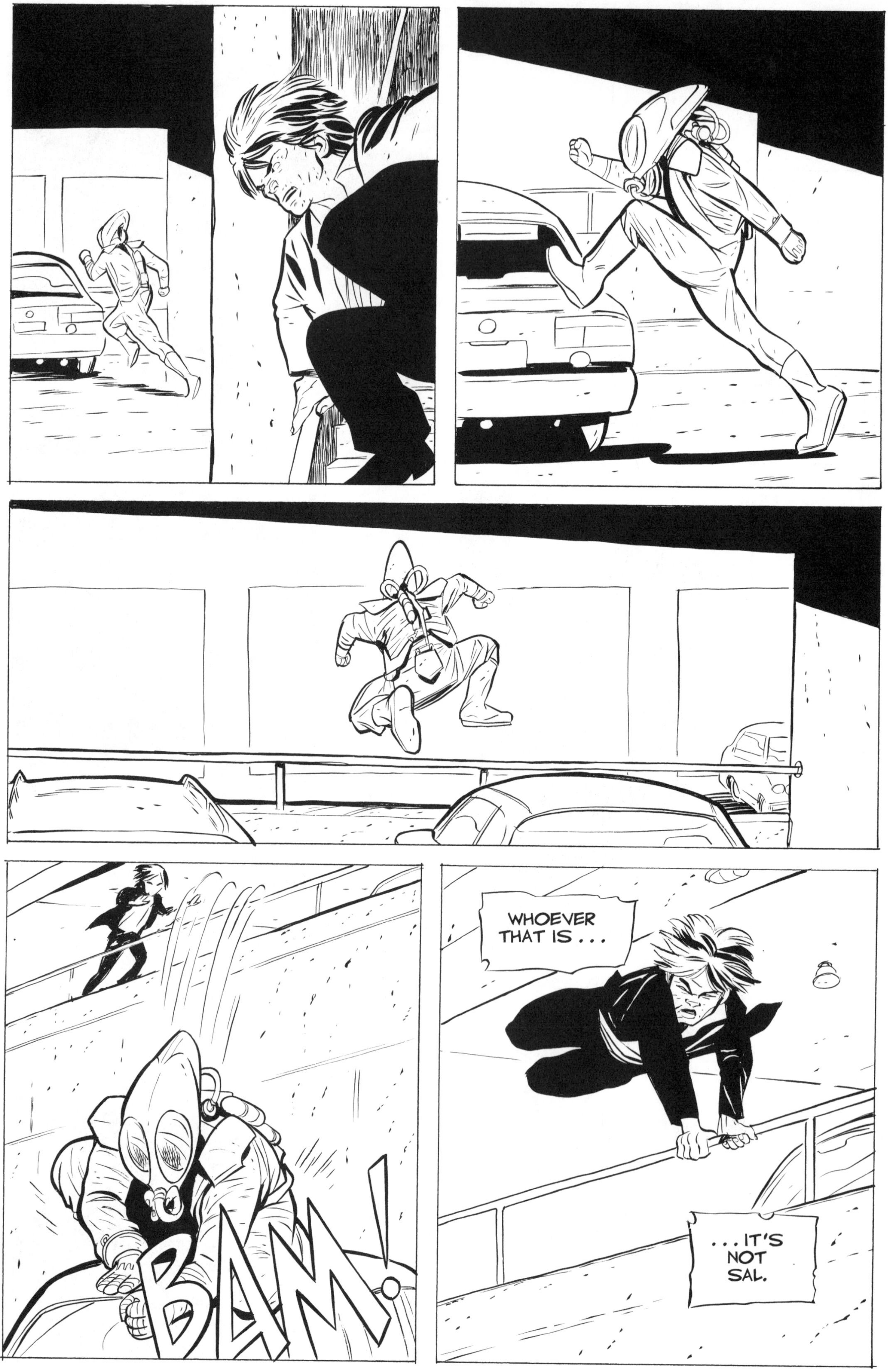
BAM!
WHOEVER THAT IS . . .
. . . IT'S NOT SAL.

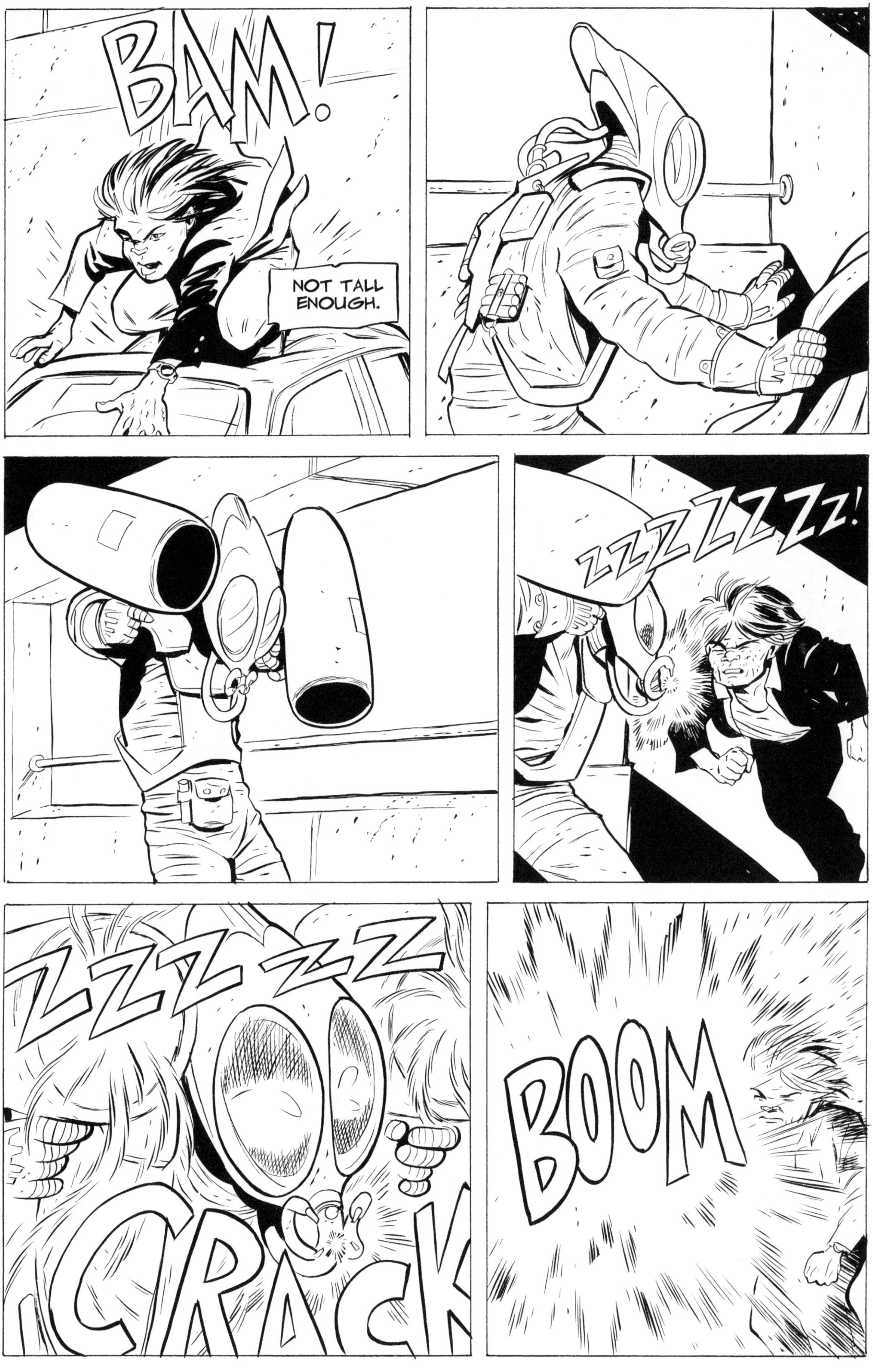
BAM!
NOT TALL ENOUGH.
ZZZZZZZZ!
ZZZZZZ
CRACK
BOOM

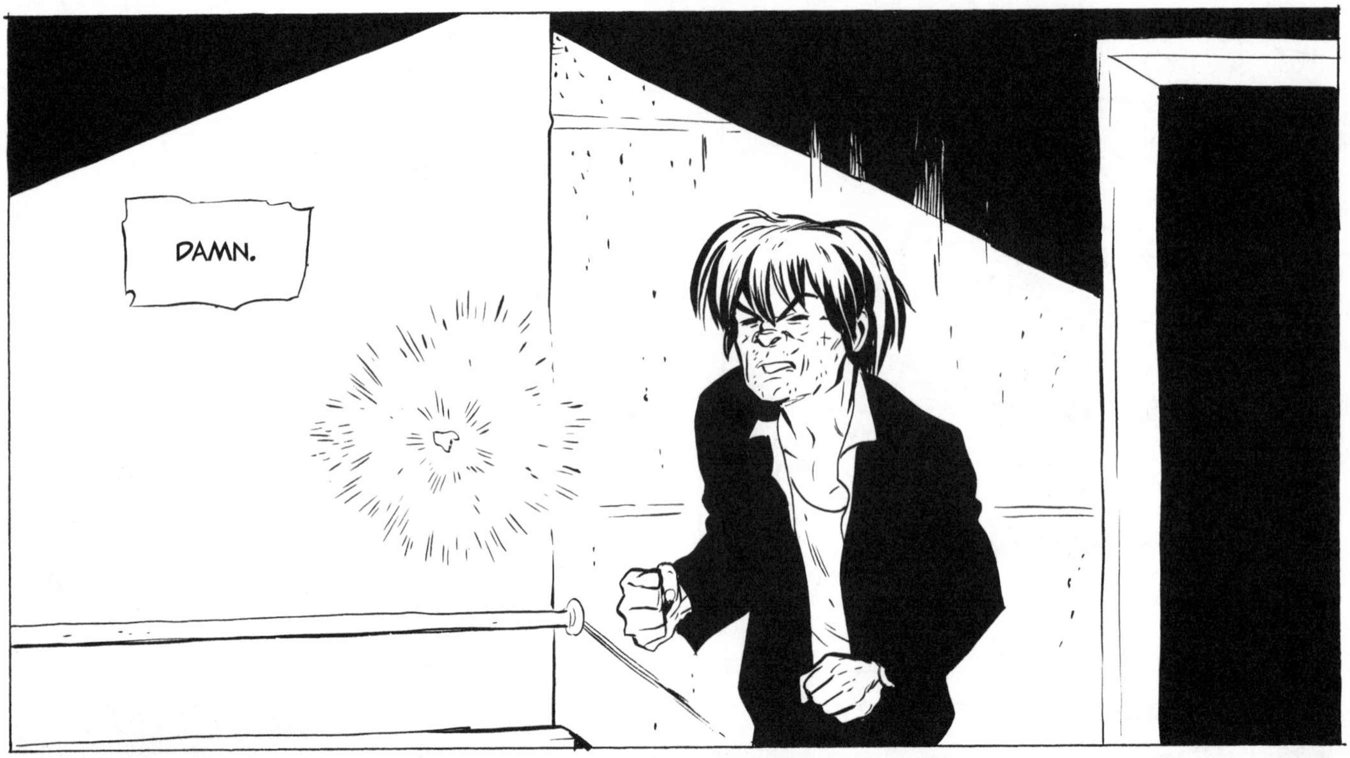
DAMN.

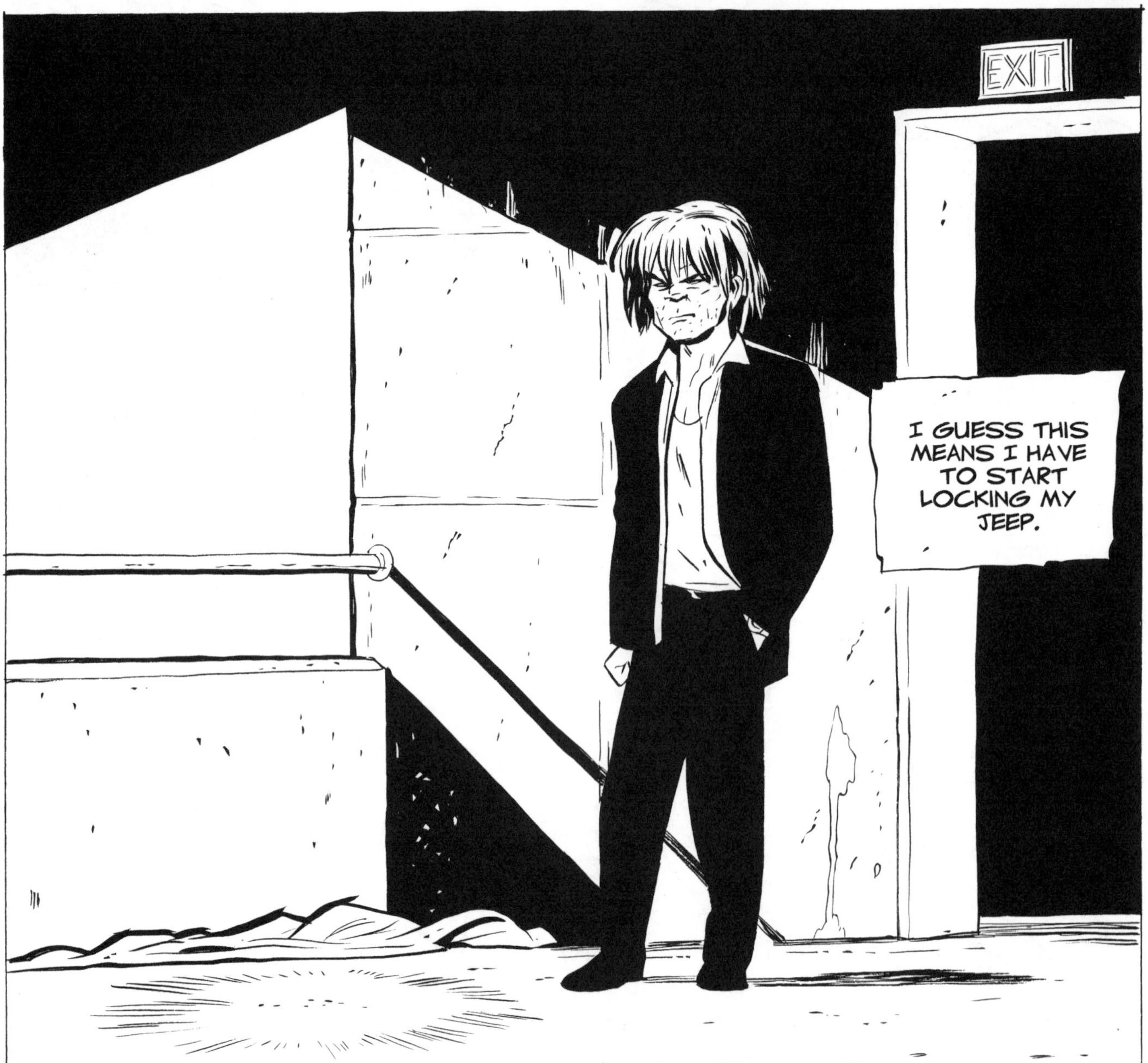
EXIT
I GUESS THIS MEANS I HAVE TO START LOCKING MY JEEP.

# 10.
# BEST LAID PLANS

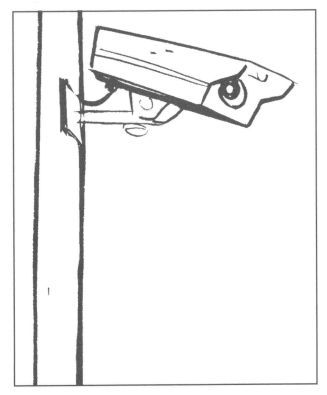

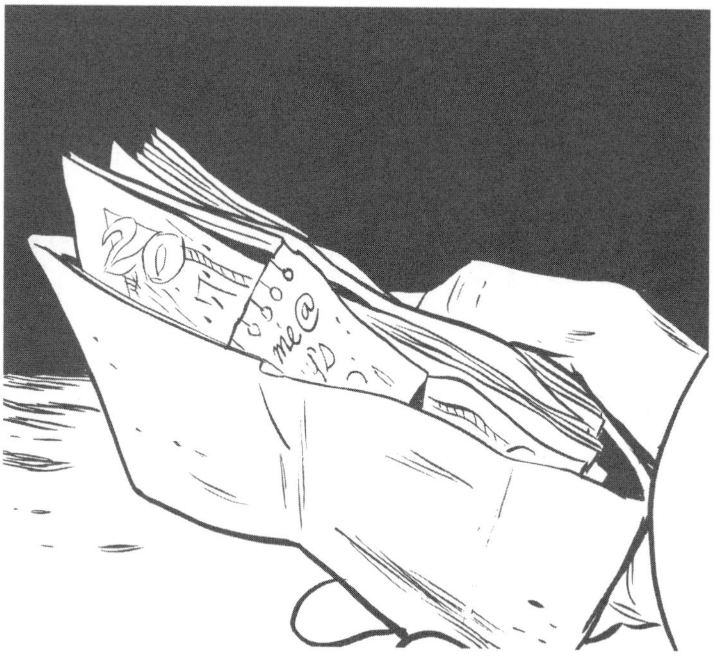
20
me@

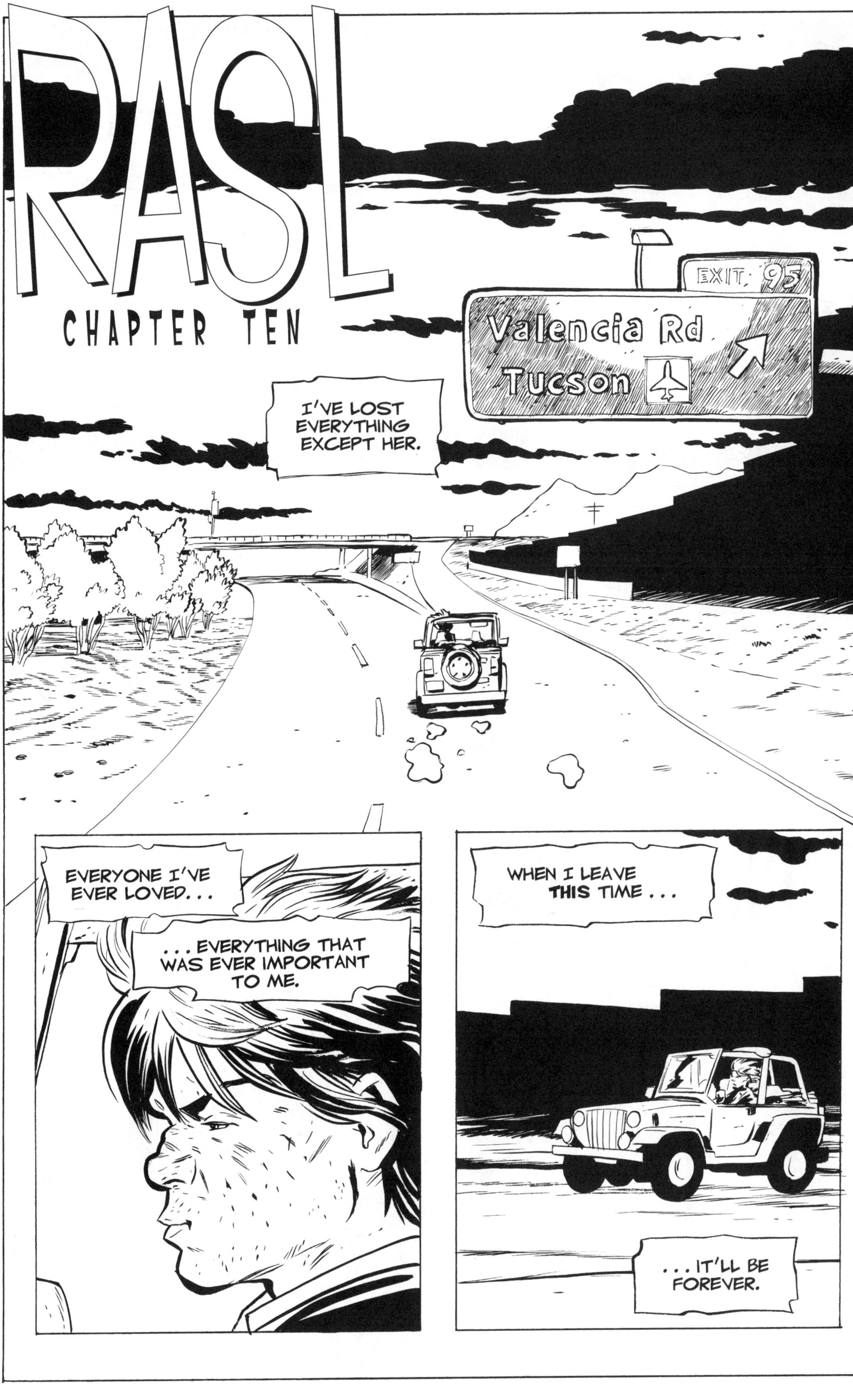
RASL
CHAPTER TEN
EXIT 95
Valencia Rd
Tucson
I'VE LOST EVERYTHING EXCEPT HER.
EVERYONE I'VE EVER LOVED...
...EVERYTHING THAT WAS EVER IMPORTANT TO ME.
WHEN I LEAVE **THIS** TIME...
...IT'LL BE FOREVER.

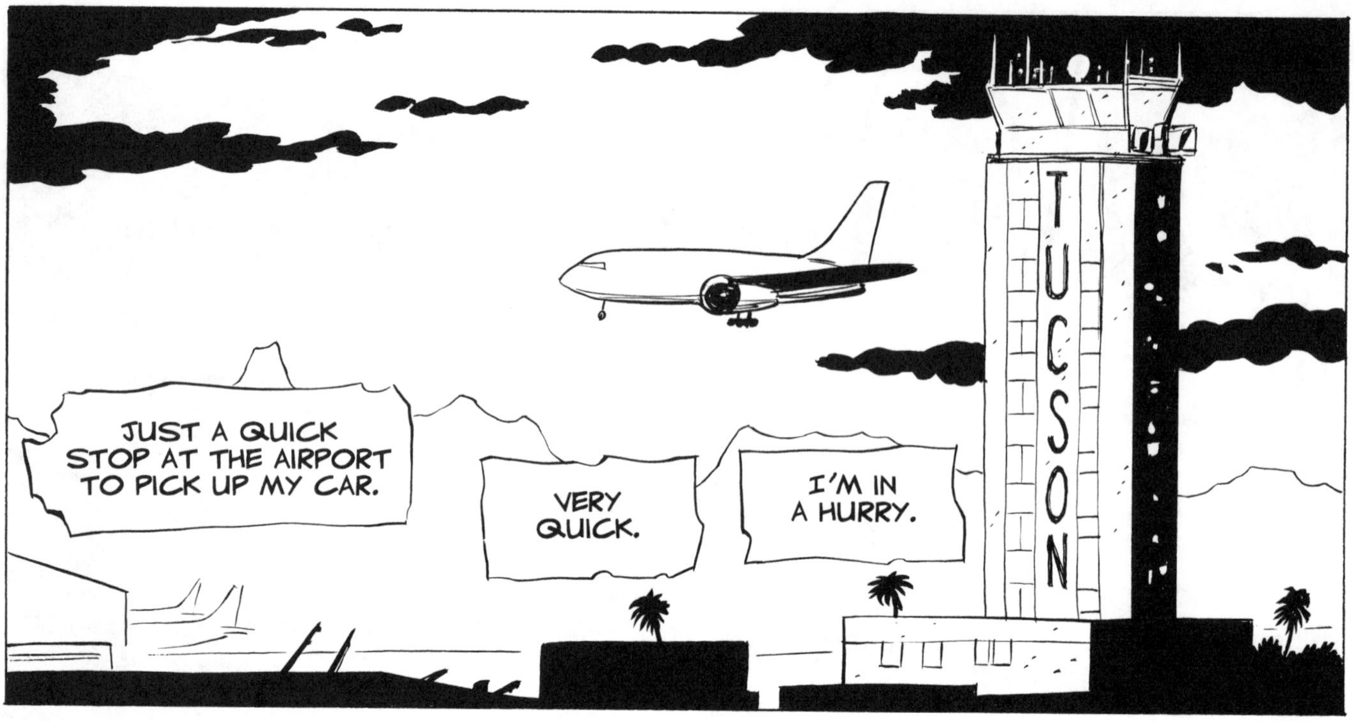
JUST A QUICK STOP AT THE AIRPORT TO PICK UP MY CAR.
VERY QUICK.
I'M IN A HURRY.
TUCSON

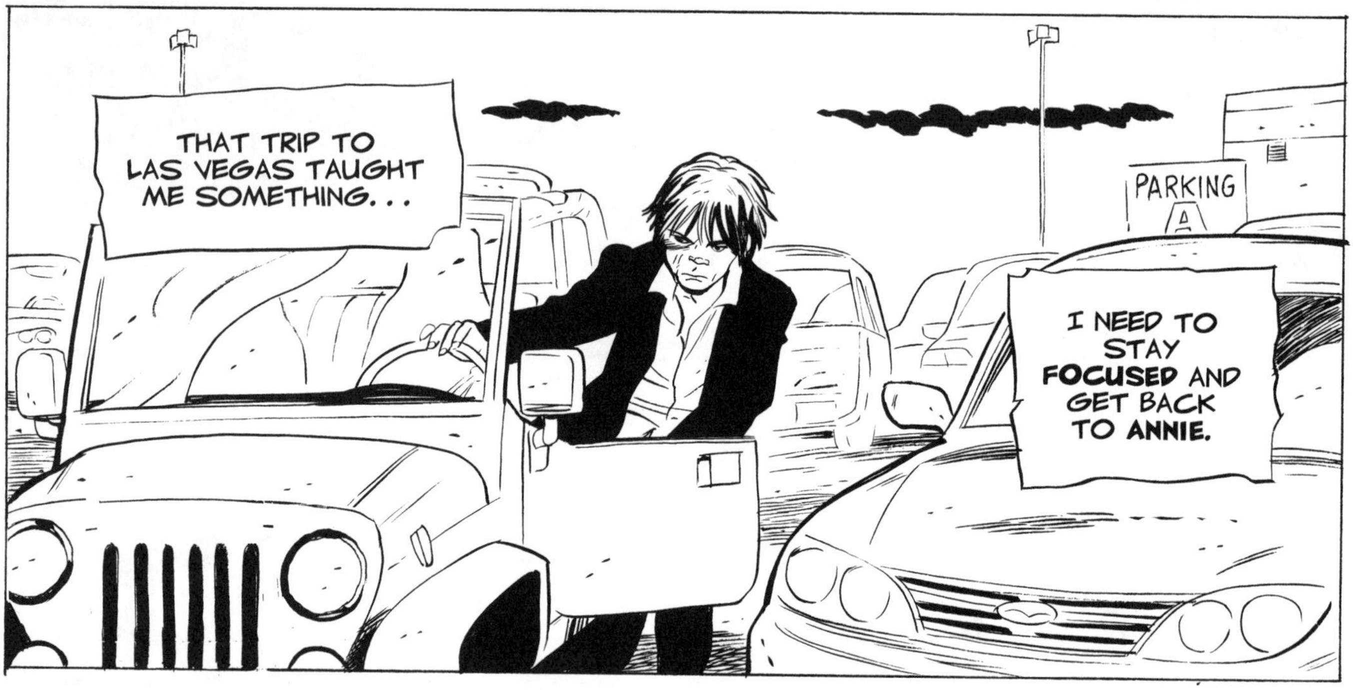
THAT TRIP TO LAS VEGAS TAUGHT ME SOMETHING. . .
PARKING A
I NEED TO STAY **FOCUSED** AND GET BACK TO **ANNIE.**

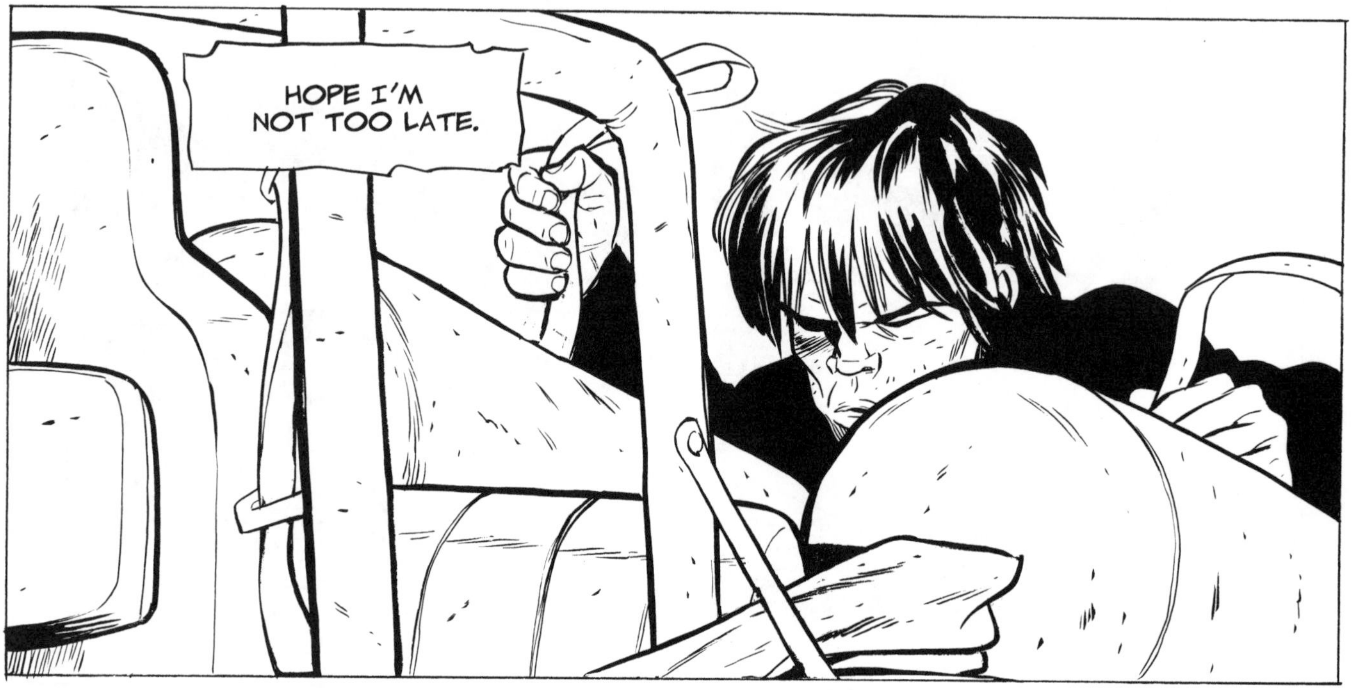
HOPE I'M NOT TOO LATE.

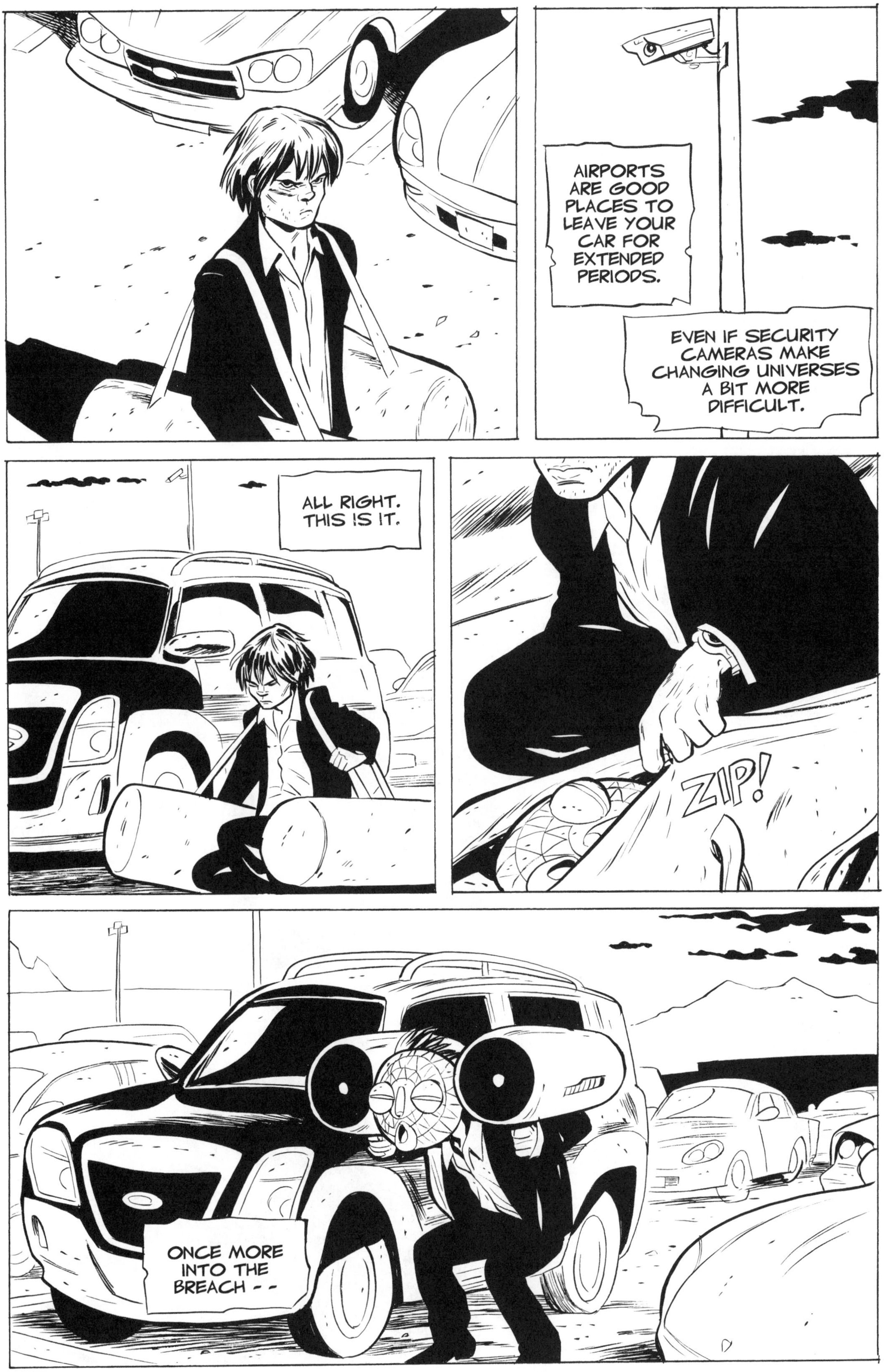
AIRPORTS ARE GOOD PLACES TO LEAVE YOUR CAR FOR EXTENDED PERIODS.
EVEN IF SECURITY CAMERAS MAKE CHANGING UNIVERSES A BIT MORE DIFFICULT.
ALL RIGHT. THIS IS IT.
ZIP!
ONCE MORE INTO THE BREACH - -

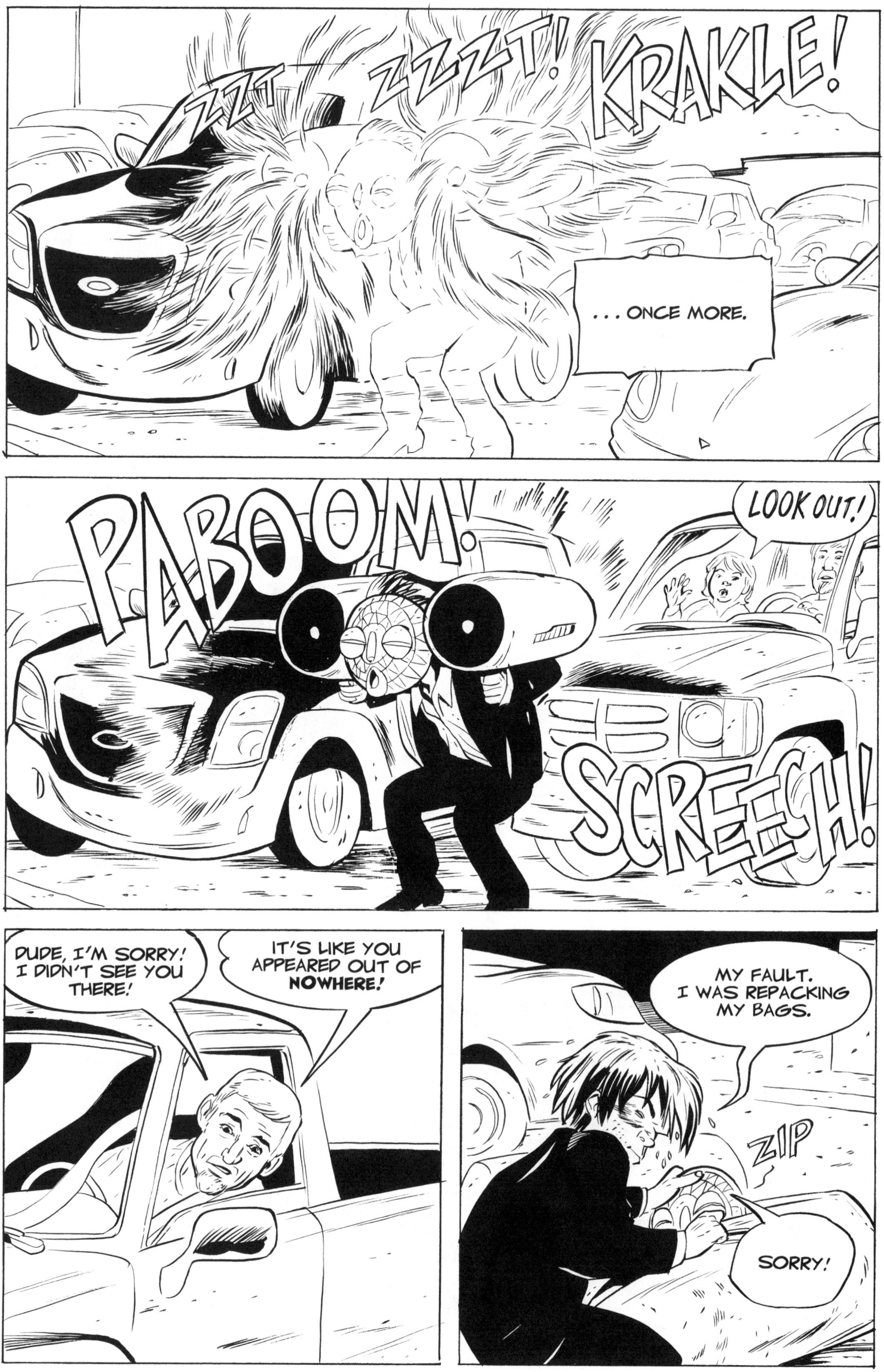
ZZZT ZZZZT! KRAKLE!
. . . ONCE MORE.
PABOOM!
LOOK OUT!
SCREECH!
DUDE, I'M SORRY! I DIDN'T SEE YOU THERE!
IT'S LIKE YOU APPEARED OUT OF NOWHERE!
MY FAULT. I WAS REPACKING MY BAGS.
ZIP
SORRY!

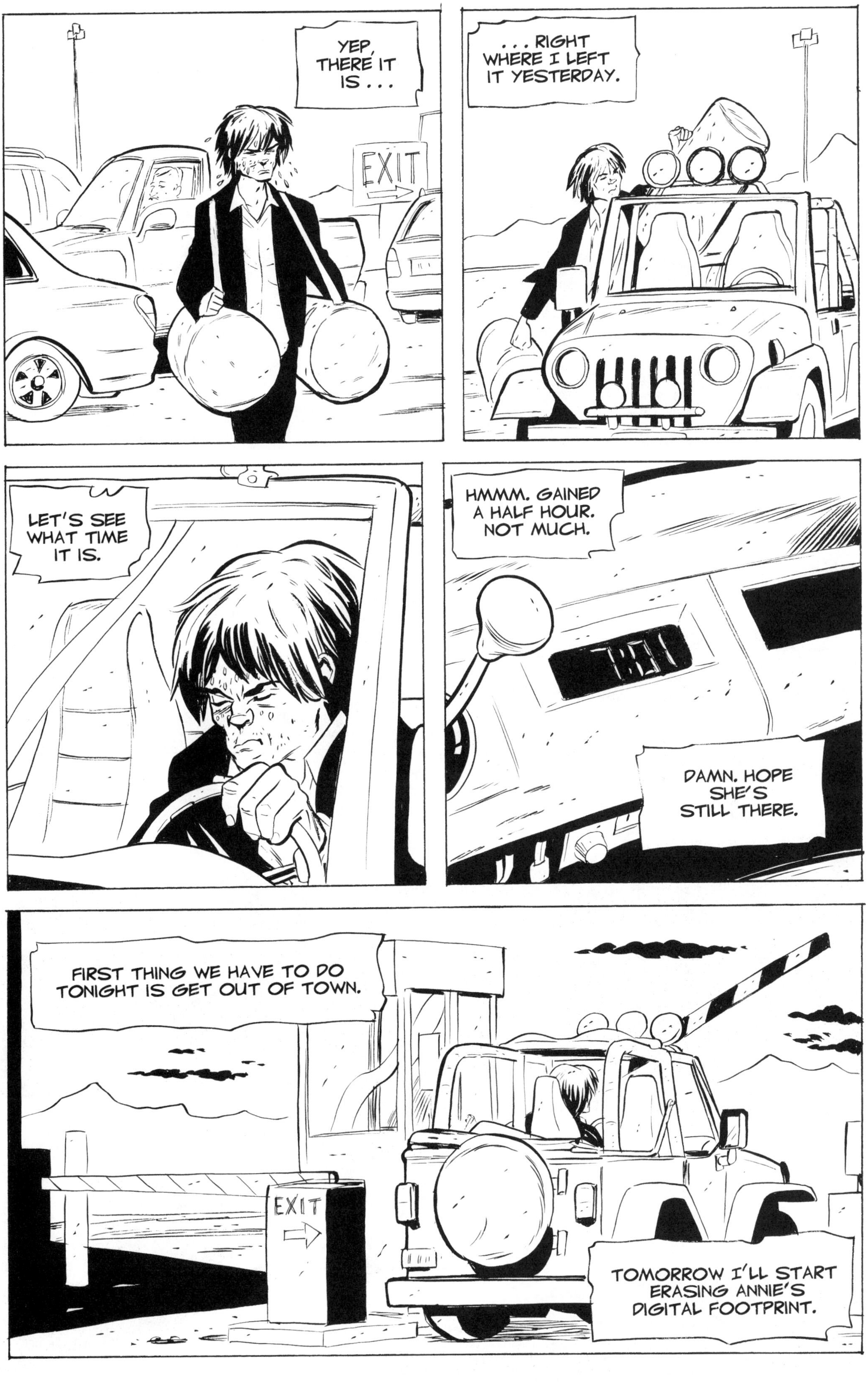

YEP, THERE IT IS . . .
EXIT
. . . RIGHT WHERE I LEFT IT YESTERDAY.
LET'S SEE WHAT TIME IT IS.
HMMM. GAINED A HALF HOUR. NOT MUCH.
DAMN. HOPE SHE'S STILL THERE.
FIRST THING WE HAVE TO DO TONIGHT IS GET OUT OF TOWN.
EXIT
TOMORROW I'LL START ERASING ANNIE'S DIGITAL FOOTPRINT.

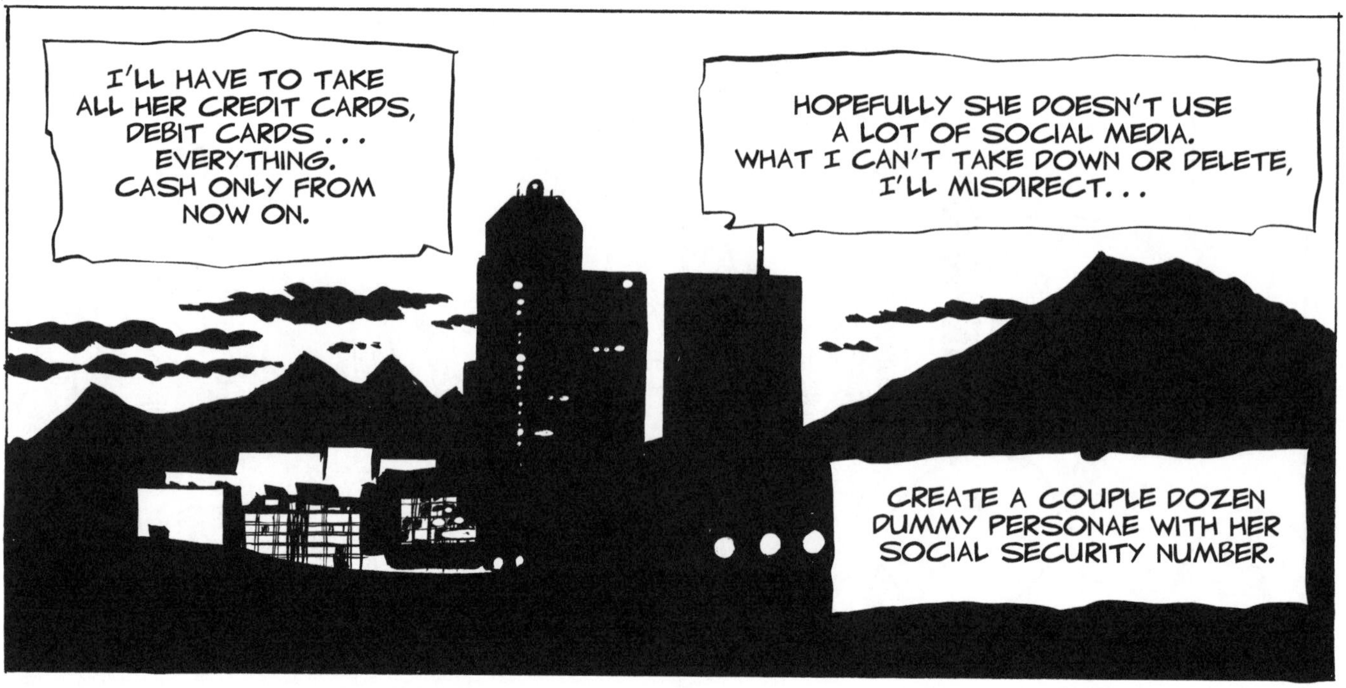
I'LL HAVE TO TAKE ALL HER CREDIT CARDS, DEBIT CARDS . . . EVERYTHING. CASH ONLY FROM NOW ON.
HOPEFULLY SHE DOESN'T USE A LOT OF SOCIAL MEDIA. WHAT I CAN'T TAKE DOWN OR DELETE, I'LL MISDIRECT. . .
CREATE A COUPLE DOZEN DUMMY PERSONAE WITH HER SOCIAL SECURITY NUMBER.

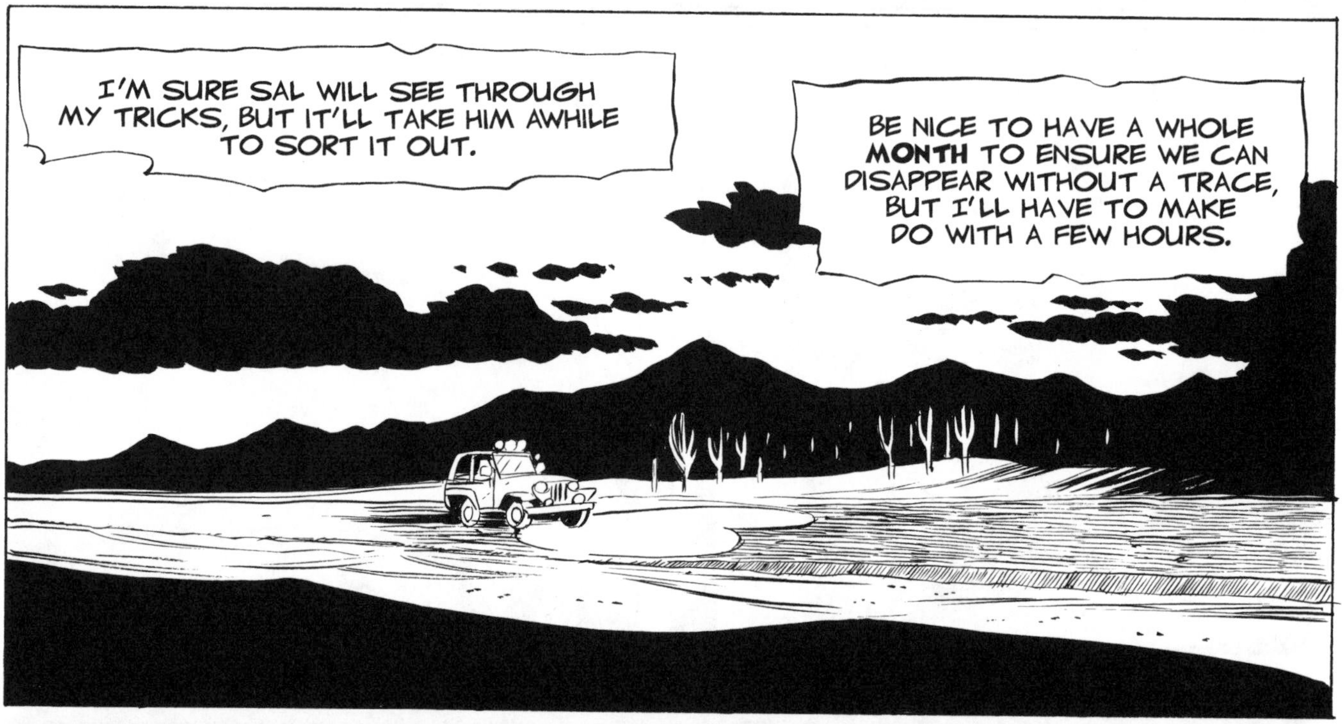
I'M SURE SAL WILL SEE THROUGH MY TRICKS, BUT IT'LL TAKE HIM AWHILE TO SORT IT OUT.
BE NICE TO HAVE A WHOLE **MONTH** TO ENSURE WE CAN DISAPPEAR WITHOUT A TRACE, BUT I'LL HAVE TO MAKE DO WITH A FEW HOURS.

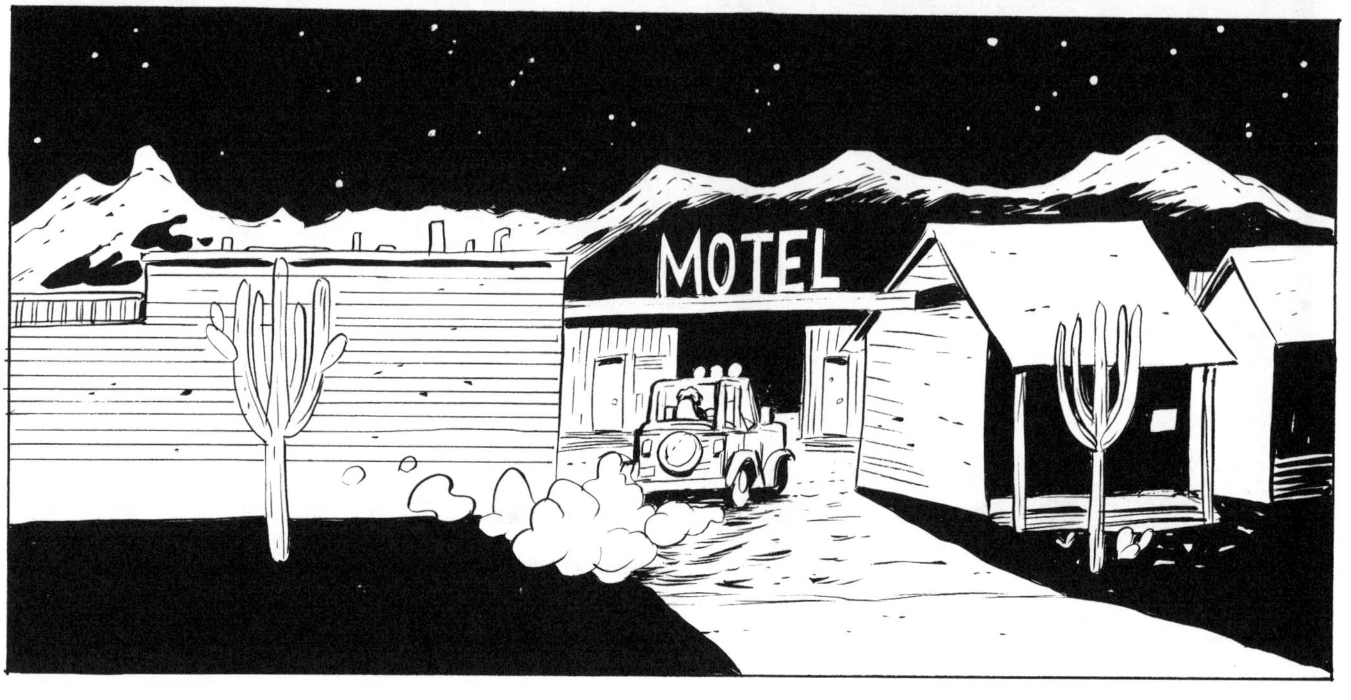
MOTEL

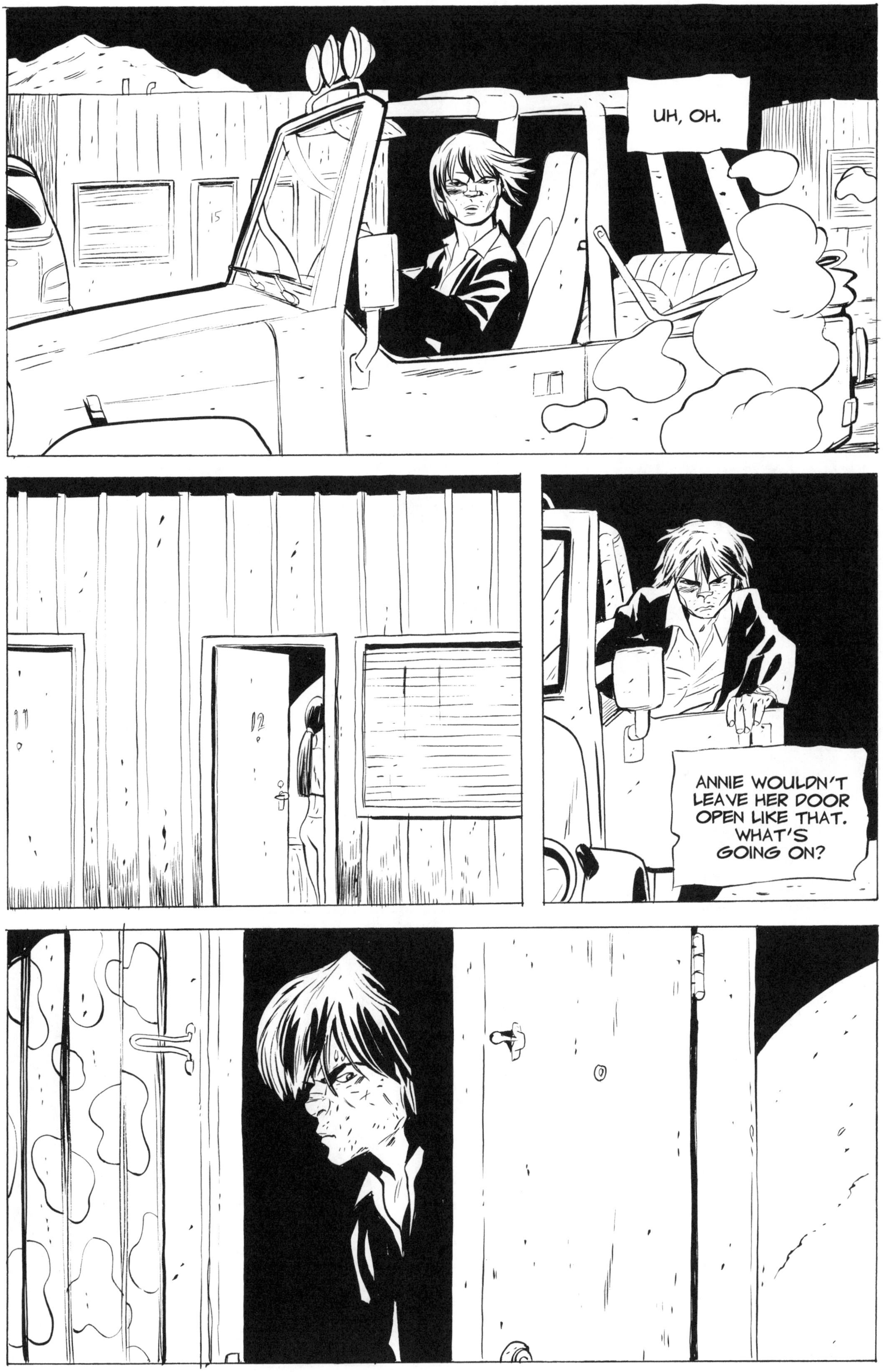
UH, OH.
ANNIE WOULDN'T LEAVE HER DOOR OPEN LIKE THAT. WHAT'S GOING ON?

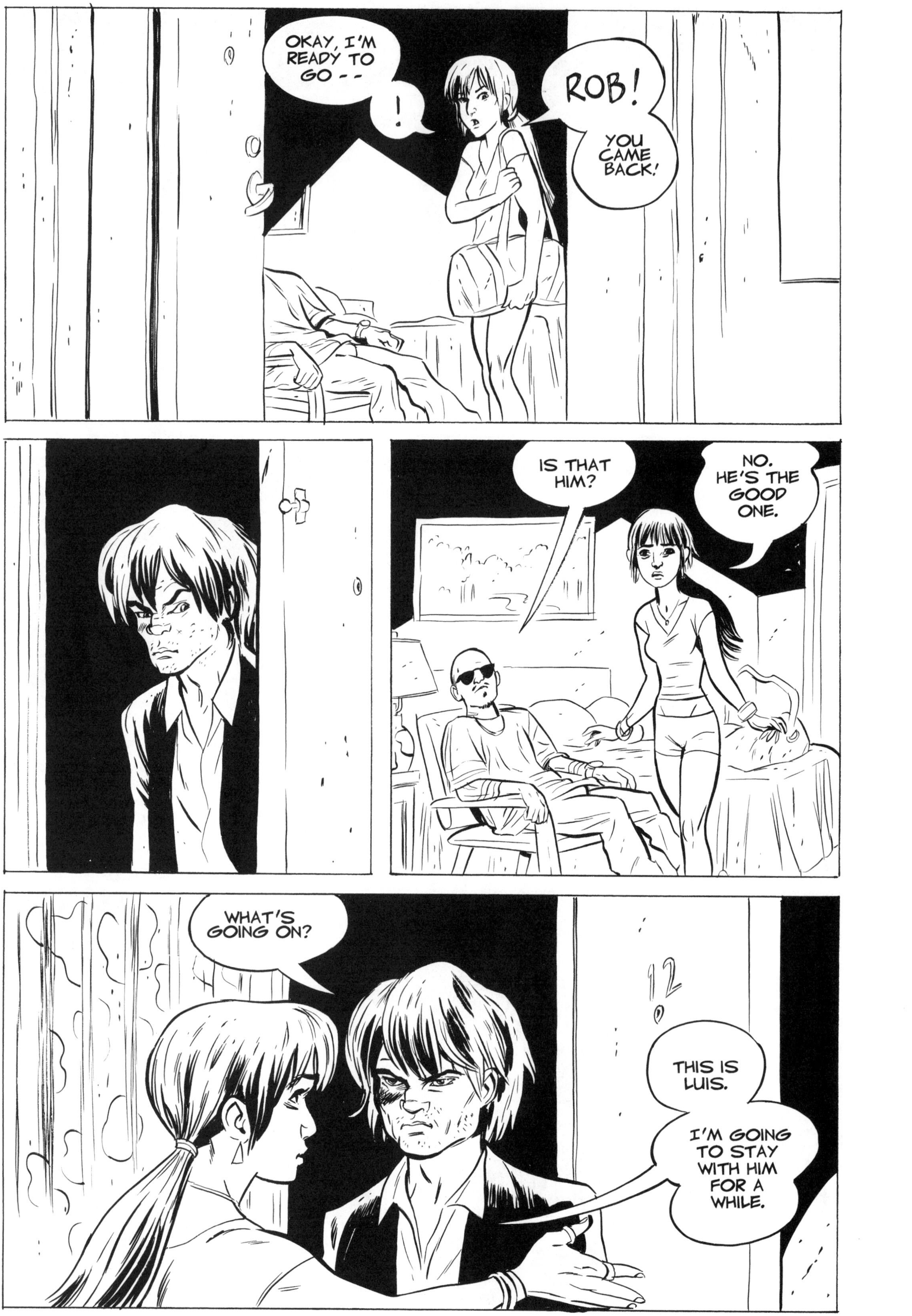
OKAY, I'M READY TO GO --
!
ROB!
YOU CAME BACK!
IS THAT HIM?
NO. HE'S THE GOOD ONE.
WHAT'S GOING ON?
12
THIS IS LUIS.
I'M GOING TO STAY WITH HIM FOR A WHILE.

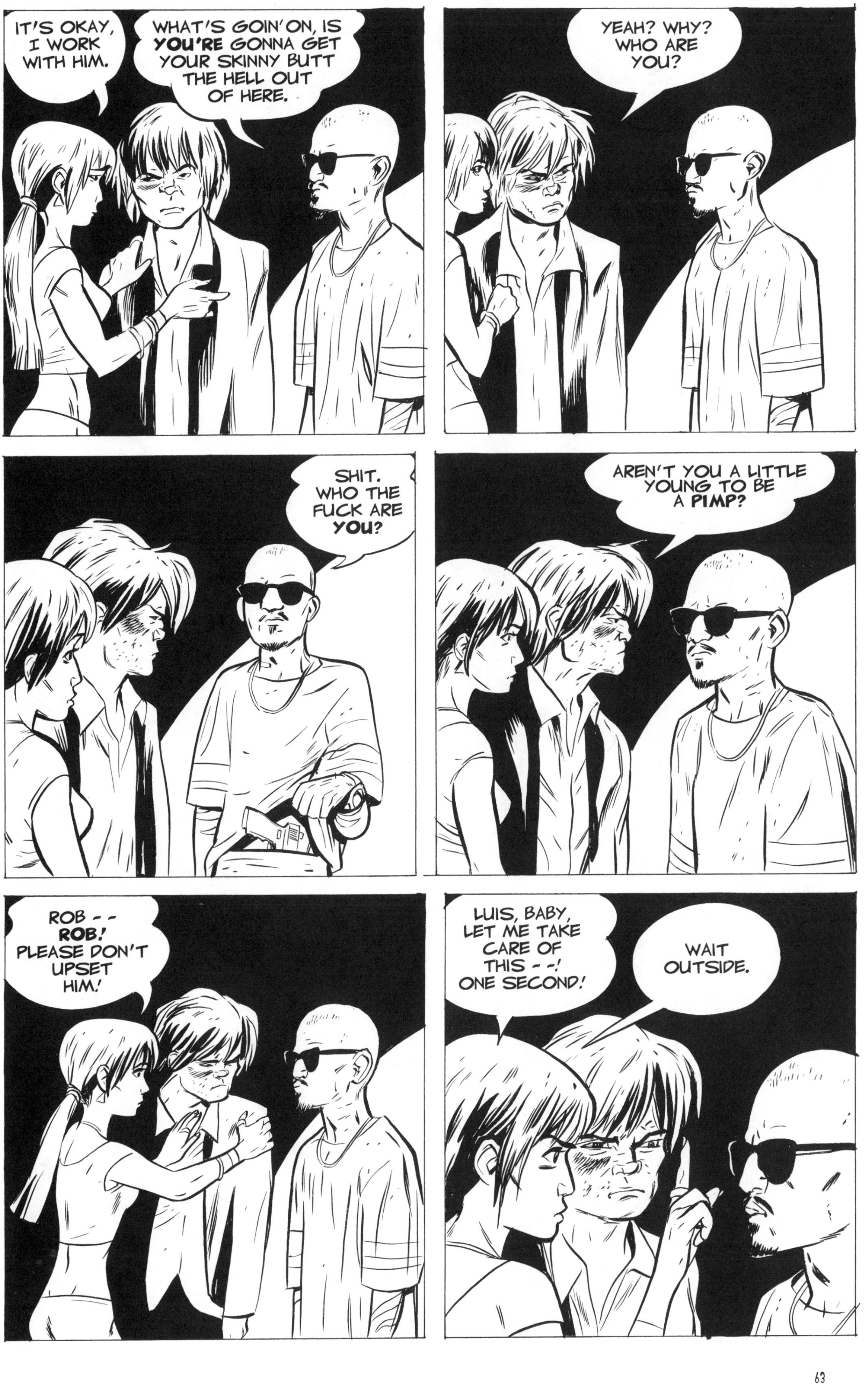
IT'S OKAY, I WORK WITH HIM.
WHAT'S GOIN' ON, IS YOU'RE GONNA GET YOUR SKINNY BUTT THE HELL OUT OF HERE.
YEAH? WHY? WHO ARE YOU?
SHIT. WHO THE FUCK ARE YOU?
AREN'T YOU A LITTLE YOUNG TO BE A PIMP?
ROB - - ROB! PLEASE DON'T UPSET HIM!
LUIS, BABY, LET ME TAKE CARE OF THIS - -! ONE SECOND!
WAIT OUTSIDE.

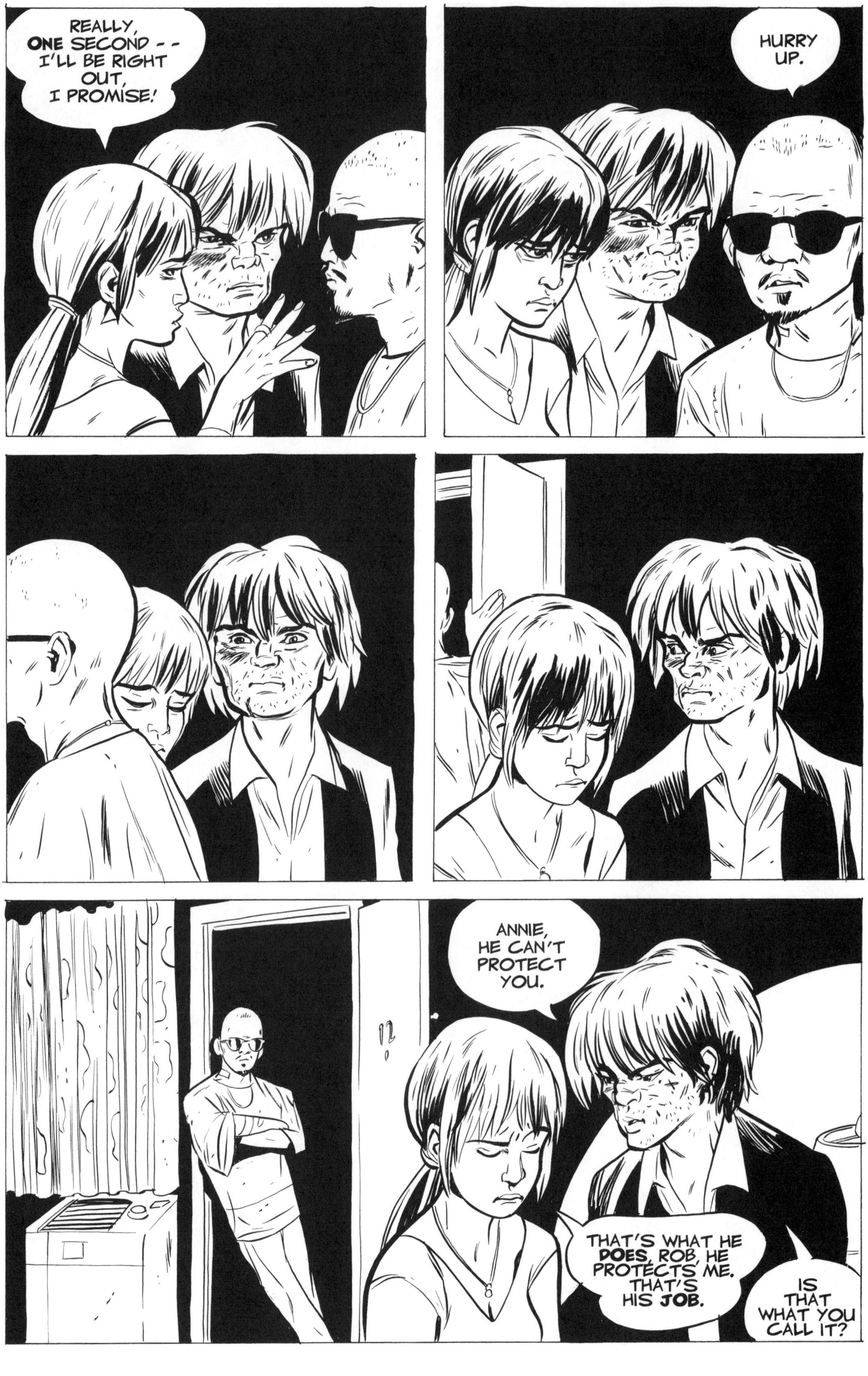
REALLY, ONE SECOND - - I'LL BE RIGHT OUT, I PROMISE!
HURRY UP.
ANNIE, HE CAN'T PROTECT YOU.
THAT'S WHAT HE DOES, ROB, HE PROTECTS ME. THAT'S HIS JOB.
IS THAT WHAT YOU CALL IT?

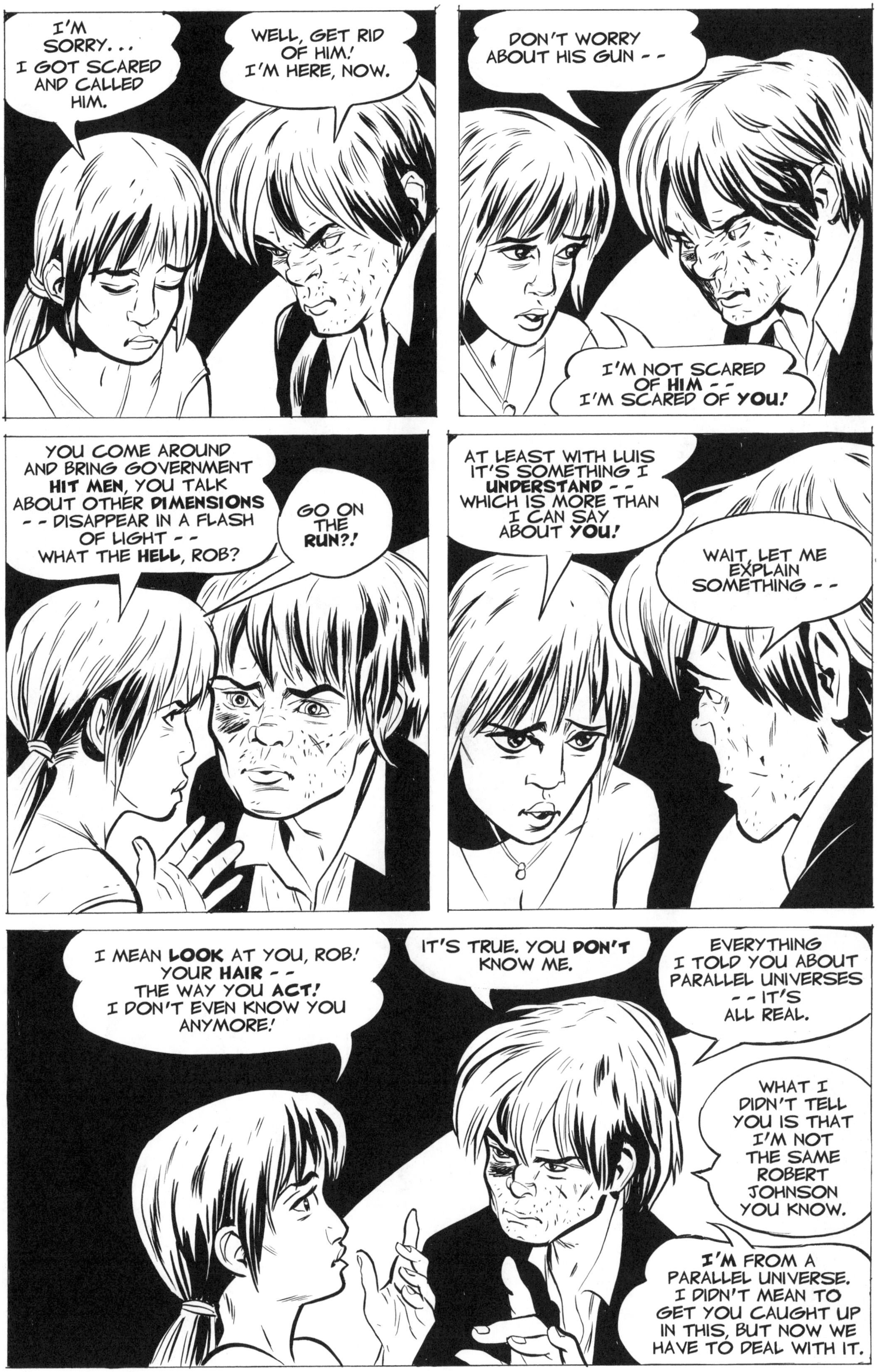
I'M SORRY... I GOT SCARED AND CALLED HIM.
WELL, GET RID OF HIM! I'M HERE, NOW.
DON'T WORRY ABOUT HIS GUN --
I'M NOT SCARED OF HIM -- I'M SCARED OF YOU!
YOU COME AROUND AND BRING GOVERNMENT HIT MEN, YOU TALK ABOUT OTHER DIMENSIONS -- DISAPPEAR IN A FLASH OF LIGHT -- WHAT THE HELL, ROB?
GO ON THE RUN?!
AT LEAST WITH LUIS IT'S SOMETHING I UNDERSTAND -- WHICH IS MORE THAN I CAN SAY ABOUT YOU!
WAIT, LET ME EXPLAIN SOMETHING --
I MEAN LOOK AT YOU, ROB! YOUR HAIR -- THE WAY YOU ACT! I DON'T EVEN KNOW YOU ANYMORE!
IT'S TRUE. YOU DON'T KNOW ME.
EVERYTHING I TOLD YOU ABOUT PARALLEL UNIVERSES -- IT'S ALL REAL.
WHAT I DIDN'T TELL YOU IS THAT I'M NOT THE SAME ROBERT JOHNSON YOU KNOW.
I'M FROM A PARALLEL UNIVERSE. I DIDN'T MEAN TO GET YOU CAUGHT UP IN THIS, BUT NOW WE HAVE TO DEAL WITH IT.

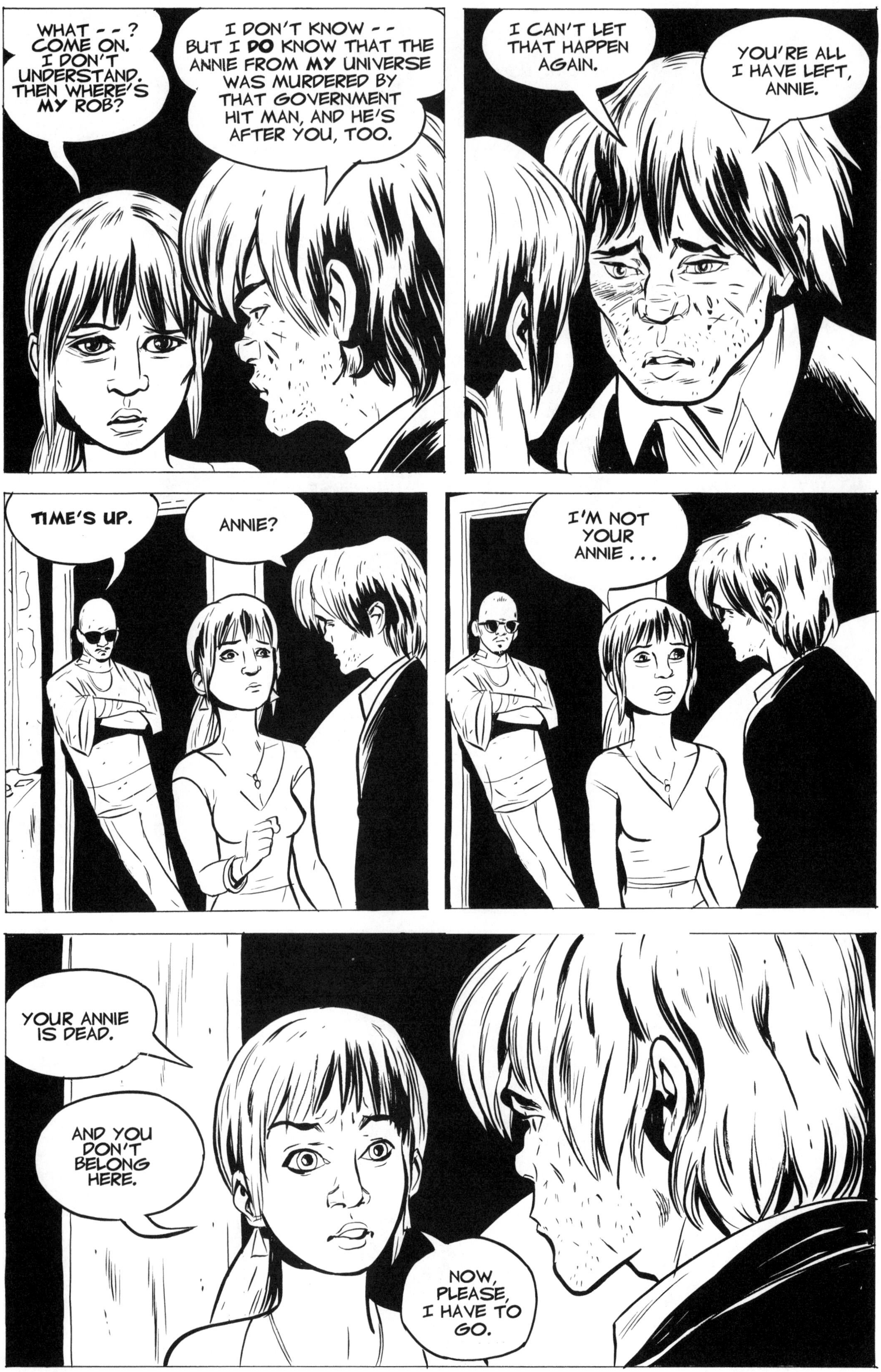

WHAT - - ? COME ON. I DON'T UNDERSTAND. THEN WHERE'S MY ROB?
I DON'T KNOW - - BUT I DO KNOW THAT THE ANNIE FROM MY UNIVERSE WAS MURDERED BY THAT GOVERNMENT HIT MAN, AND HE'S AFTER YOU, TOO.
I CAN'T LET THAT HAPPEN AGAIN.
YOU'RE ALL I HAVE LEFT, ANNIE.
TIME'S UP.
ANNIE?
I'M NOT YOUR ANNIE . . .
YOUR ANNIE IS DEAD.
AND YOU DON'T BELONG HERE.
NOW, PLEASE, I HAVE TO GO.

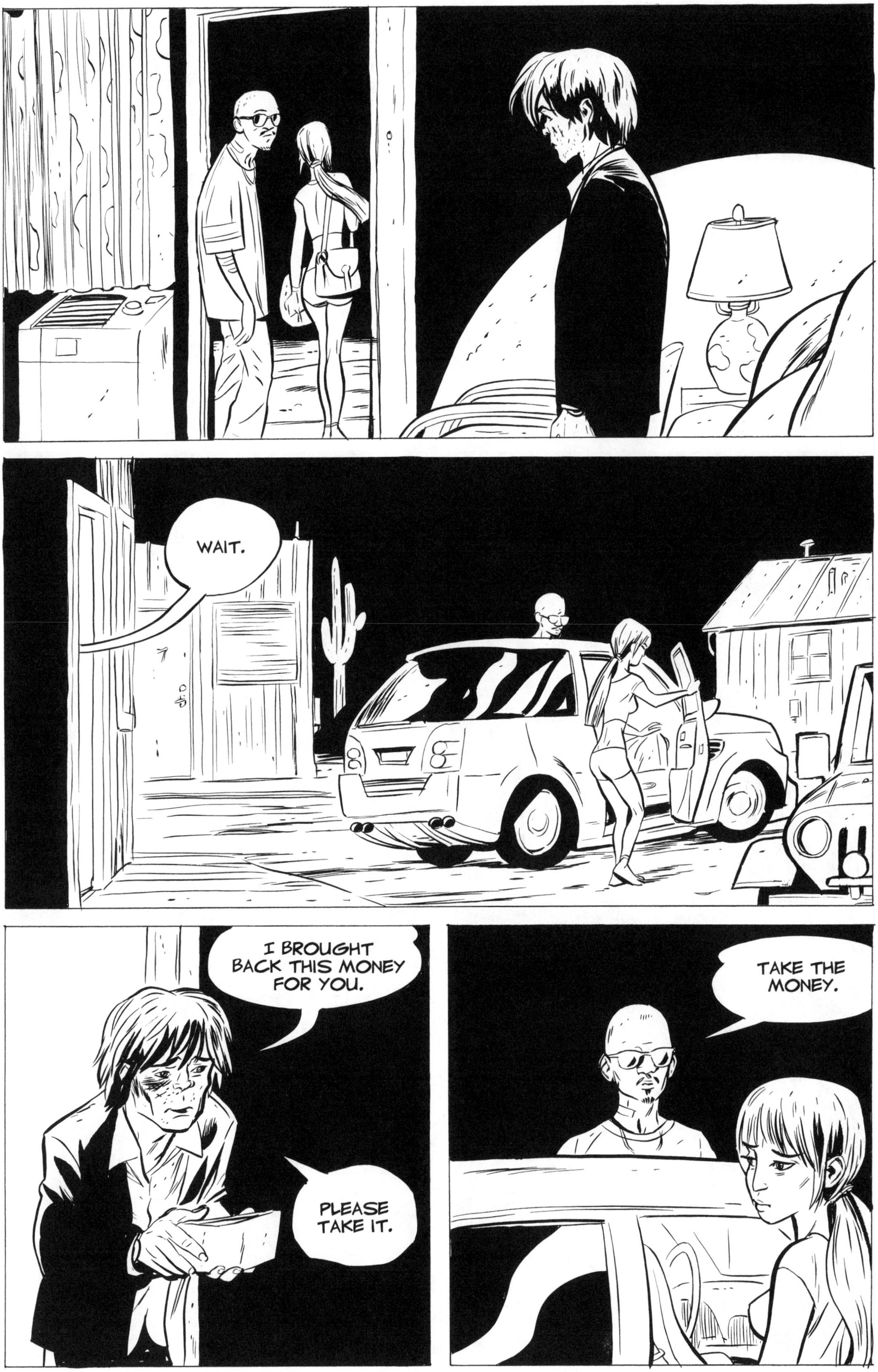
WAIT.
I BROUGHT BACK THIS MONEY FOR YOU.
PLEASE TAKE IT.
TAKE THE MONEY.

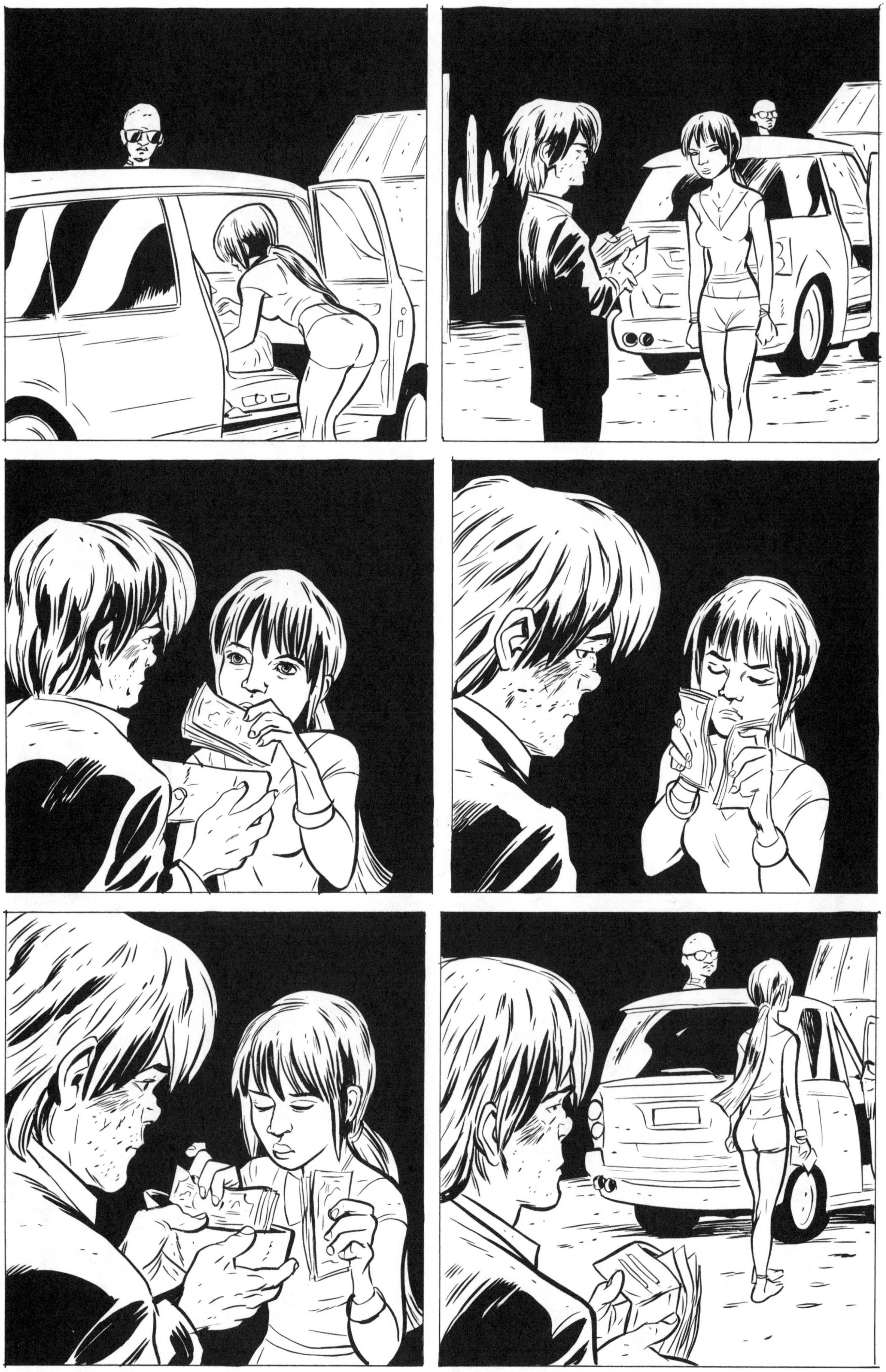

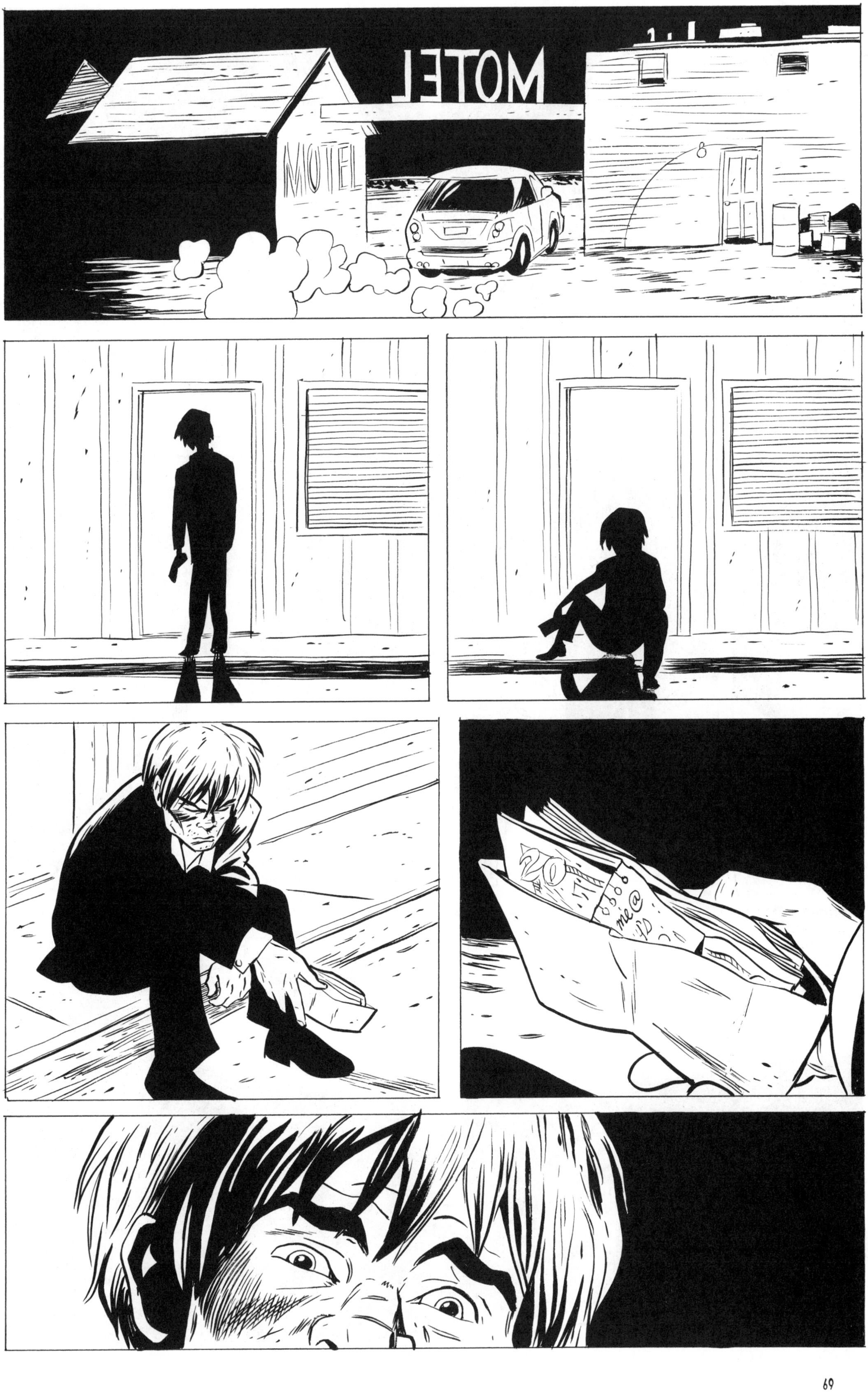
MOTEL
MOTEL

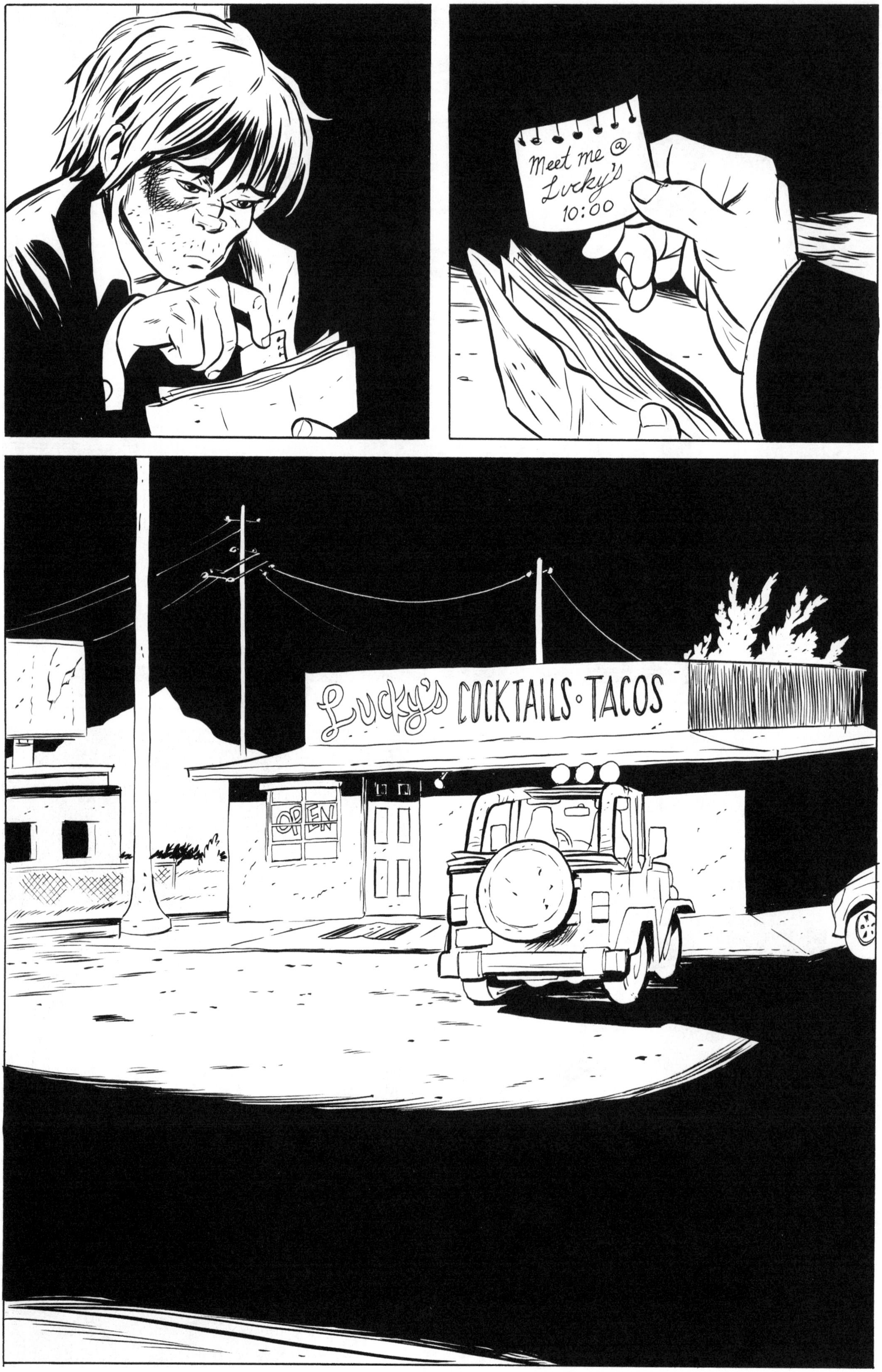

Meet me @
Lucky's
10:00
Lucky's COCKTAILS • TACOS
OPEN

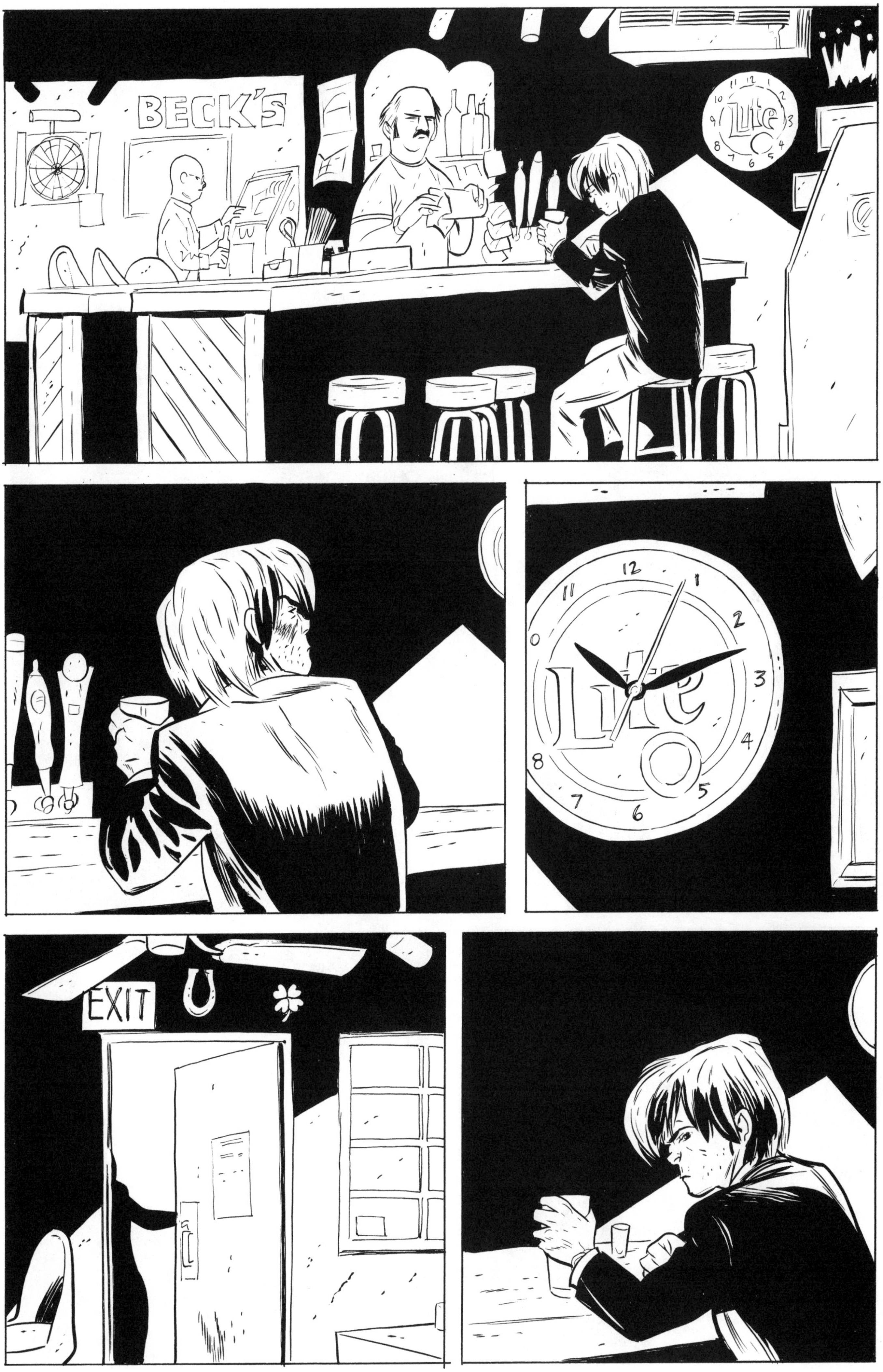
BECK'S
Lite
Lite
EXIT

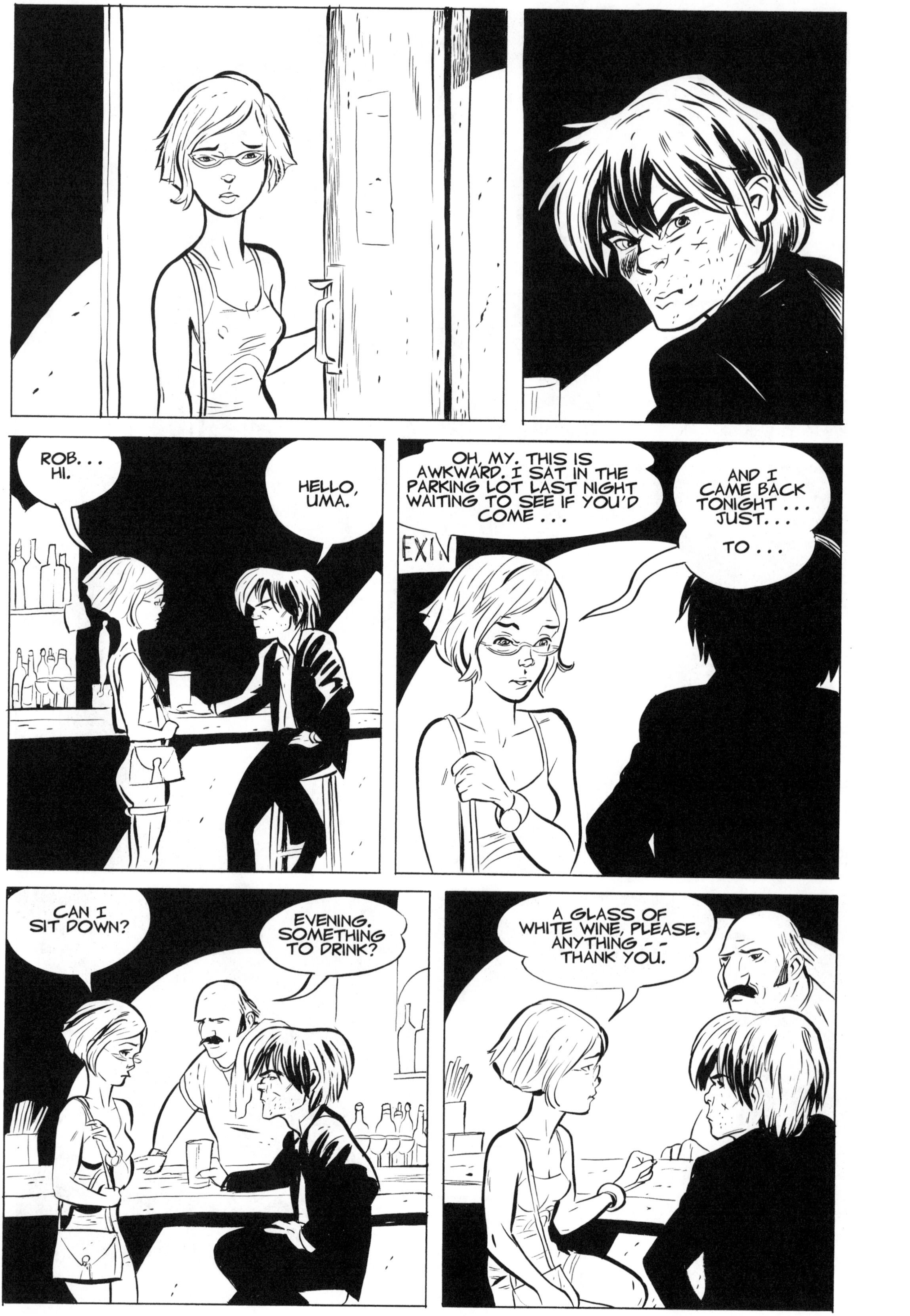
ROB. . . HI.
HELLO, UMA.
OH, MY. THIS IS AWKWARD. I SAT IN THE PARKING LOT LAST NIGHT WAITING TO SEE IF YOU'D COME . . .
AND I CAME BACK TONIGHT . . . JUST. . .
TO . . .
CAN I SIT DOWN?
EVENING. SOMETHING TO DRINK?
A GLASS OF WHITE WINE, PLEASE. ANYTHING - - THANK YOU.

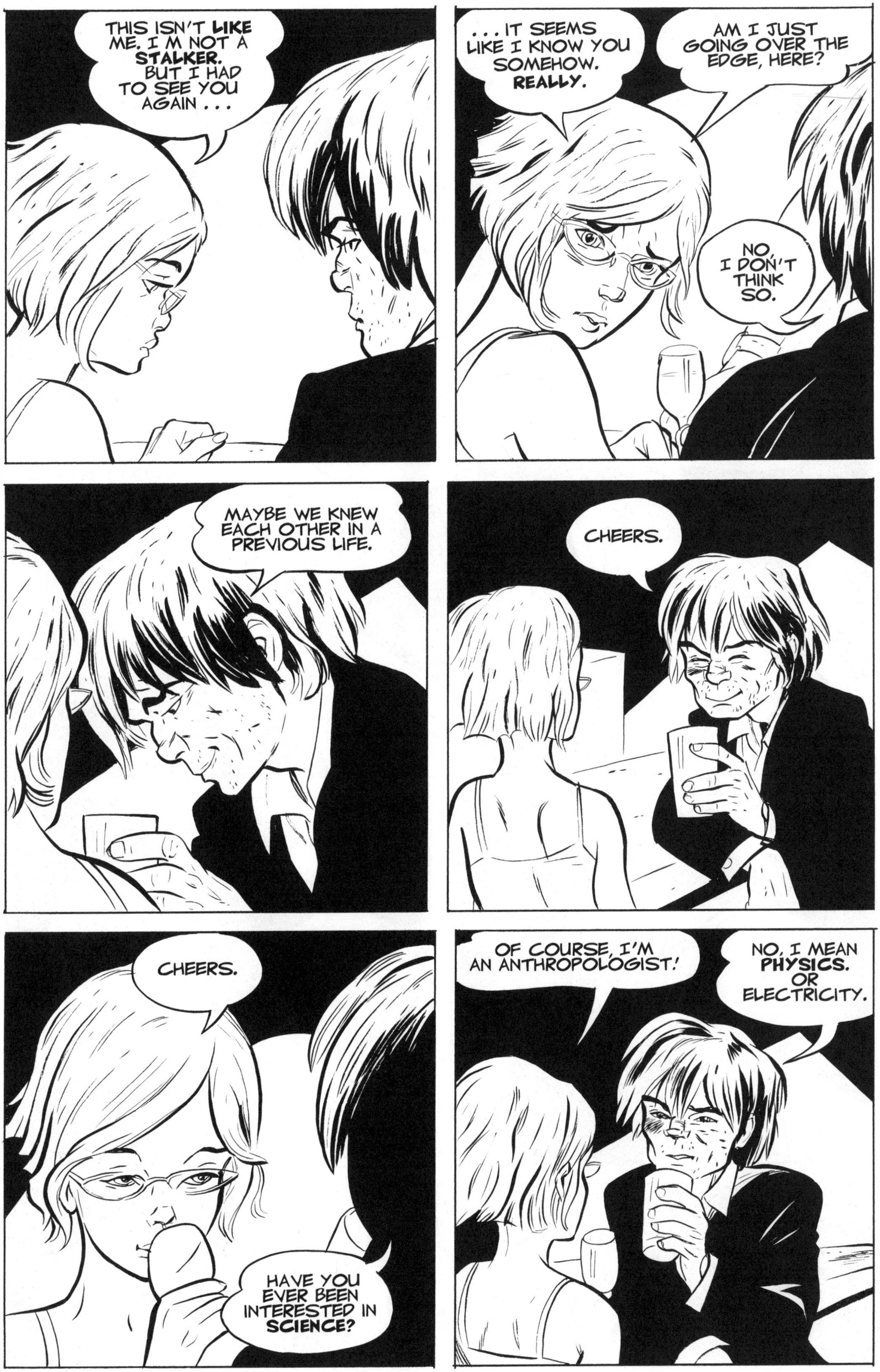
THIS ISN'T LIKE ME. I M NOT A STALKER. BUT I HAD TO SEE YOU AGAIN . . .
. . . IT SEEMS LIKE I KNOW YOU SOMEHOW. REALLY.
AM I JUST GOING OVER THE EDGE, HERE?
NO, I DON'T THINK SO.
MAYBE WE KNEW EACH OTHER IN A PREVIOUS LIFE.
CHEERS.
CHEERS.
HAVE YOU EVER BEEN INTERESTED IN SCIENCE?
OF COURSE, I'M AN ANTHROPOLOGIST!
NO, I MEAN PHYSICS. OR ELECTRICITY.

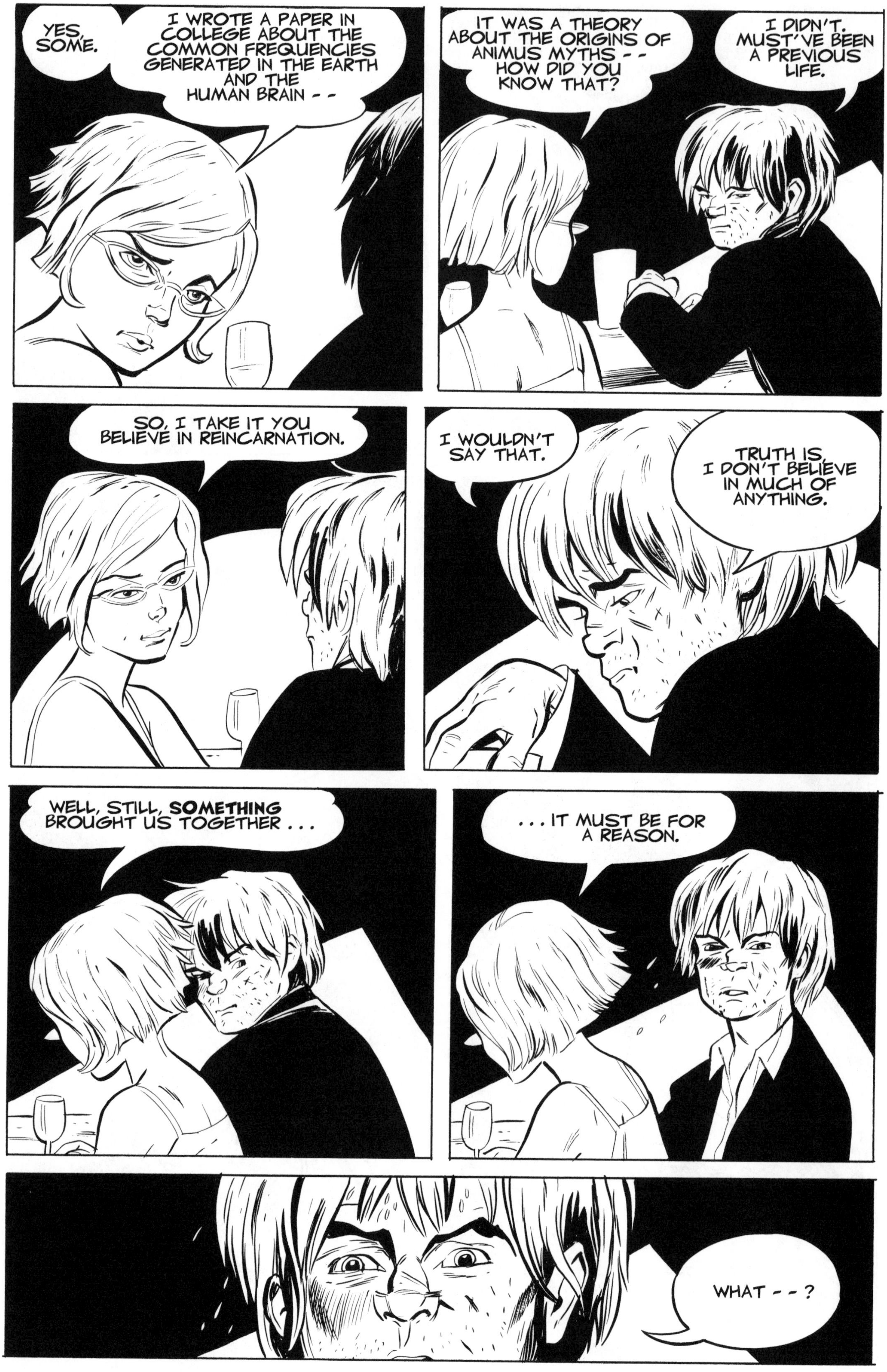
YES, SOME.
I WROTE A PAPER IN COLLEGE ABOUT THE COMMON FREQUENCIES GENERATED IN THE EARTH AND THE HUMAN BRAIN - -
IT WAS A THEORY ABOUT THE ORIGINS OF ANIMUS MYTHS - - HOW DID YOU KNOW THAT?
I DIDN'T. MUST'VE BEEN A PREVIOUS LIFE.
SO, I TAKE IT YOU BELIEVE IN REINCARNATION.
I WOULDN'T SAY THAT.
TRUTH IS, I DON'T BELIEVE IN MUCH OF ANYTHING.
WELL, STILL, SOMETHING BROUGHT US TOGETHER . . .
. . . IT MUST BE FOR A REASON.
WHAT - - ?

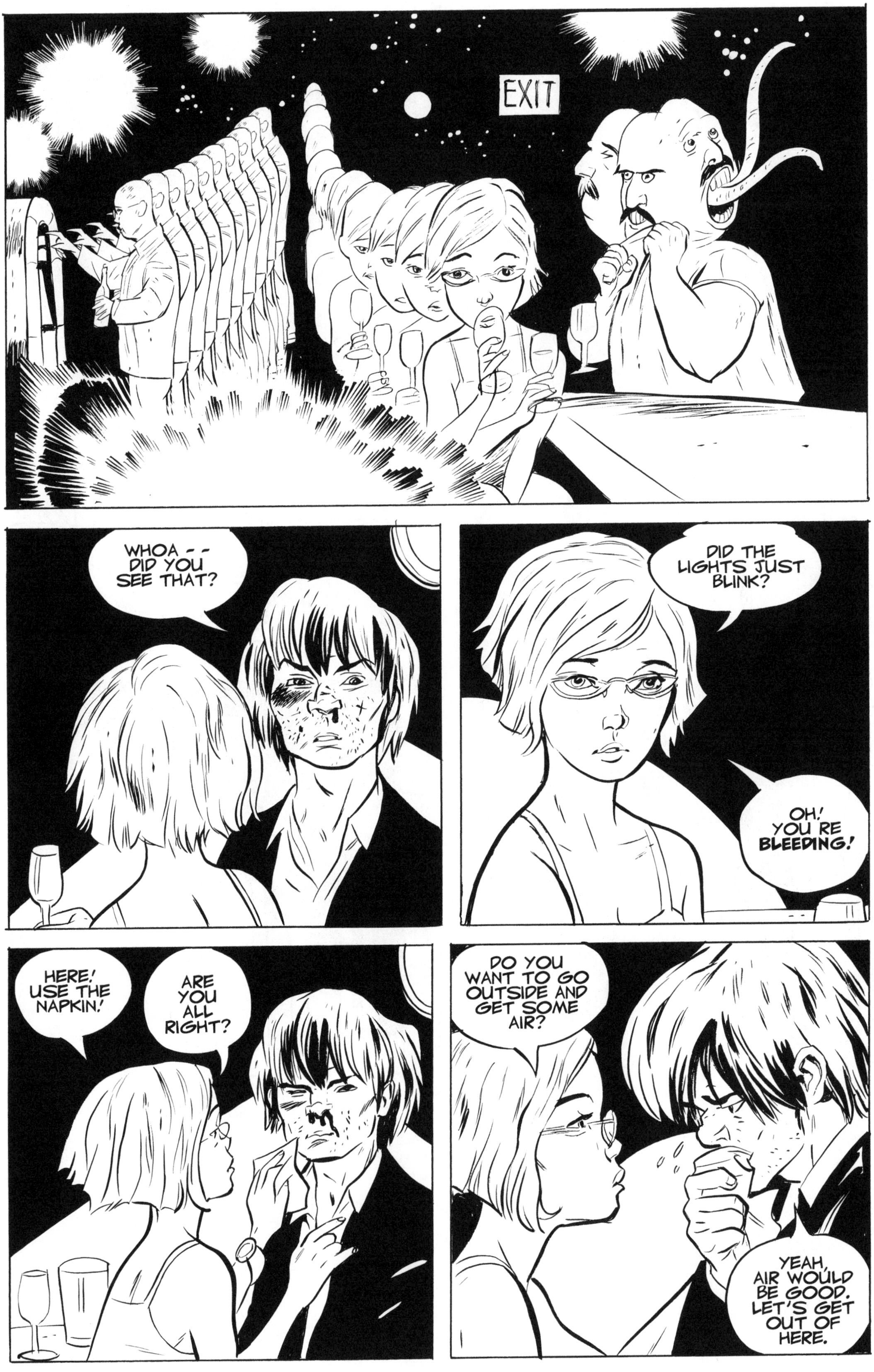
EXIT
WHOA -- DID YOU SEE THAT?
DID THE LIGHTS JUST BLINK?
OH! YOU'RE BLEEDING!
HERE! USE THE NAPKIN!
ARE YOU ALL RIGHT?
DO YOU WANT TO GO OUTSIDE AND GET SOME AIR?
YEAH, AIR WOULD BE GOOD. LET'S GET OUT OF HERE.

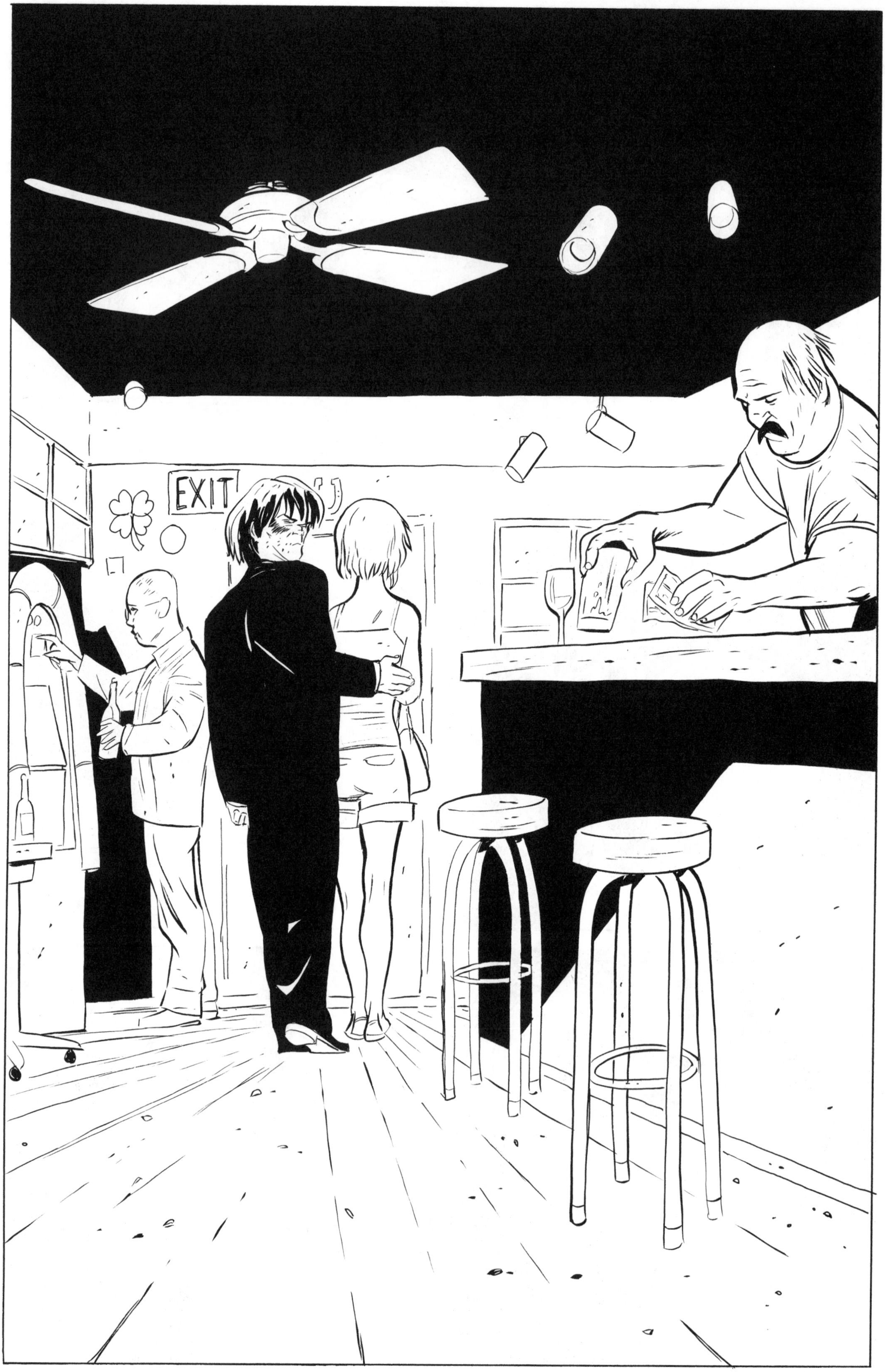
EXIT

# 11.
# THE EVENT

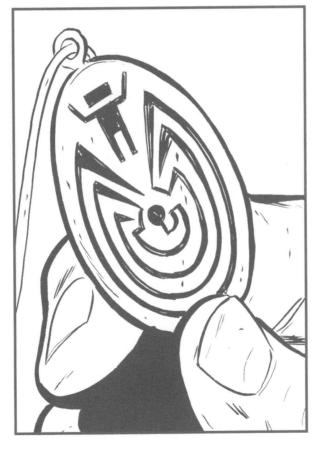

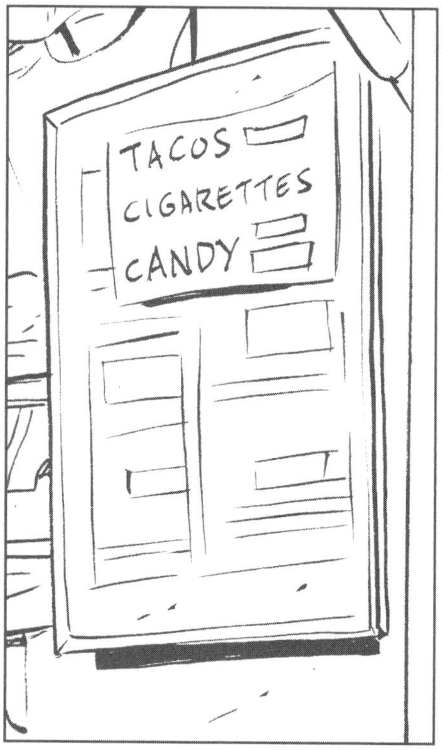
TACOS
CIGARETTES
CANDY

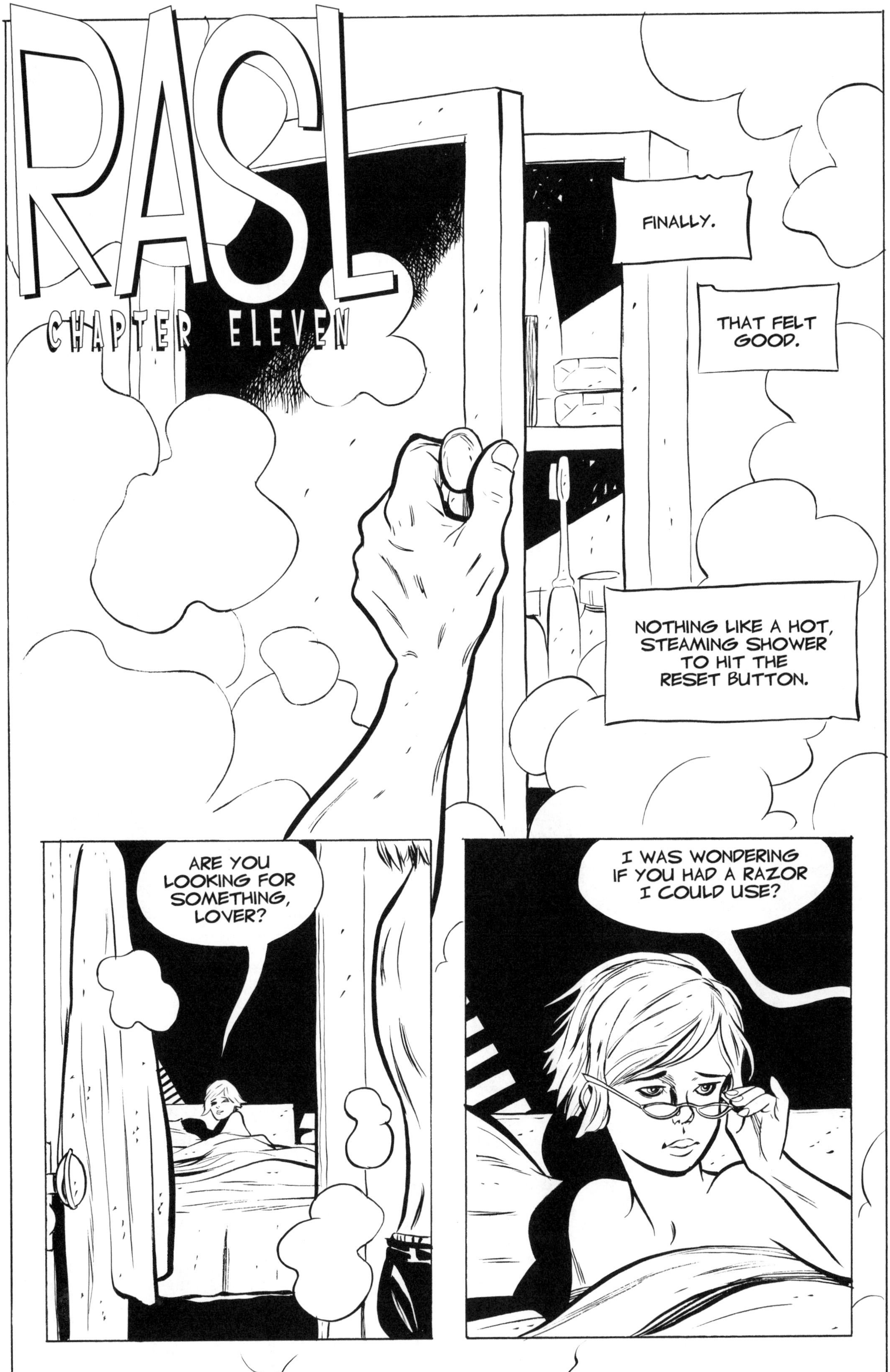
RASL
CHAPTER ELEVEN
FINALLY.
THAT FELT GOOD.
NOTHING LIKE A HOT, STEAMING SHOWER TO HIT THE RESET BUTTON.
ARE YOU LOOKING FOR SOMETHING, LOVER?
I WAS WONDERING IF YOU HAD A RAZOR I COULD USE?

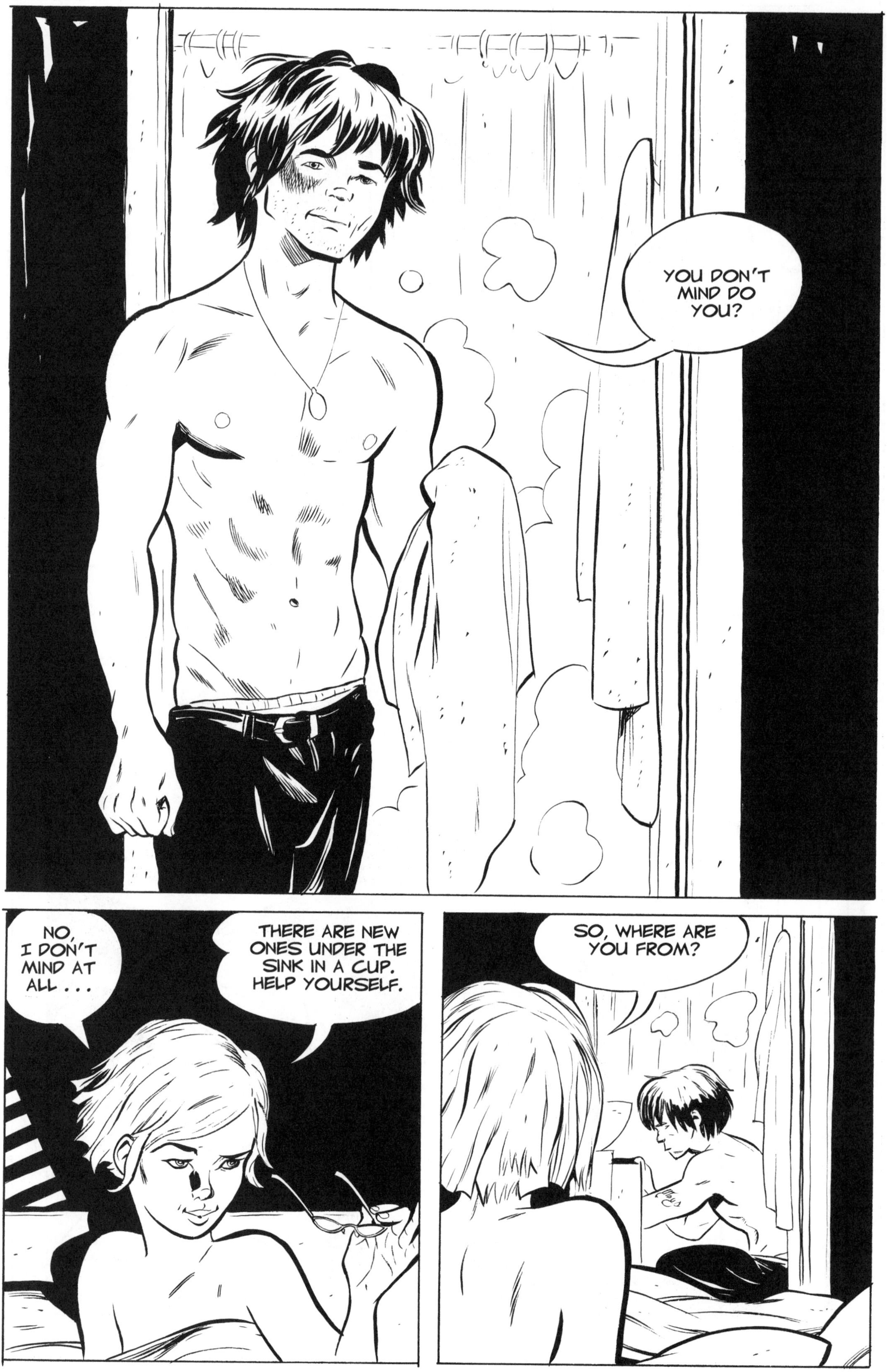
YOU DON'T MIND DO YOU?
NO, I DON'T MIND AT ALL . . .
THERE ARE NEW ONES UNDER THE SINK IN A CUP. HELP YOURSELF.
SO, WHERE ARE YOU FROM?

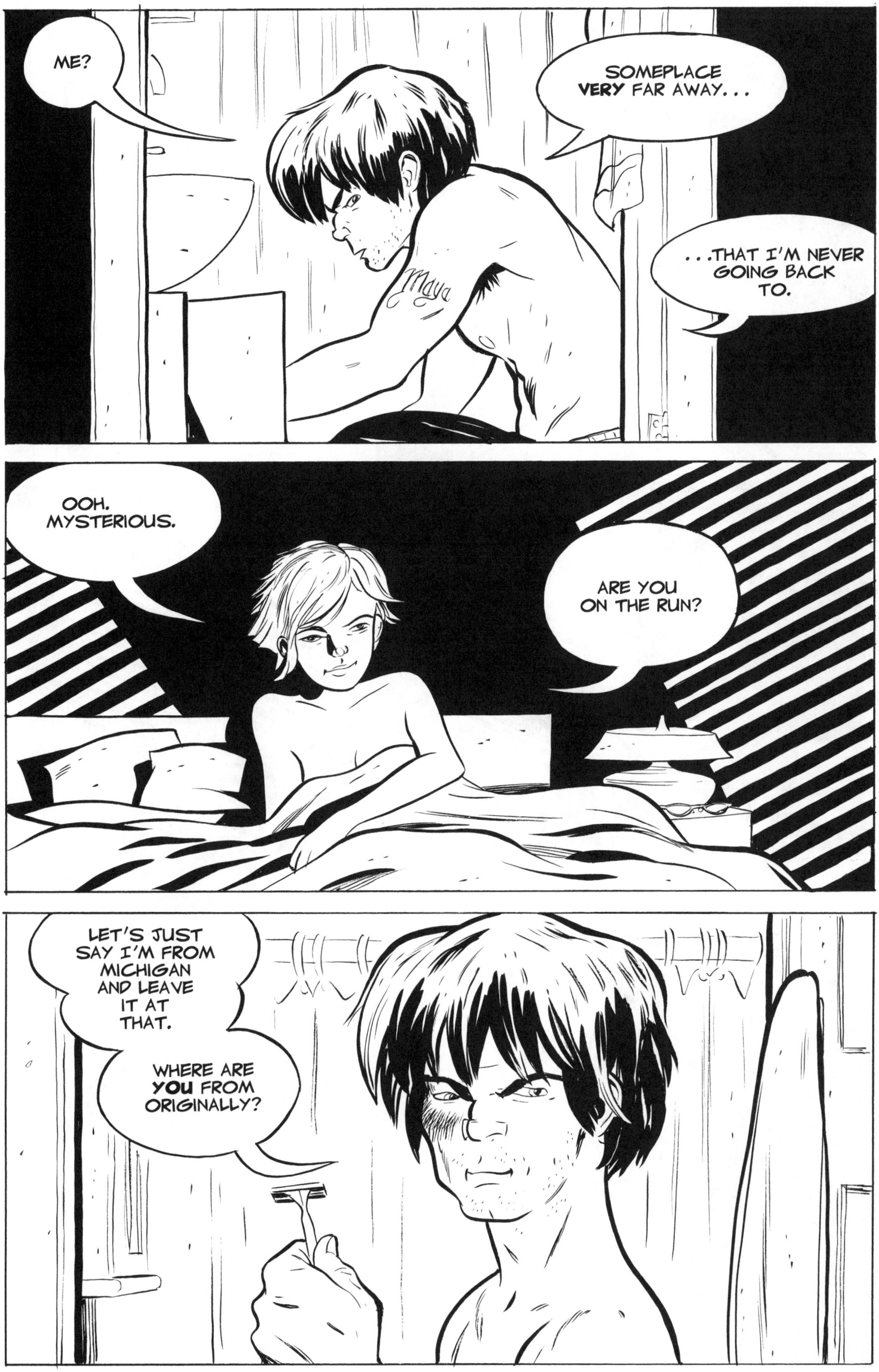
ME?
SOMEPLACE VERY FAR AWAY...
...THAT I'M NEVER GOING BACK TO.
OOH. MYSTERIOUS.
ARE YOU ON THE RUN?
LET'S JUST SAY I'M FROM MICHIGAN AND LEAVE IT AT THAT.
WHERE ARE YOU FROM ORIGINALLY?

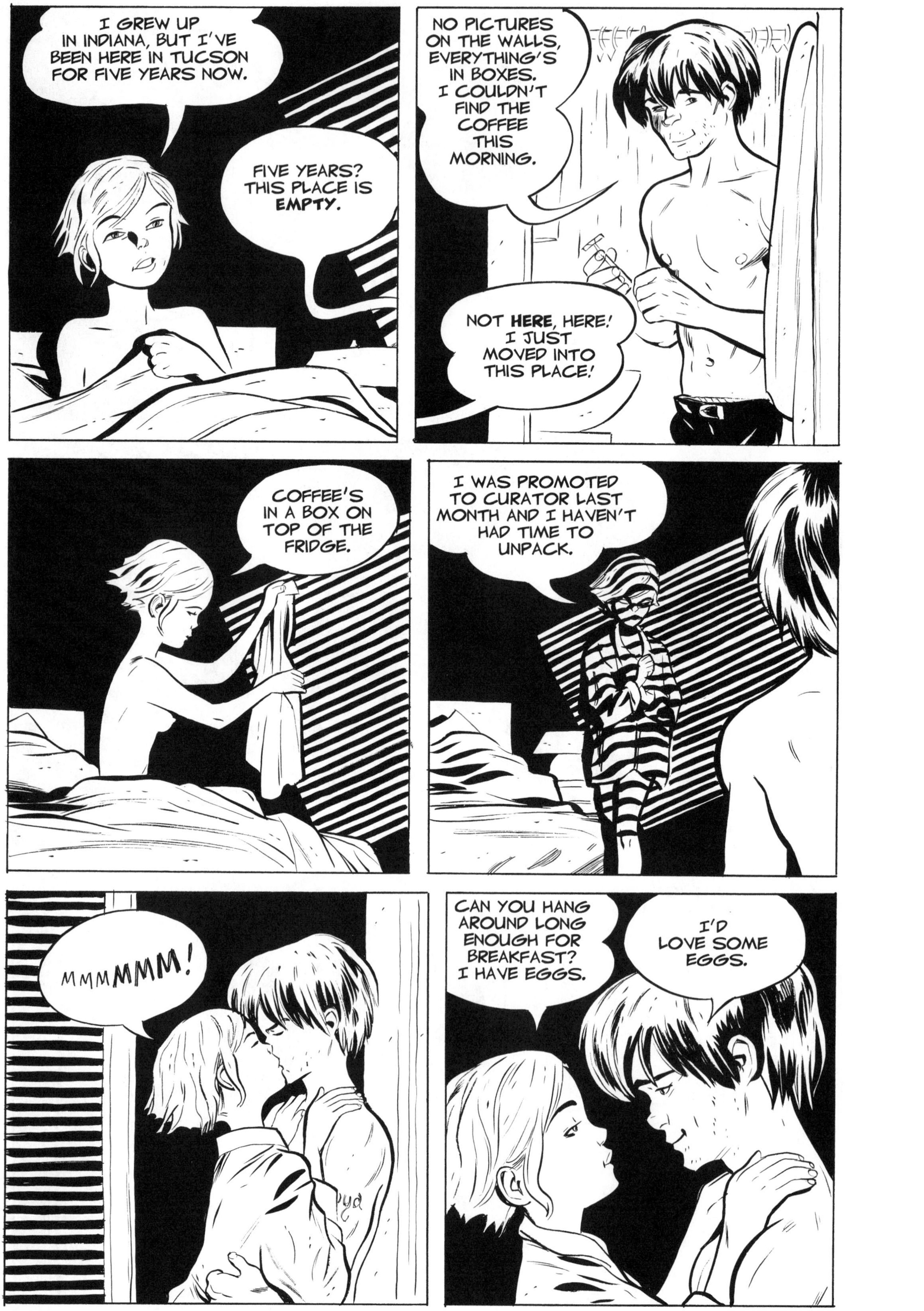
I GREW UP IN INDIANA, BUT I'VE BEEN HERE IN TUCSON FOR FIVE YEARS NOW.
FIVE YEARS? THIS PLACE IS EMPTY.
NO PICTURES ON THE WALLS, EVERYTHING'S IN BOXES. I COULDN'T FIND THE COFFEE THIS MORNING.
NOT HERE, HERE! I JUST MOVED INTO THIS PLACE!
COFFEE'S IN A BOX ON TOP OF THE FRIDGE.
I WAS PROMOTED TO CURATOR LAST MONTH AND I HAVEN'T HAD TIME TO UNPACK.
MMMMMM!
CAN YOU HANG AROUND LONG ENOUGH FOR BREAKFAST? I HAVE EGGS.
I'D LOVE SOME EGGS.

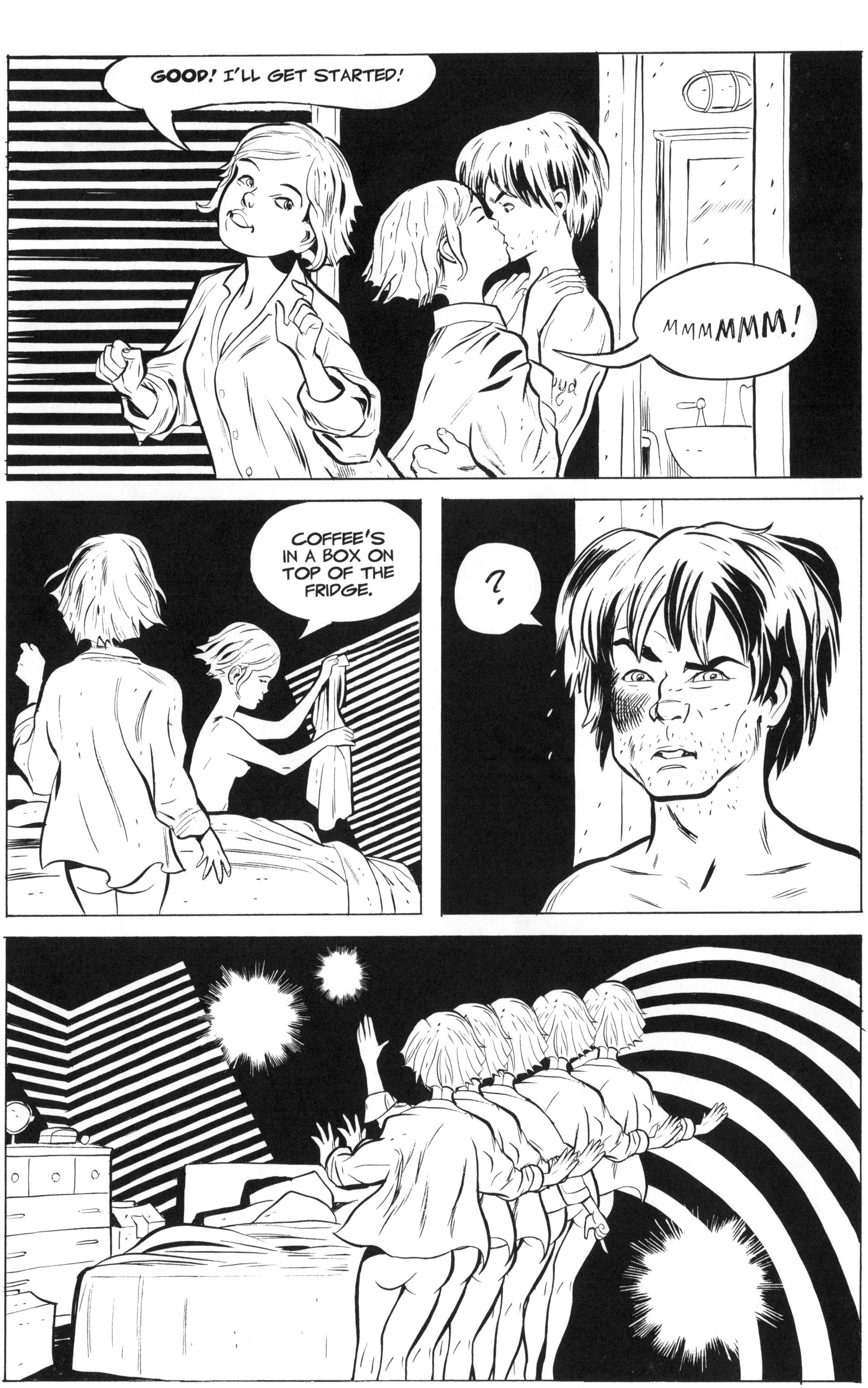
GOOD! I'LL GET STARTED!
MMMMMM!
COFFEE'S IN A BOX ON TOP OF THE FRIDGE.
?

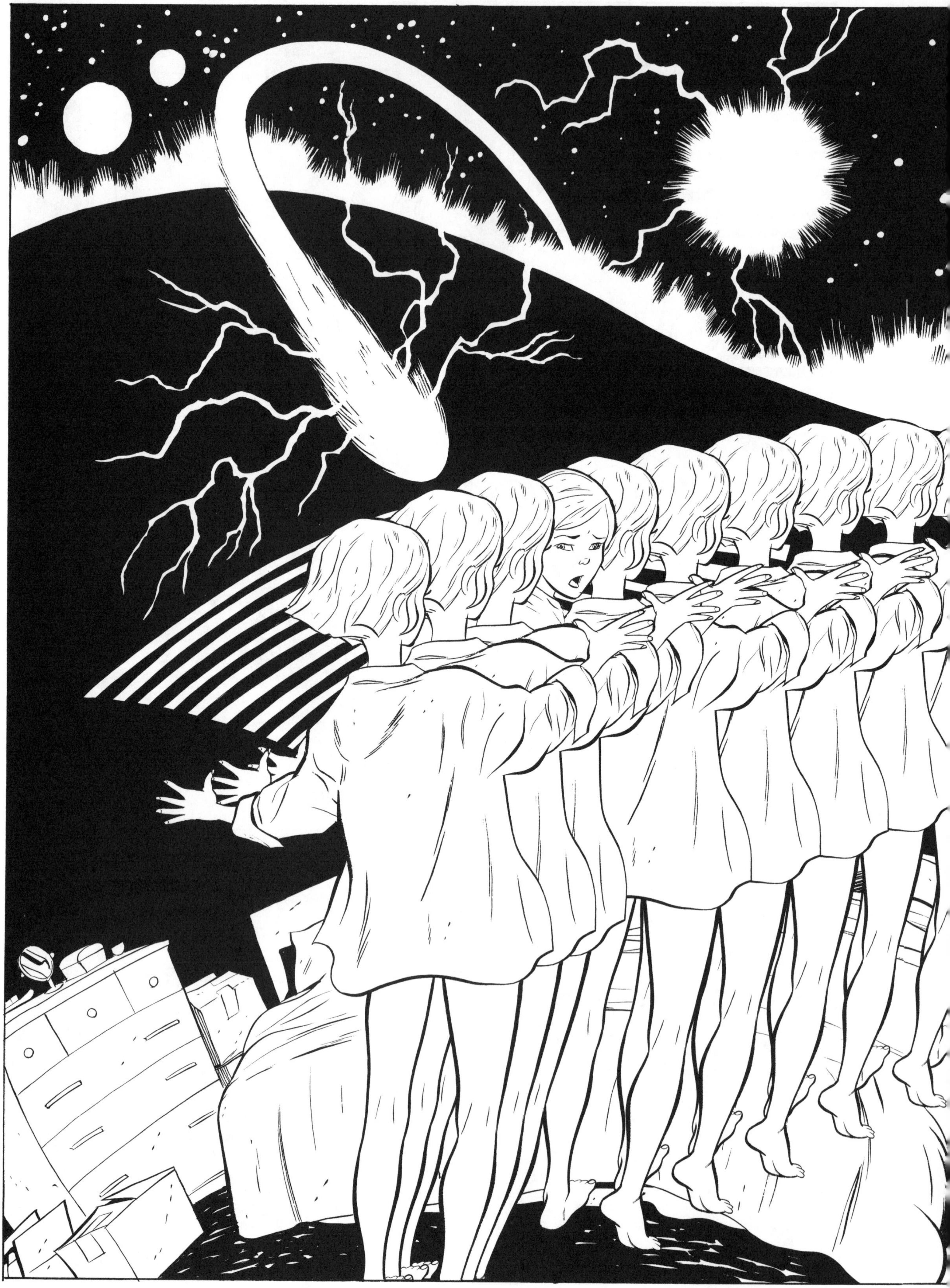

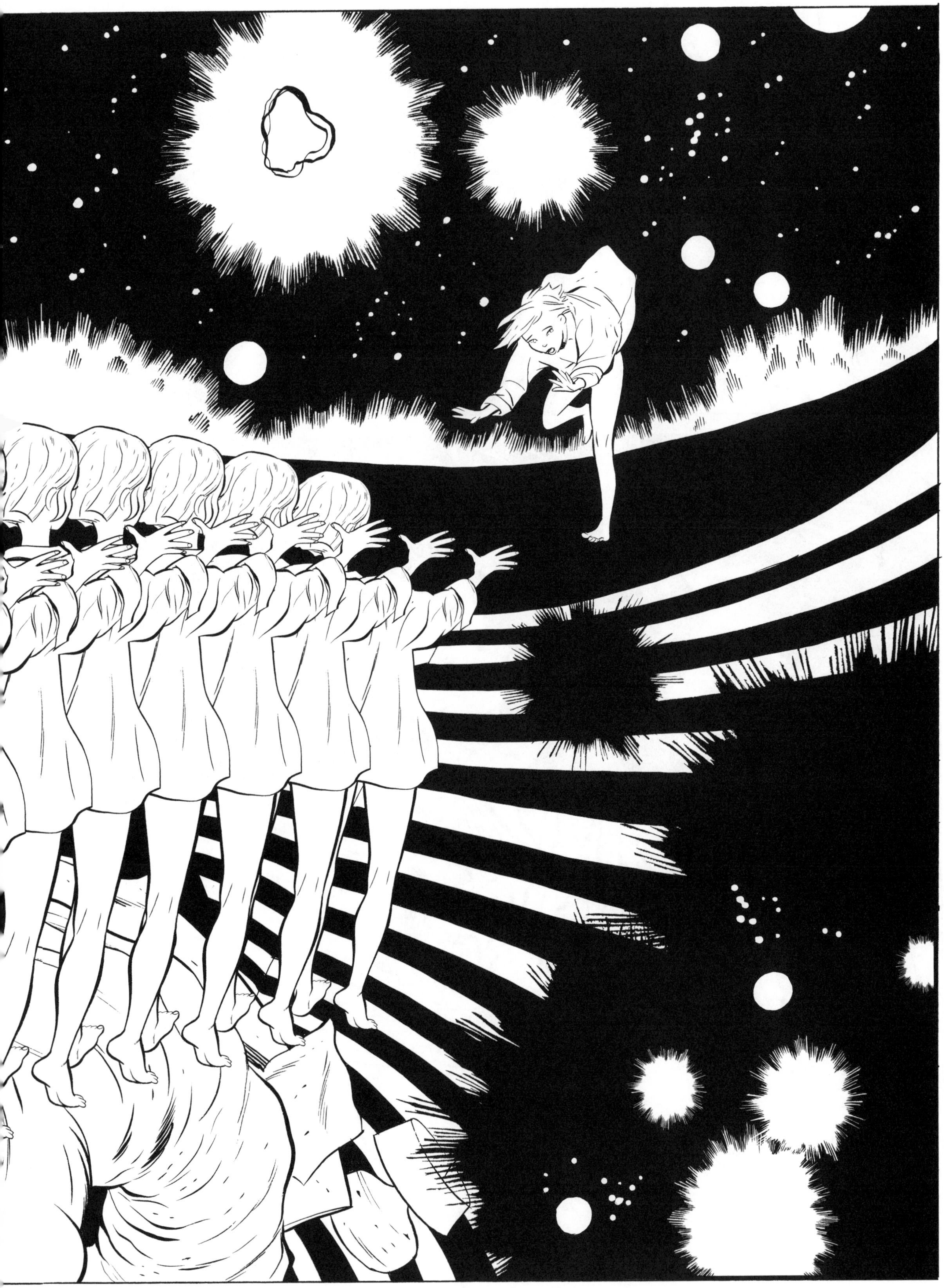

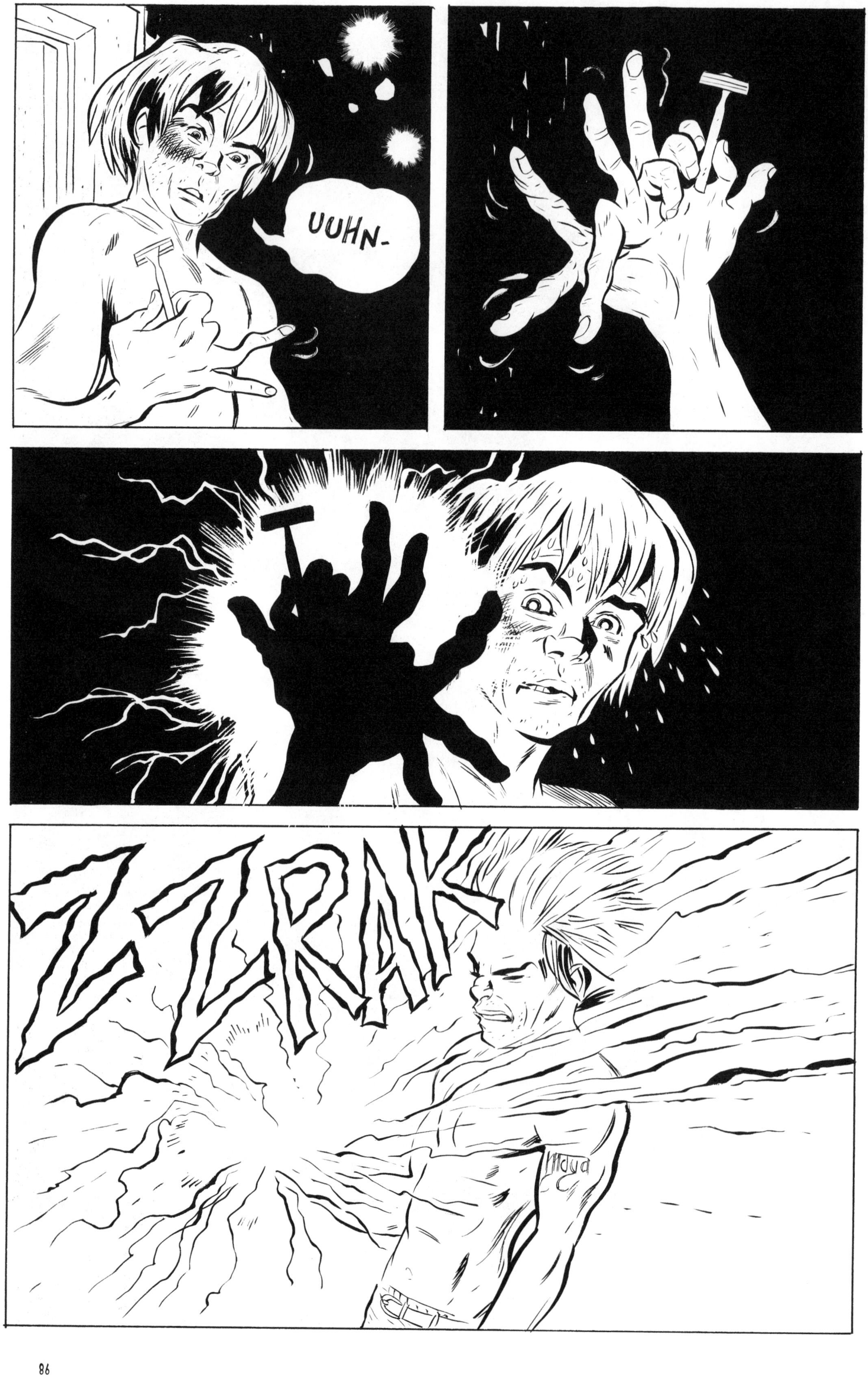
UUHN-
ZZRAK
Maya

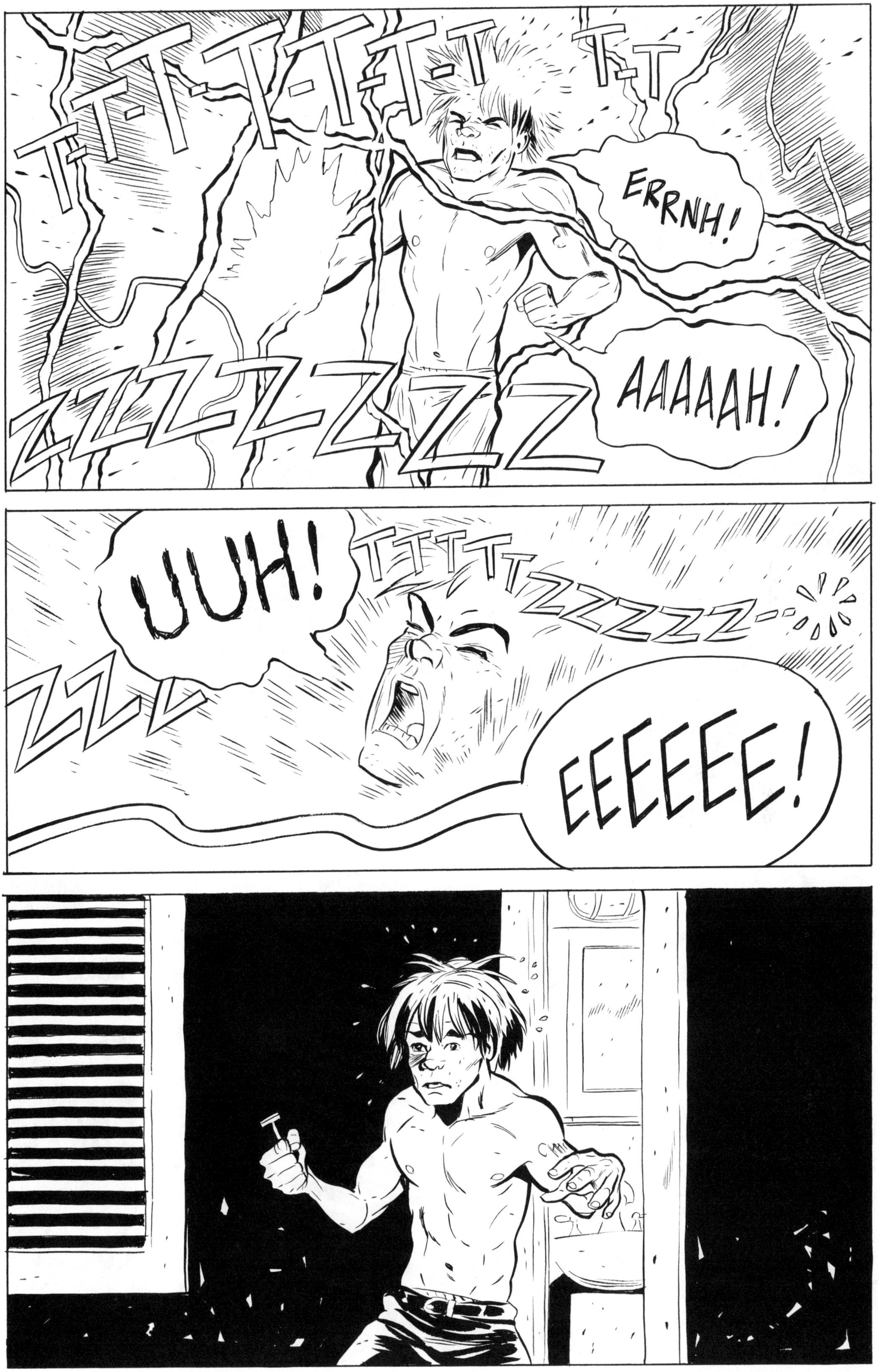
T-T-T-T-T-T-T-T
T-T
ERRNH!
ZZZZZZZZZ
AAAAAH!
UUH!
TTTTTZZZZZZ
ZZZ
EEEEEE!

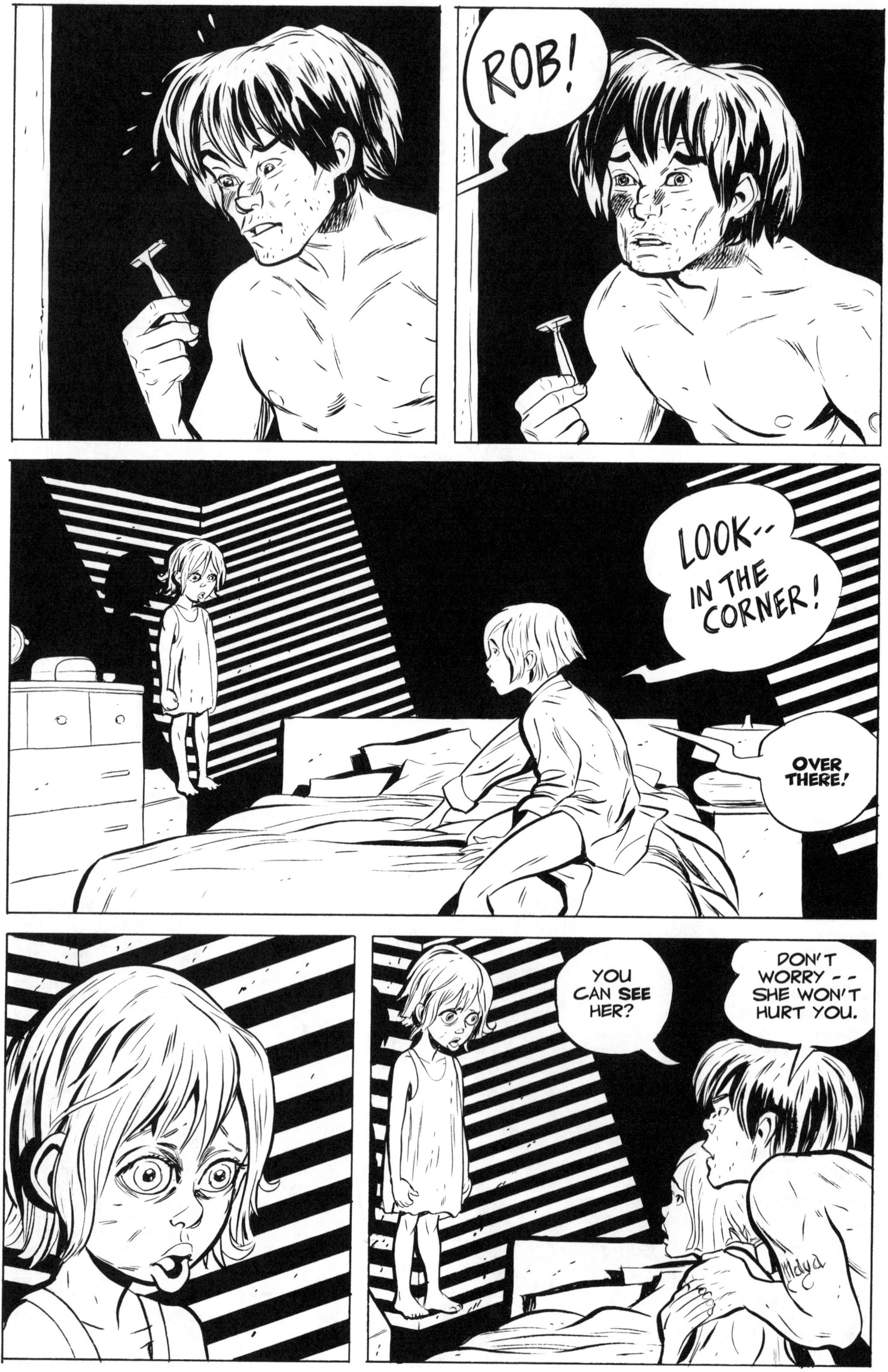
ROB!
LOOK-- IN THE CORNER!
OVER THERE!
YOU CAN SEE HER?
DON'T WORRY -- SHE WON'T HURT YOU.

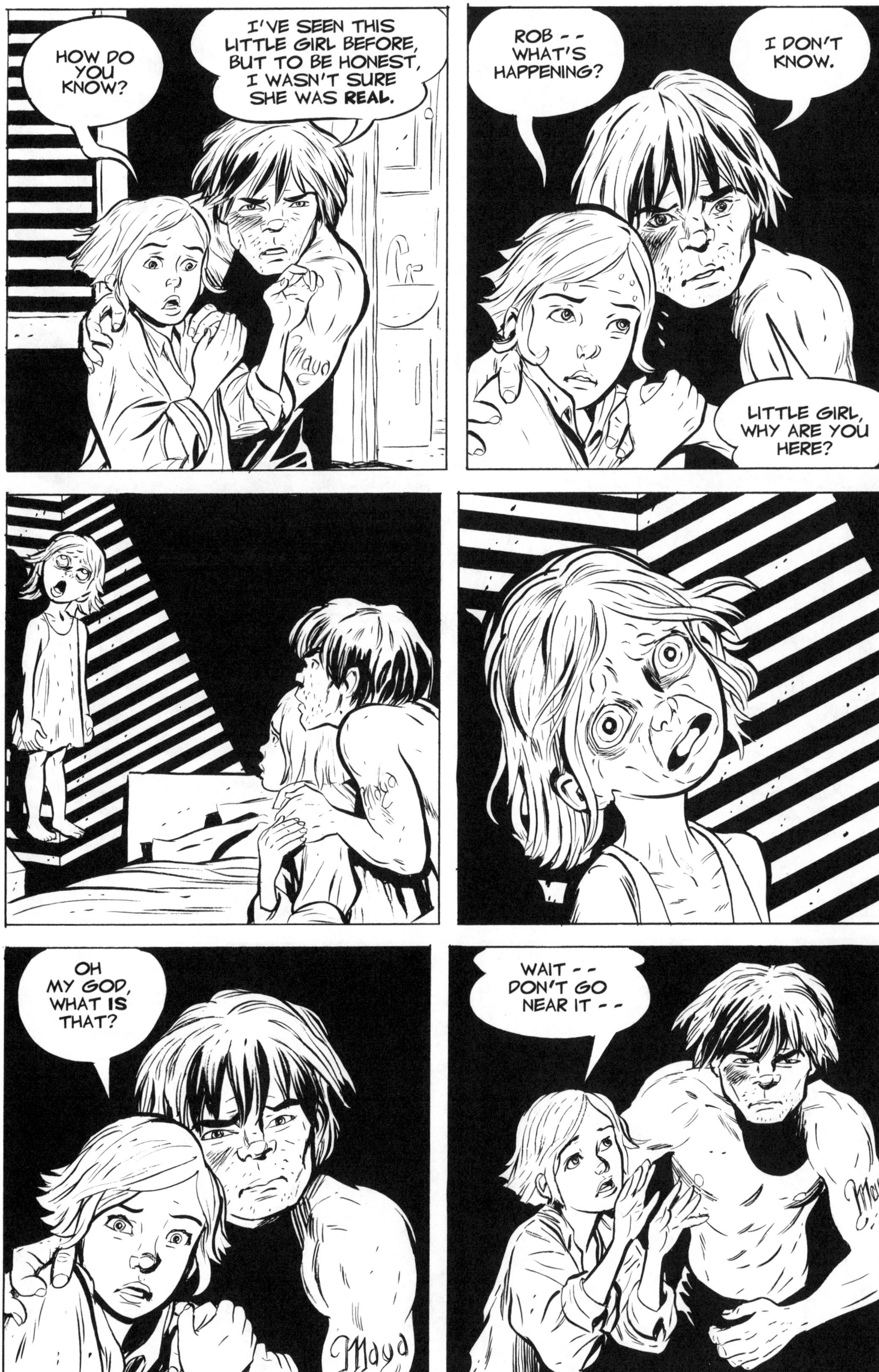
HOW DO YOU KNOW?
I'VE SEEN THIS LITTLE GIRL BEFORE, BUT TO BE HONEST, I WASN'T SURE SHE WAS **REAL.**
ROB -- WHAT'S HAPPENING?
I DON'T KNOW.
LITTLE GIRL, WHY ARE YOU HERE?
OH MY GOD, WHAT **IS** THAT?
WAIT -- DON'T GO NEAR IT --

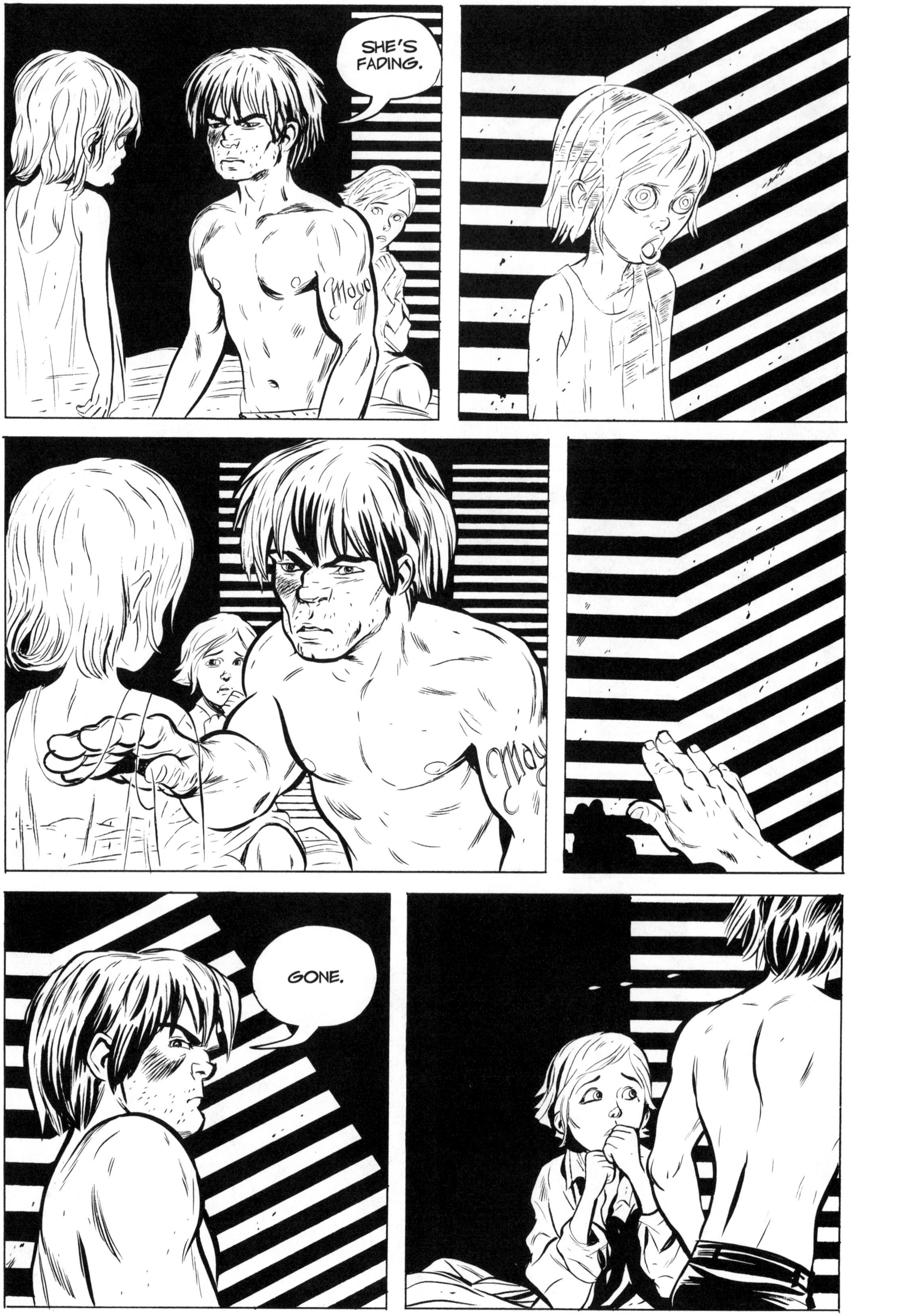
SHE'S FADING.
GONE.

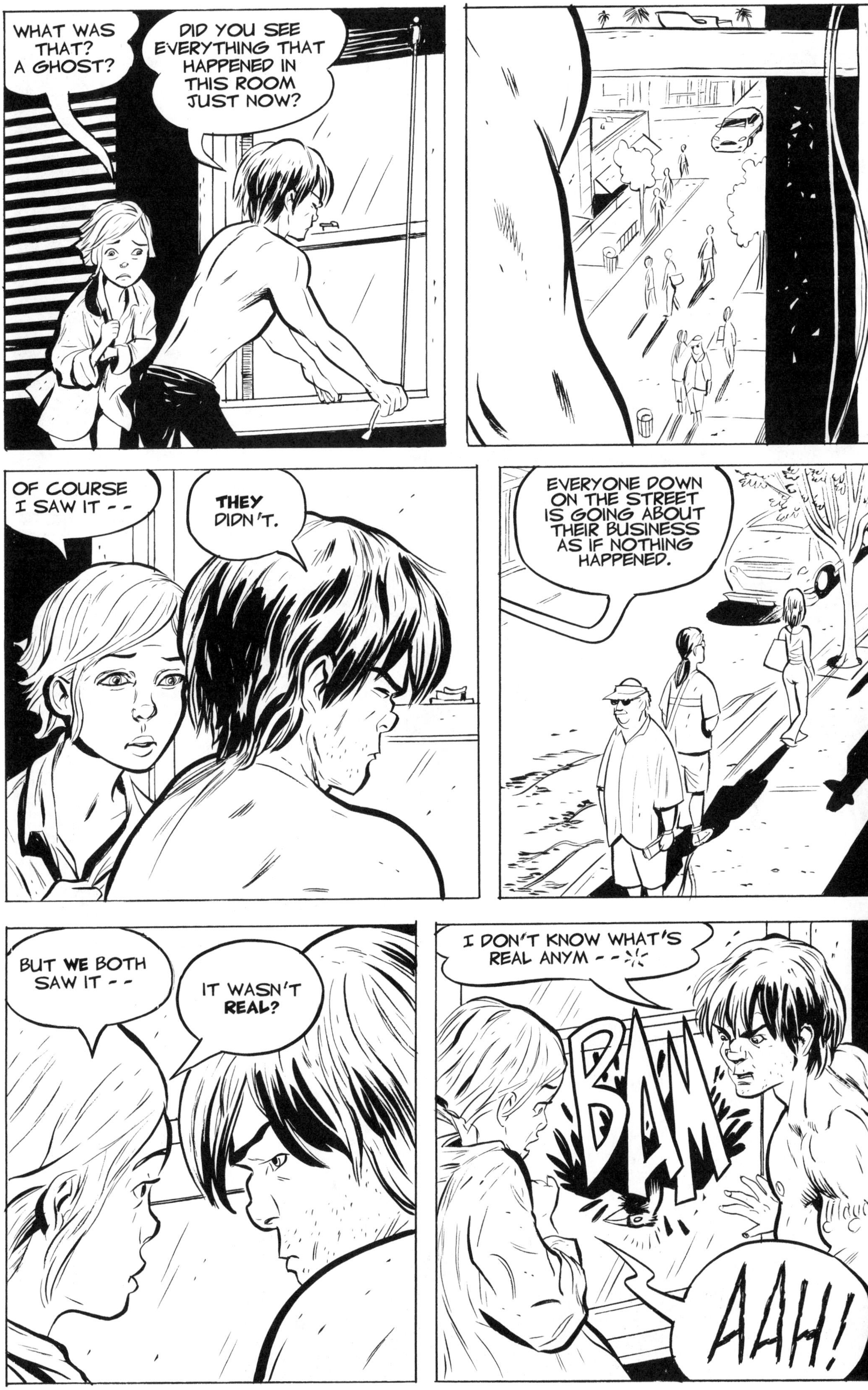
WHAT WAS THAT? A GHOST?
DID YOU SEE EVERYTHING THAT HAPPENED IN THIS ROOM JUST NOW?
OF COURSE I SAW IT --
THEY DIDN'T.
EVERYONE DOWN ON THE STREET IS GOING ABOUT THEIR BUSINESS AS IF NOTHING HAPPENED.
BUT WE BOTH SAW IT --
IT WASN'T REAL?
I DON'T KNOW WHAT'S REAL ANYM --
BAM
AAH!

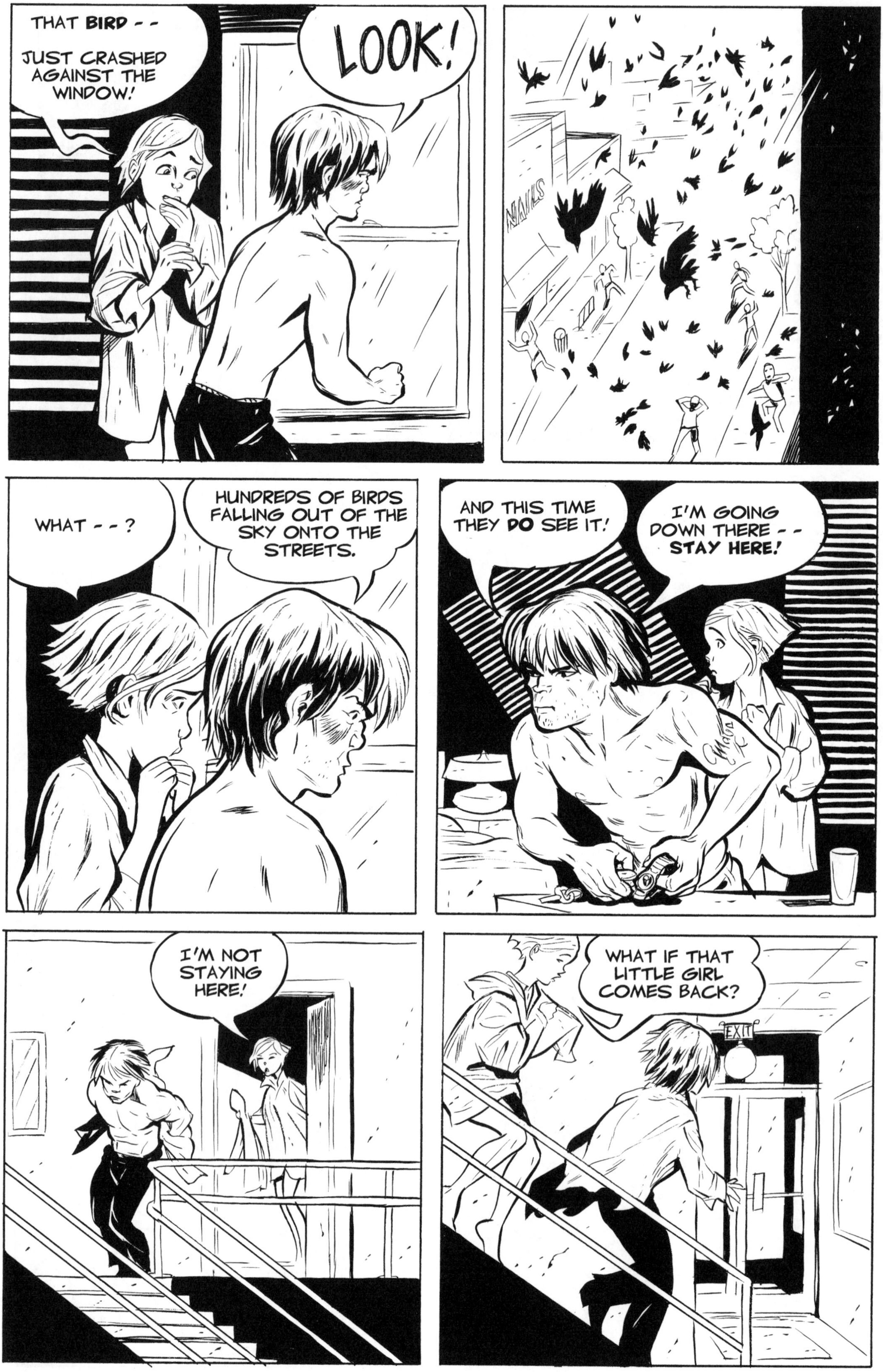

THAT BIRD - - JUST CRASHED AGAINST THE WINDOW!
LOOK!
WHAT - - ?
HUNDREDS OF BIRDS FALLING OUT OF THE SKY ONTO THE STREETS.
AND THIS TIME THEY DO SEE IT!
I'M GOING DOWN THERE - - STAY HERE!
I'M NOT STAYING HERE!
WHAT IF THAT LITTLE GIRL COMES BACK?
EXIT

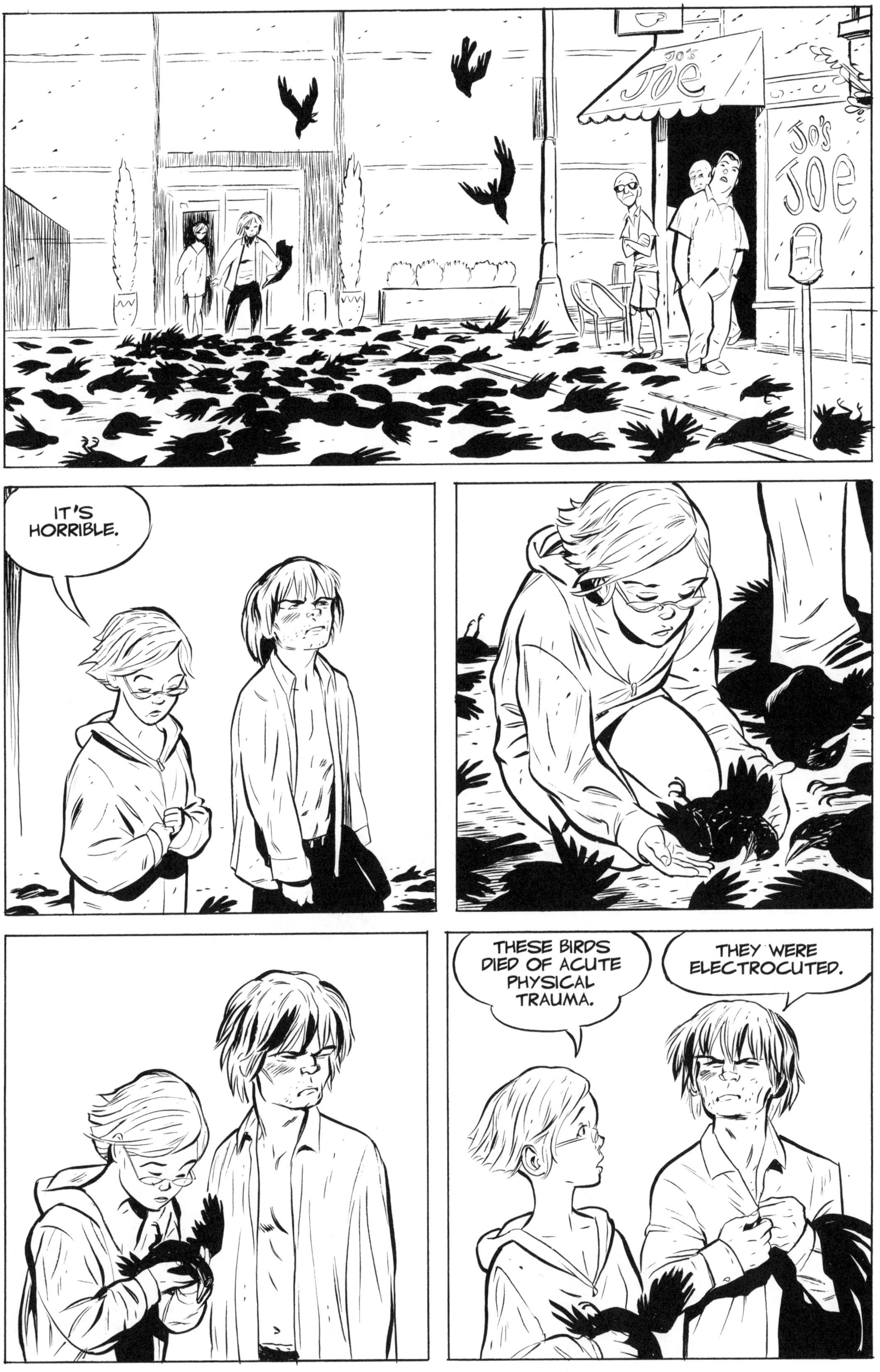
JO'S JOE
JO'S JOE
IT'S HORRIBLE.
THESE BIRDS DIED OF ACUTE PHYSICAL TRAUMA.
THEY WERE ELECTROCUTED.

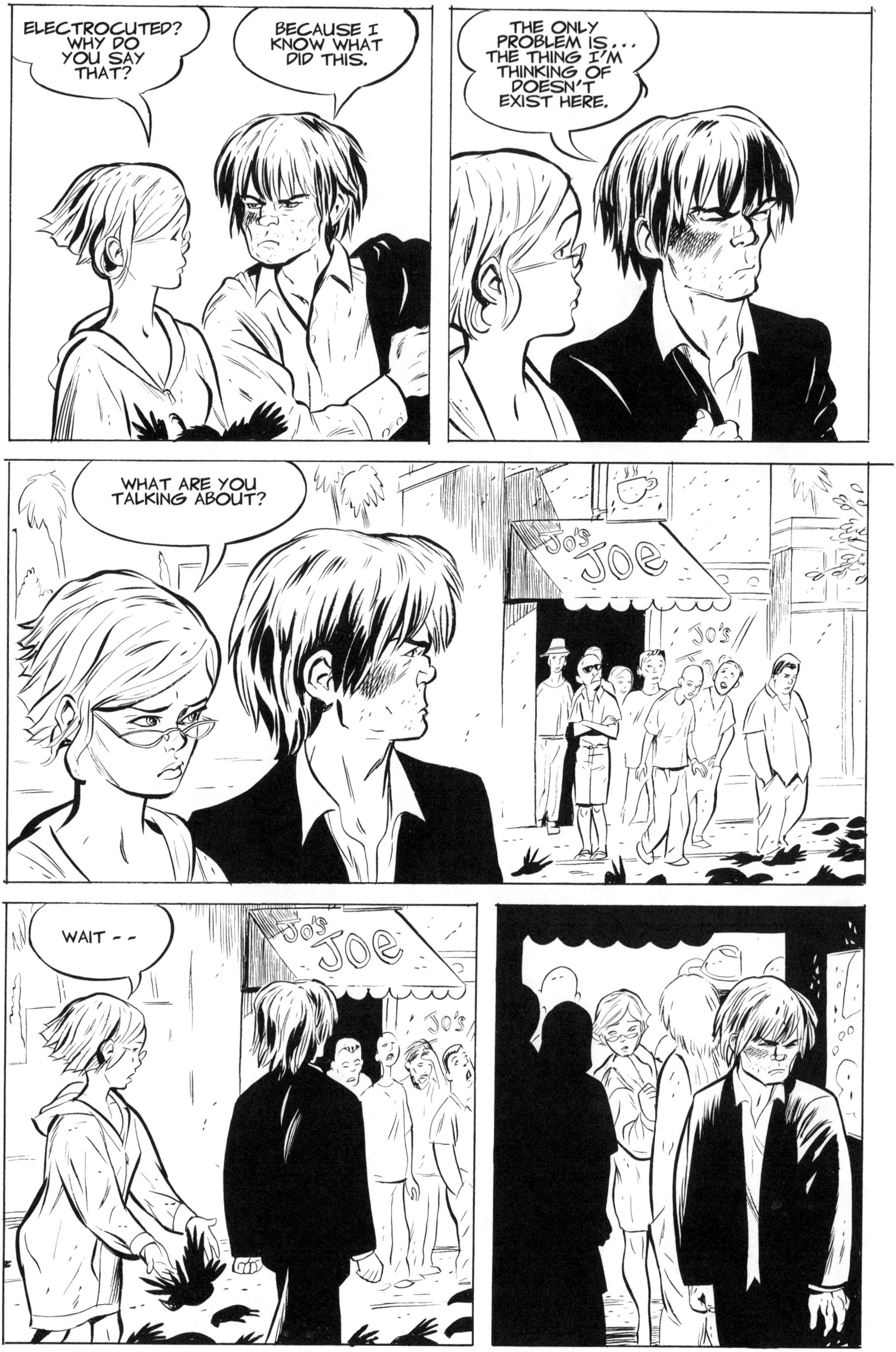
ELECTROCUTED? WHY DO YOU SAY THAT?
BECAUSE I KNOW WHAT DID THIS.
THE ONLY PROBLEM IS... THE THING I'M THINKING OF DOESN'T EXIST HERE.
WHAT ARE YOU TALKING ABOUT?
Jo's JOE
Jo's
WAIT --
Jo's JOE
Jo's

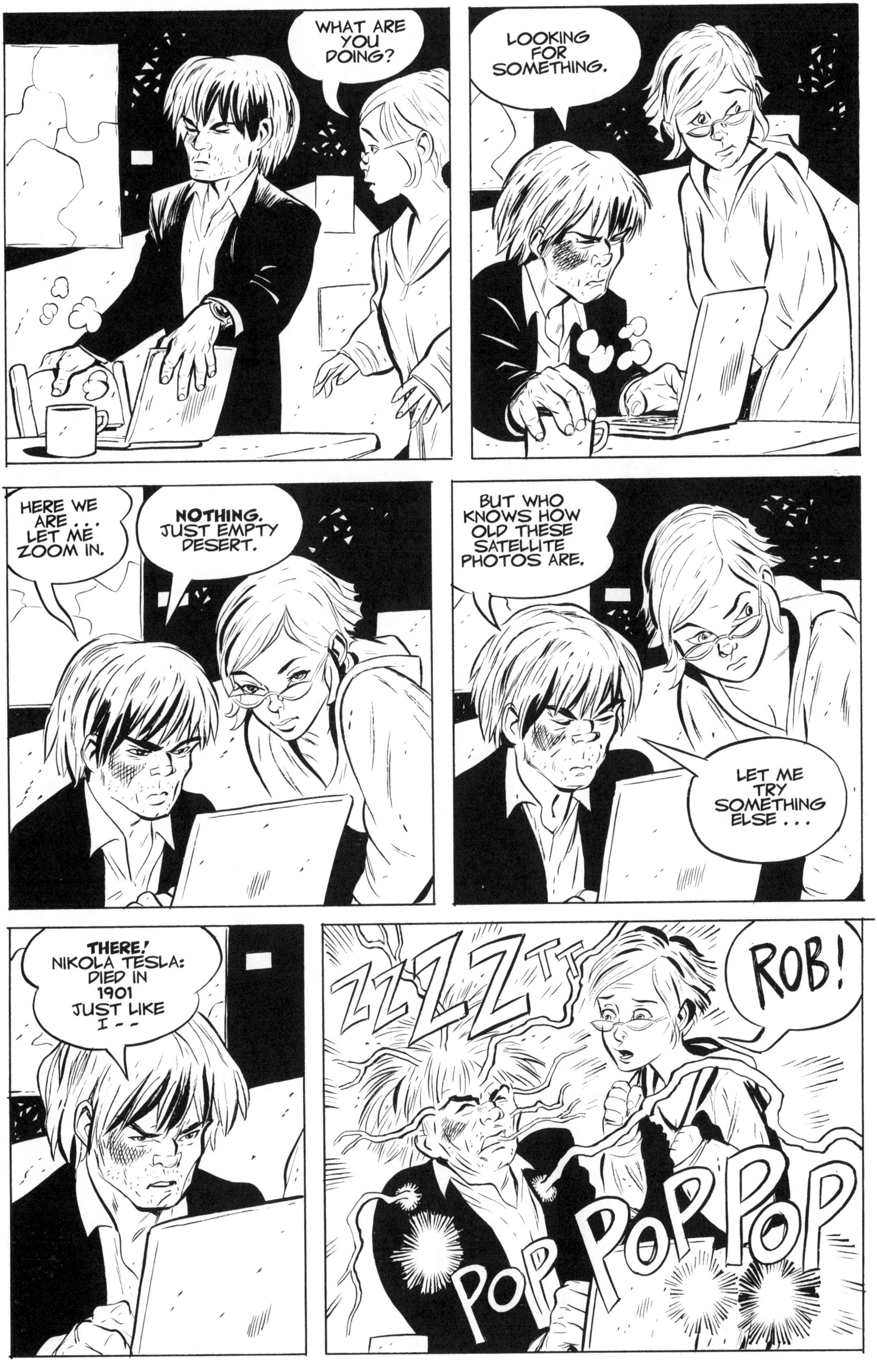
WHAT ARE YOU DOING?
LOOKING FOR SOMETHING.
HERE WE ARE . . . LET ME ZOOM IN.
NOTHING. JUST EMPTY DESERT.
BUT WHO KNOWS HOW OLD THESE SATELLITE PHOTOS ARE.
LET ME TRY SOMETHING ELSE . . .
THERE! NIKOLA TESLA: DIED IN 1901 JUST LIKE I - -
ZZZZTT
ROB!
POP POP POP POP

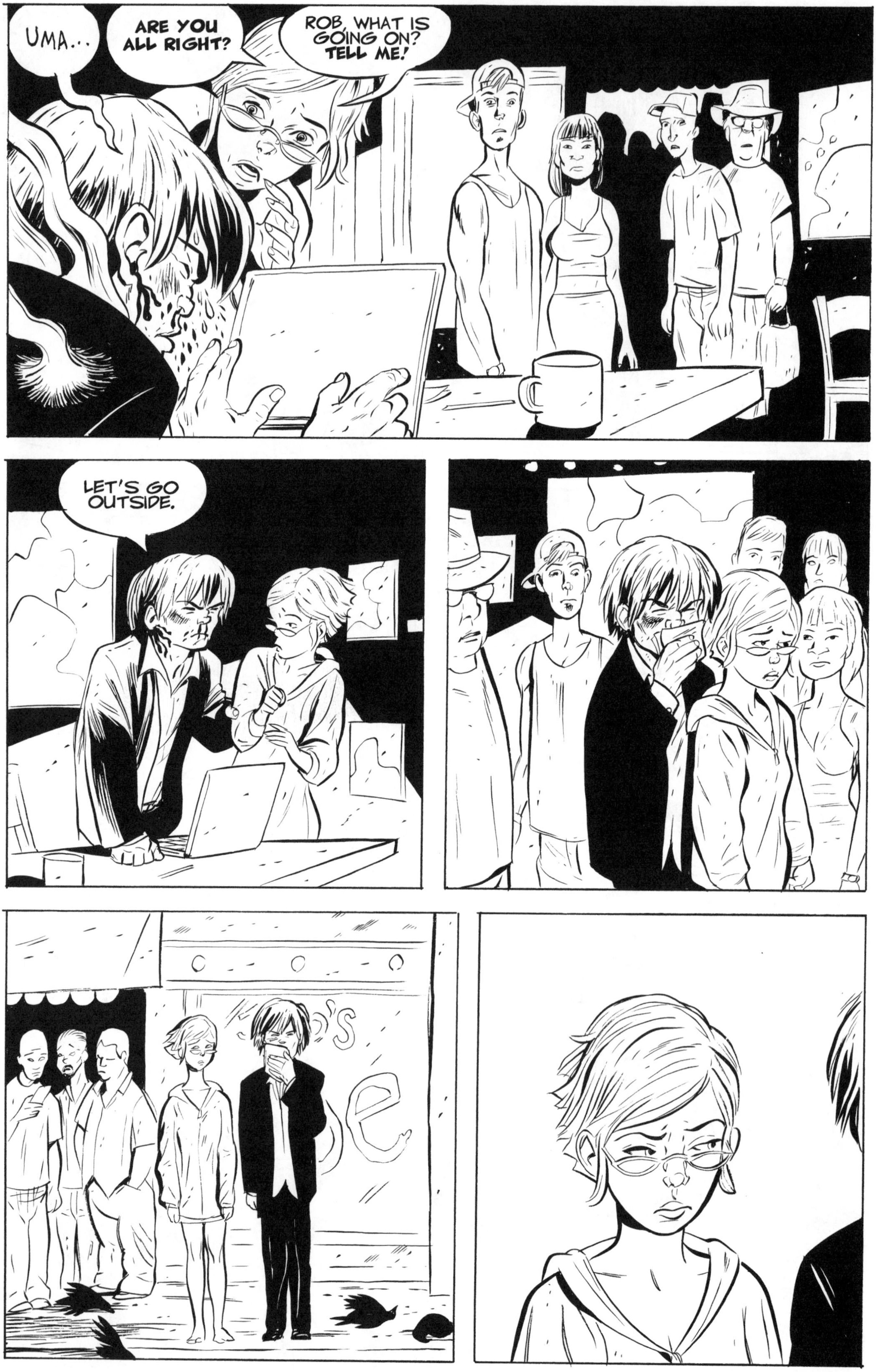
UMA...
ARE YOU ALL RIGHT?
ROB, WHAT IS GOING ON? TELL ME!
LET'S GO OUTSIDE.

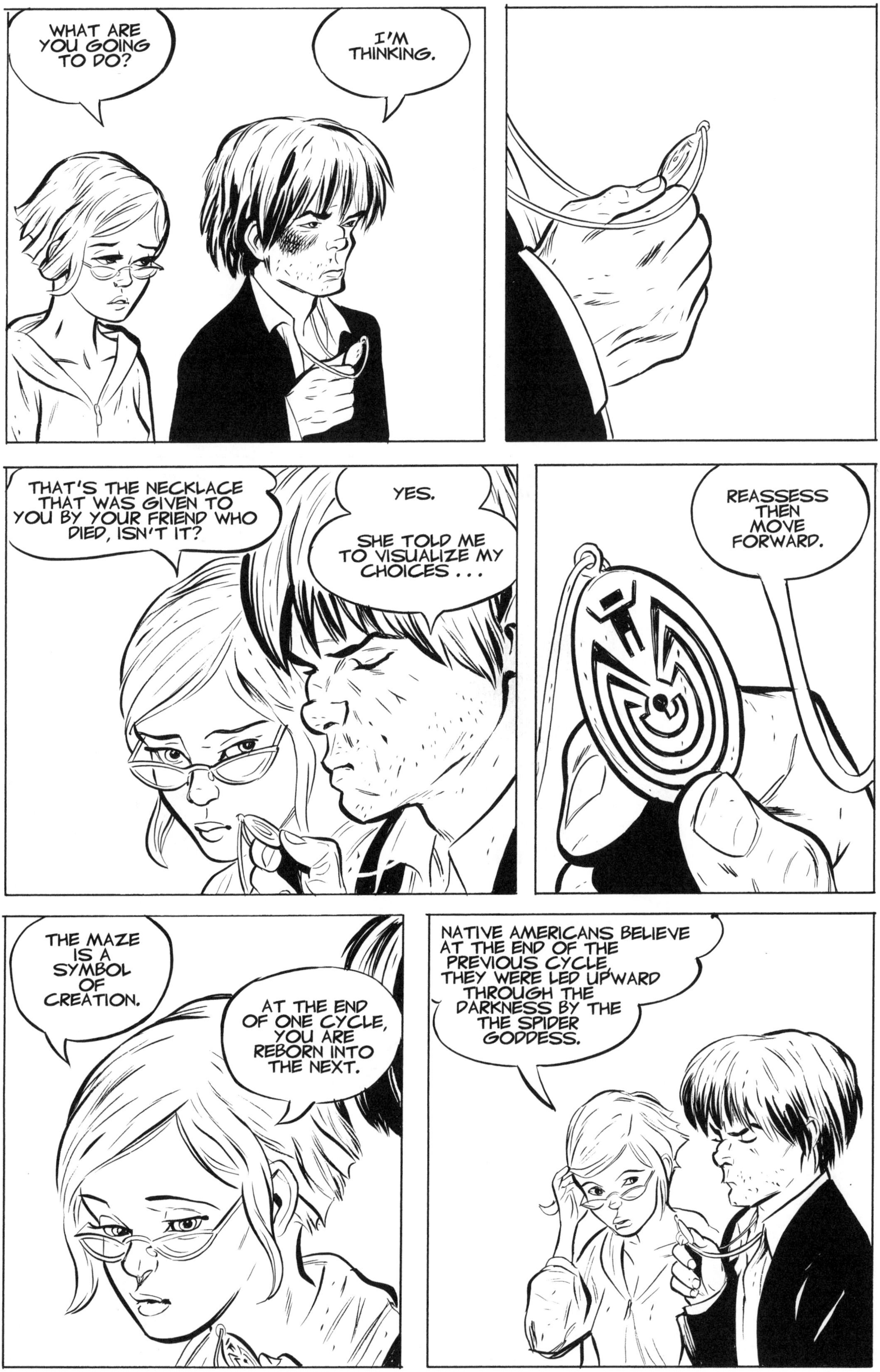
WHAT ARE YOU GOING TO DO?
I'M THINKING.
THAT'S THE NECKLACE THAT WAS GIVEN TO YOU BY YOUR FRIEND WHO DIED, ISN'T IT?
YES.
SHE TOLD ME TO VISUALIZE MY CHOICES . . .
REASSESS THEN MOVE FORWARD.
THE MAZE IS A SYMBOL OF CREATION.
AT THE END OF ONE CYCLE, YOU ARE REBORN INTO THE NEXT.
NATIVE AMERICANS BELIEVE AT THE END OF THE PREVIOUS CYCLE THEY WERE LED UPWARD THROUGH THE DARKNESS BY THE THE SPIDER GODDESS.

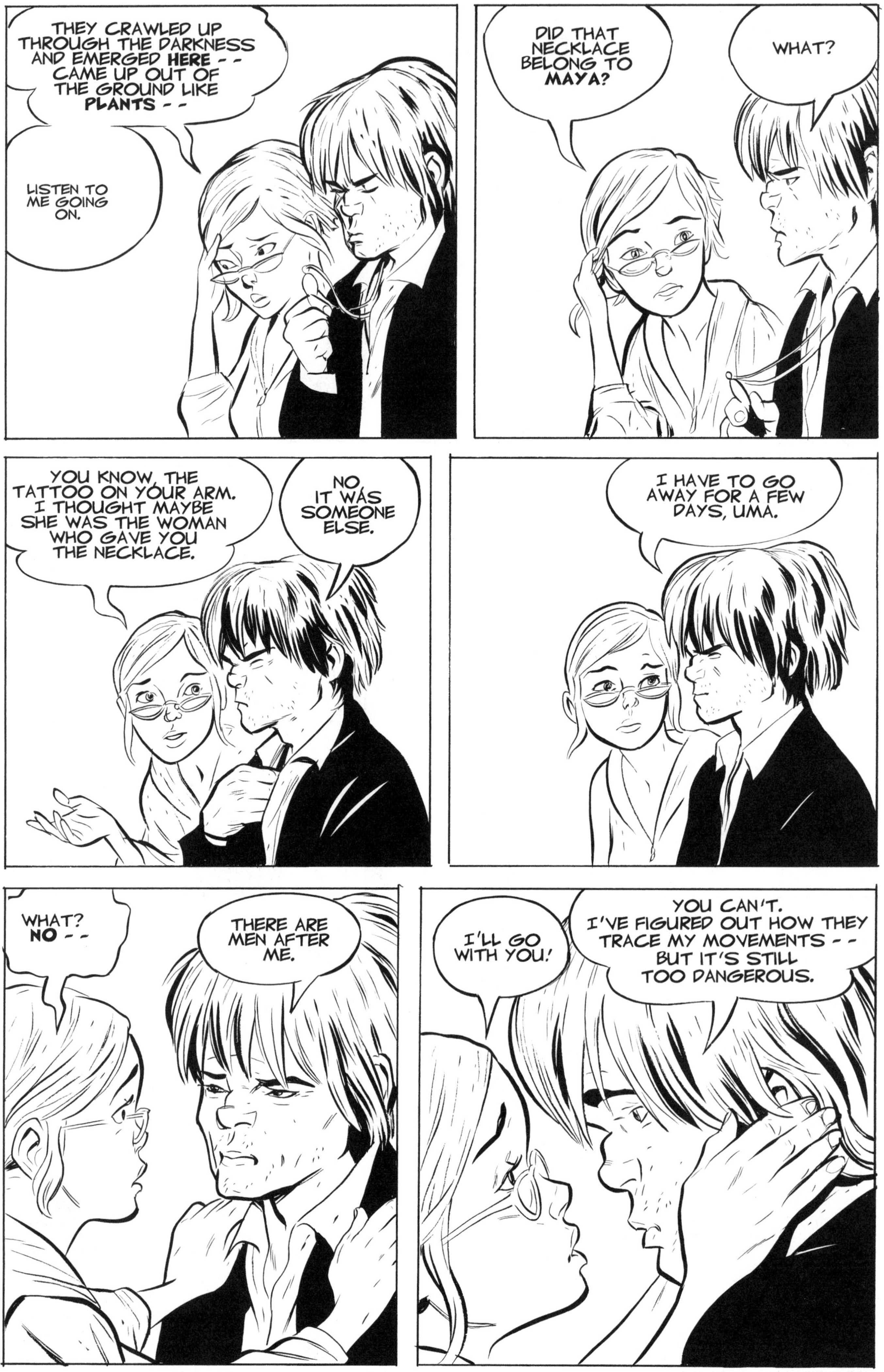
THEY CRAWLED UP THROUGH THE DARKNESS AND EMERGED HERE -- CAME UP OUT OF THE GROUND LIKE PLANTS --
LISTEN TO ME GOING ON.
DID THAT NECKLACE BELONG TO MAYA?
WHAT?
YOU KNOW, THE TATTOO ON YOUR ARM. I THOUGHT MAYBE SHE WAS THE WOMAN WHO GAVE YOU THE NECKLACE.
NO IT WAS SOMEONE ELSE.
I HAVE TO GO AWAY FOR A FEW DAYS, UMA.
THERE ARE MEN AFTER ME.
WHAT? NO --
I'LL GO WITH YOU!
YOU CAN'T. I'VE FIGURED OUT HOW THEY TRACE MY MOVEMENTS -- BUT IT'S STILL TOO DANGEROUS.

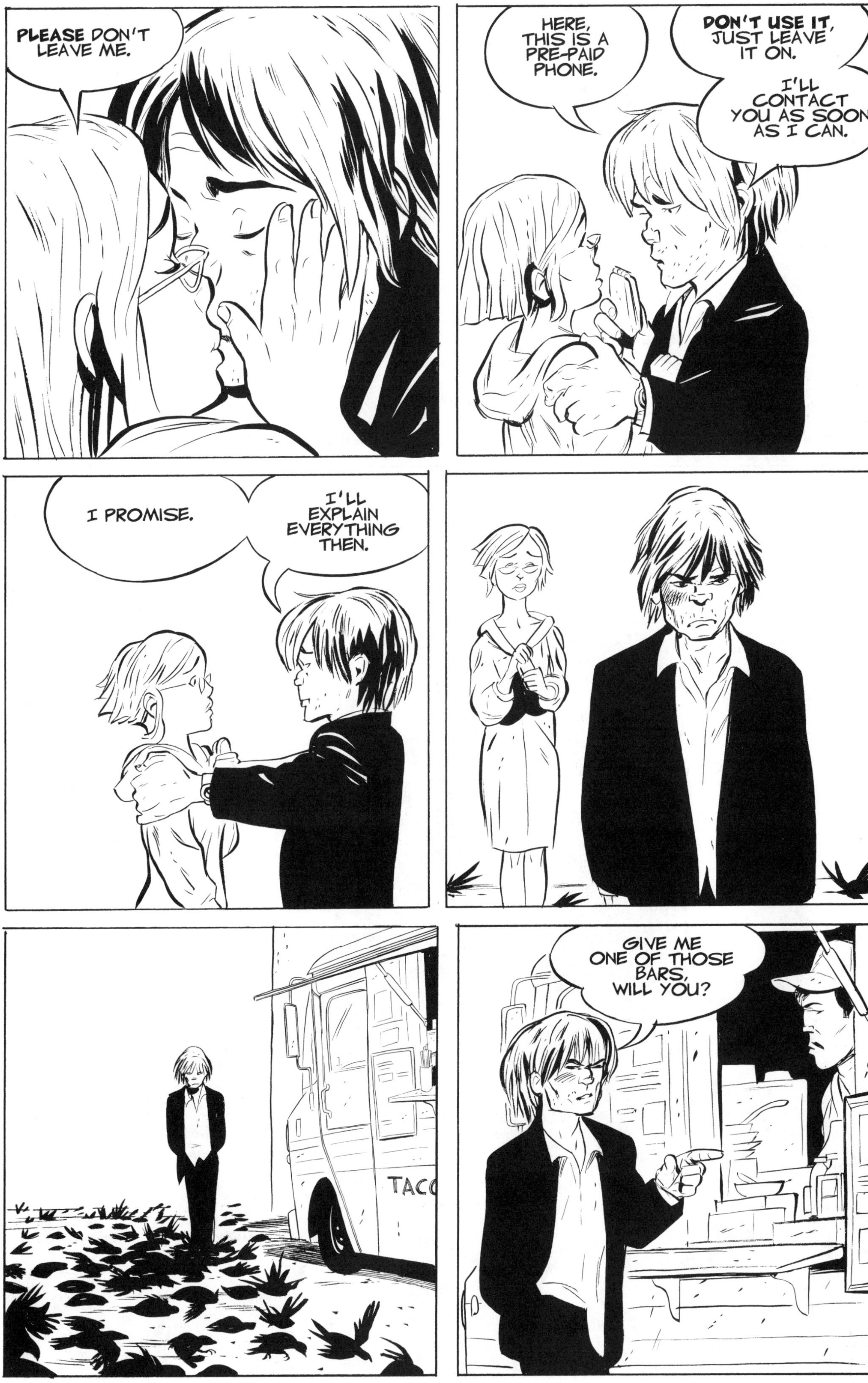
PLEASE DON'T LEAVE ME.
HERE, THIS IS A PRE-PAID PHONE.
DON'T USE IT, JUST LEAVE IT ON.
I'LL CONTACT YOU AS SOON AS I CAN.
I PROMISE.
I'LL EXPLAIN EVERYTHING THEN.
TACO
GIVE ME ONE OF THOSE BARS, WILL YOU?

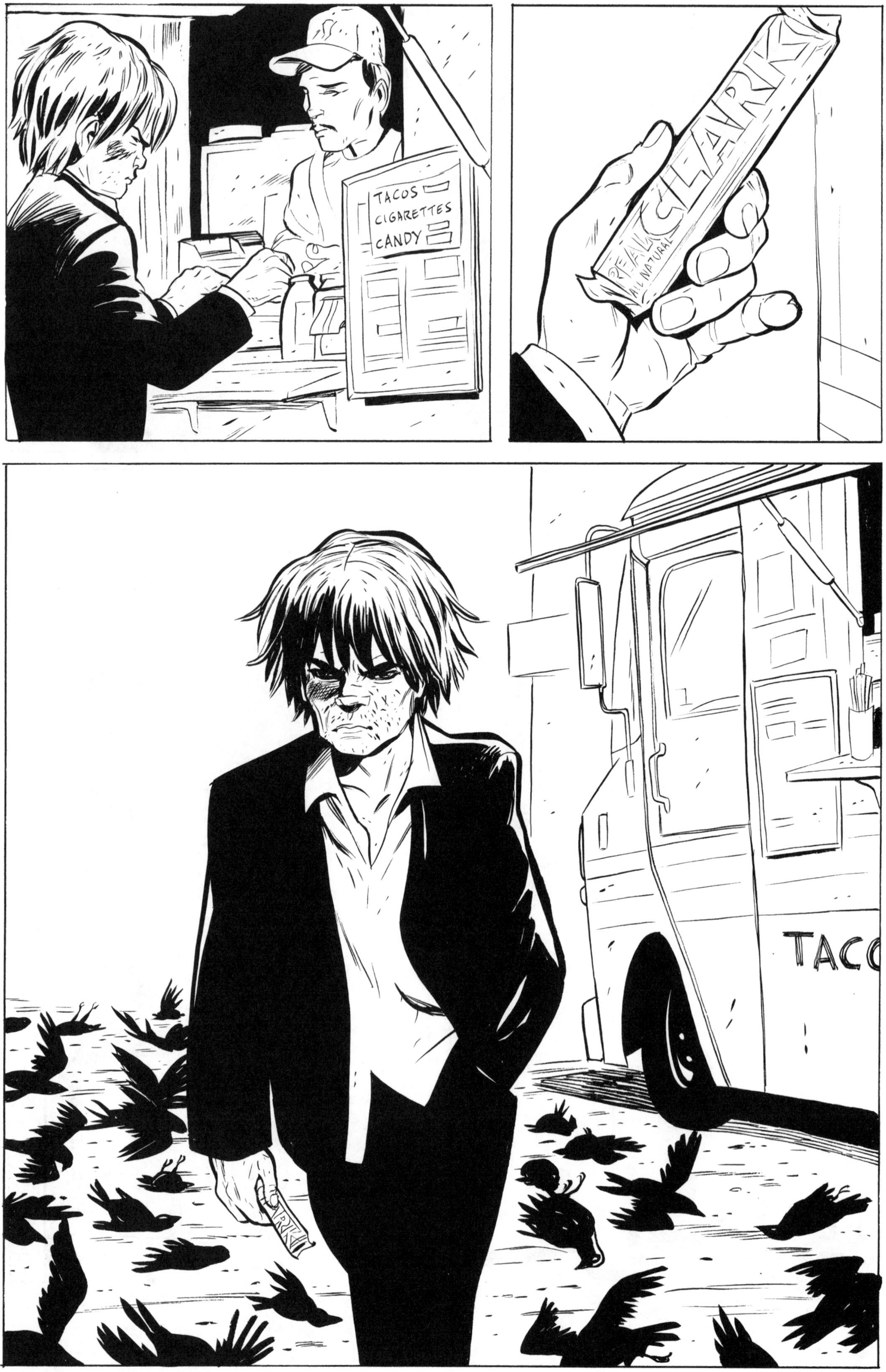
TACOS
CIGARETTES
CANDY
REAL
ALL NATURAL
CLARK
TACO

To be concluded in
RASL 4:
The Lost Journals of Nikola Tesla

# APPENDIX
# Part One

## Behind the Scenes of
## RASL Volumes One and Two

# Designing the Drift

## Behind the Scenes of RASL 1: The Drift

The idea of being able to change places with yourself in a parallel universe has always been intriguing to me. Would you have the same friends? The same career? Would you meet your girlfriend only to find she had married someone else and didn't even know you?

I read up on current scientific thinking like String Theory and "M"Theory which imply the existence of parallel universes, and then I dug deep into the underworld of fringe science; a murky world where Einstein completed his Unified Field Theory in 1928 only to cover it up, Tesla built Death Rays that fired through the earth and caused the Tunguska Event in 1908, and the Navy turned a WWII Destroyer Escort ship invisible and teleported it 300 miles.

During long, late night inking sessions on BONE, my laptop played films like *Blade Runner*, *2001: A Space Odyssey*, *The Maltese Falcon*, and *The Big Sleep*, over & over again. I'm a huge fan of science fiction and noir, so it was only a matter of time before I put the two together. I decided to make a science fiction comic that contained hard science, and fill it with hard-boiled characters. The idea that a scientist and former employee of the military industrial complex might use experimental equipment to slip into neighboring universes and steal precious artworks for dangerous clients, fit my idea of a noir world, and if this scientist's past could be littered with regrettable decisions, well, perfect! The kicker came when I discovered the infamous nineteenth century inventor Nikola Tesla, whose creations not only underlie all of modern civilization - - and form the basis of RASL's technology - - but whose own history is strewn with the kinds of bad choices that fuel conspiracy theories. With a pair of hand-held Thermal-magnetic warp engines on his shoulders and a shot of rye whisky in his gut, RASL was born.

In the Fall of 2007, I was ready to start work on my new project. I had a lot of ideas, and a pretty good inkling where the story was headed, but it needed organizing. I spent two weeks in Arizona, taking trips into the desert with nothing to distract me but the sounds of insects, the occasional birdcall, and the wind blowing through the drying bones of ancient saguaros.

As I sat in 110° temperatures, the torrid tale of RASL, inter-dimensional art thief came to life.

The Special Oversized Edition you hold in your hands includes some behind the scenes sketches, photos, script pages and even a couple of unused covers. I hope you enjoyed the first volume of the tale, and if you haven't already, pop on Robert Zimmerman's *Blonde on Blonde* and kick back.

*Jeff Smith*
*March 2009*

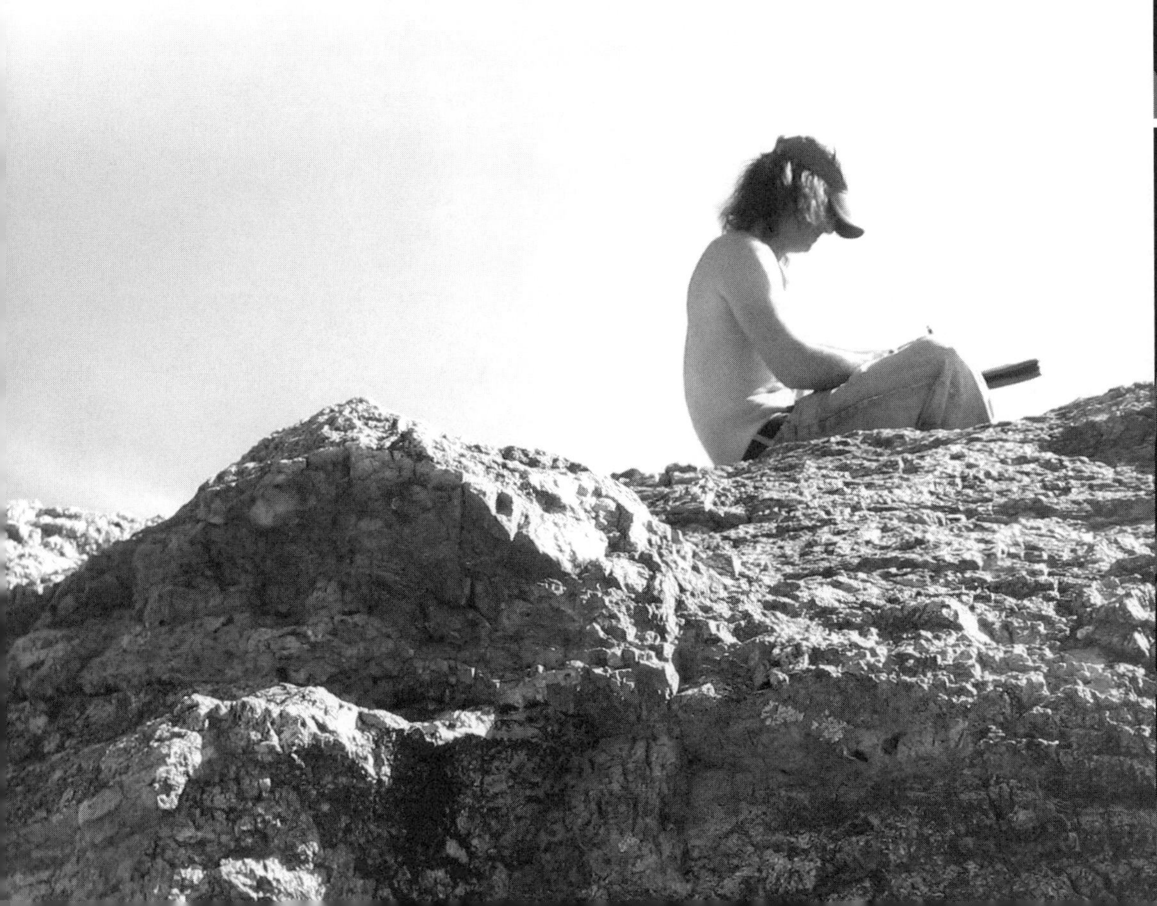

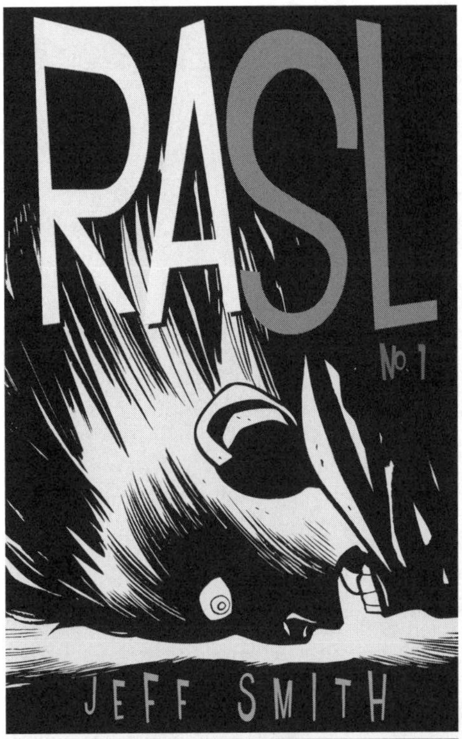
RASL
No. 1
JEFF SMITH

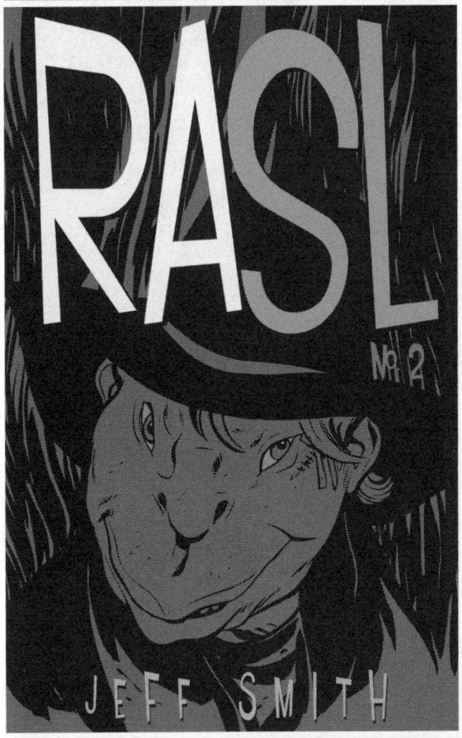
RASL
No. 2
JEFF SMITH

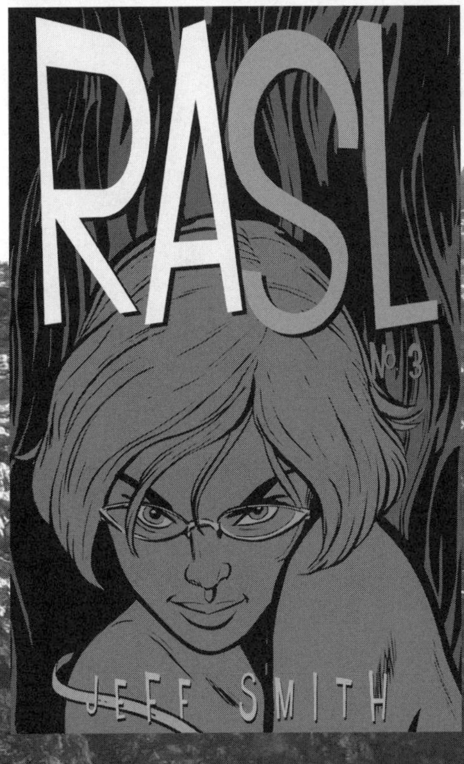
RASL
No. 3
JEFF SMITH

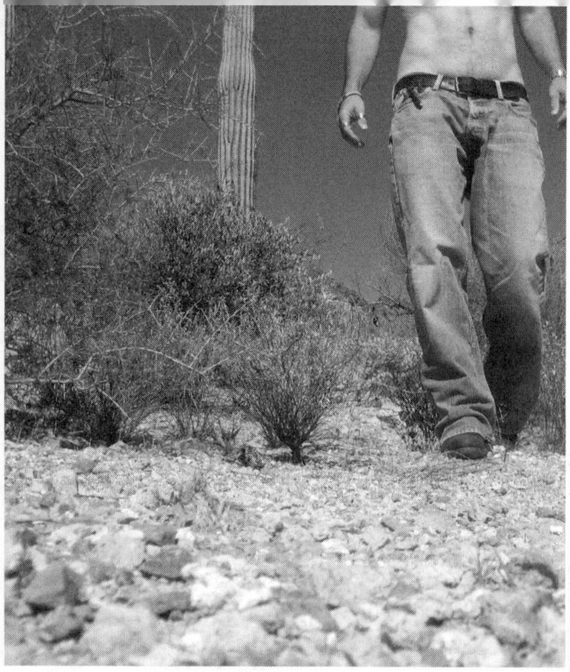

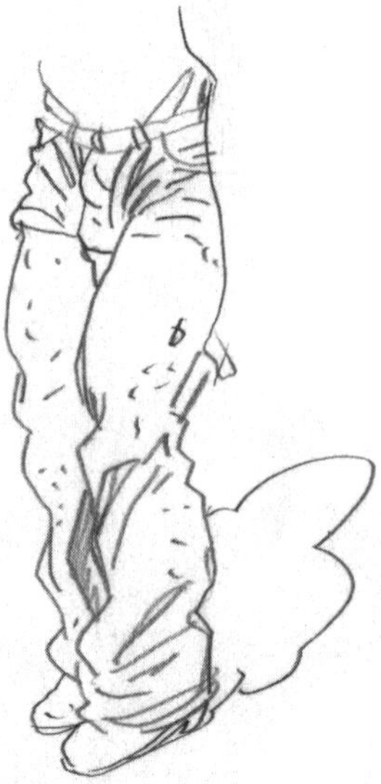

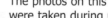

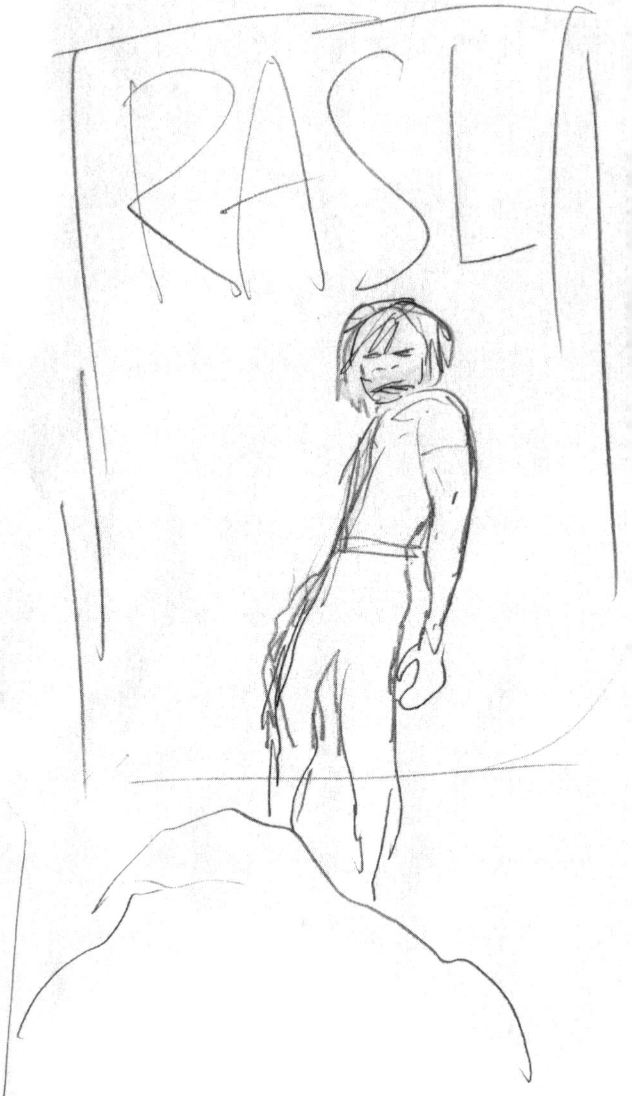
RASL

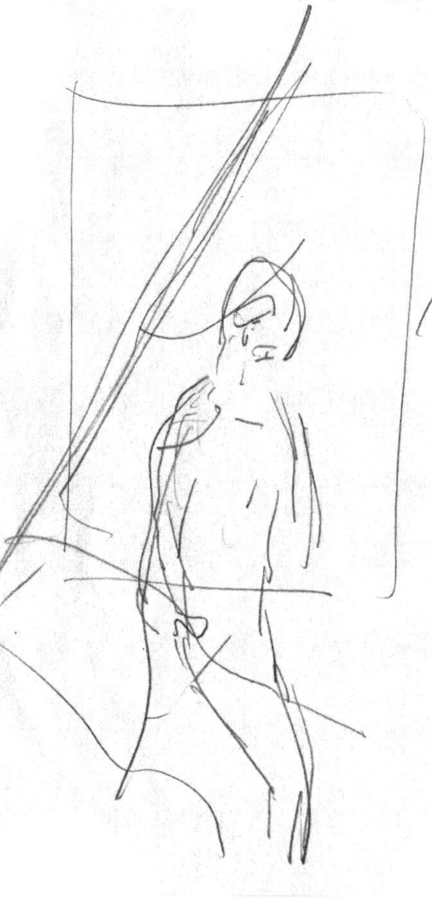

**Photo reference:**
The photos on this and the following pages were taken during my two weeks in Arizona, and were used to create the opening desert scene of RASL #1.

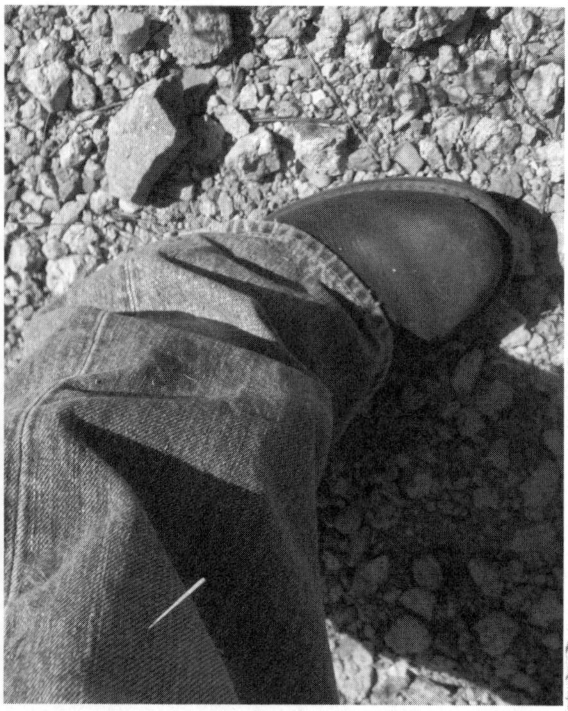

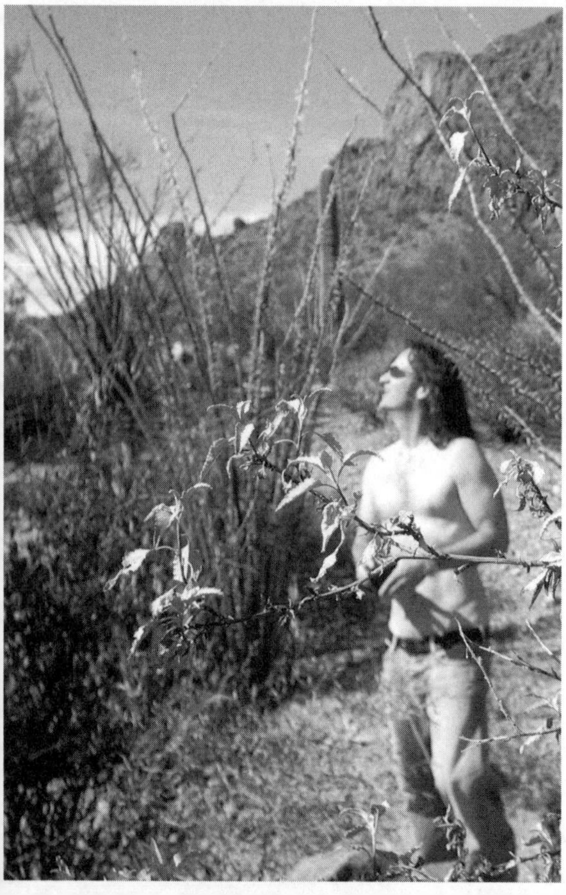

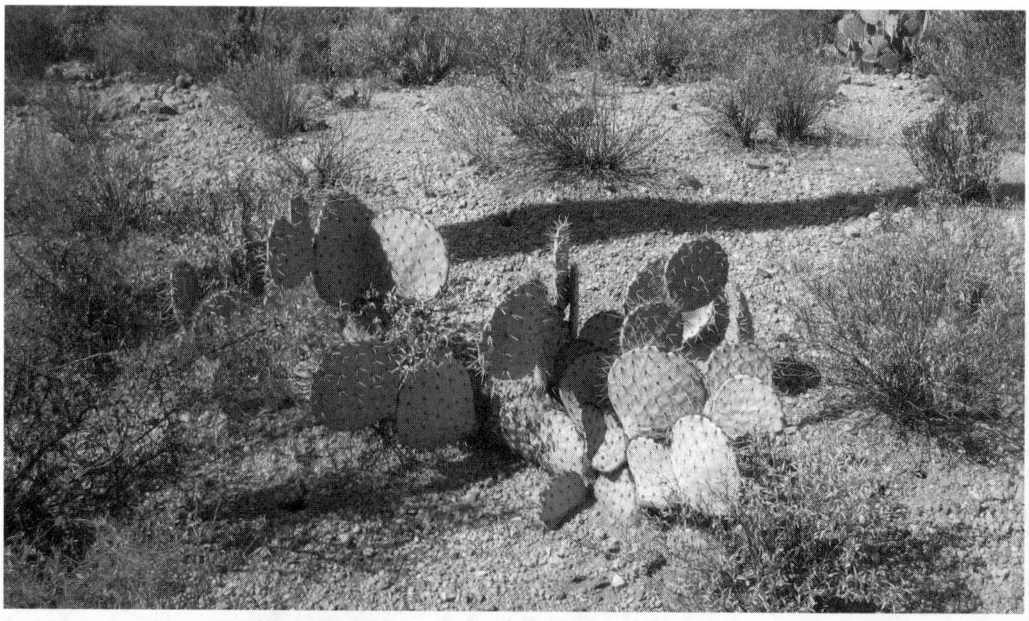

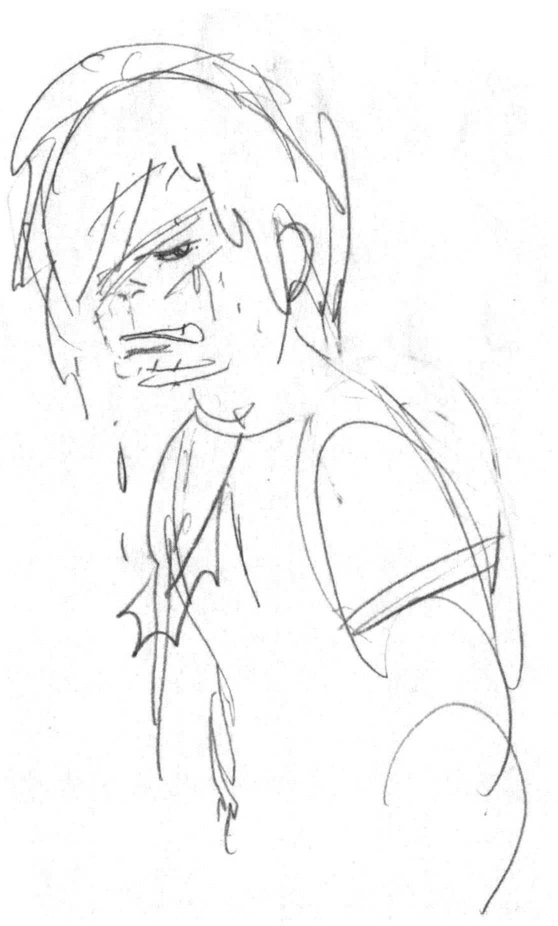

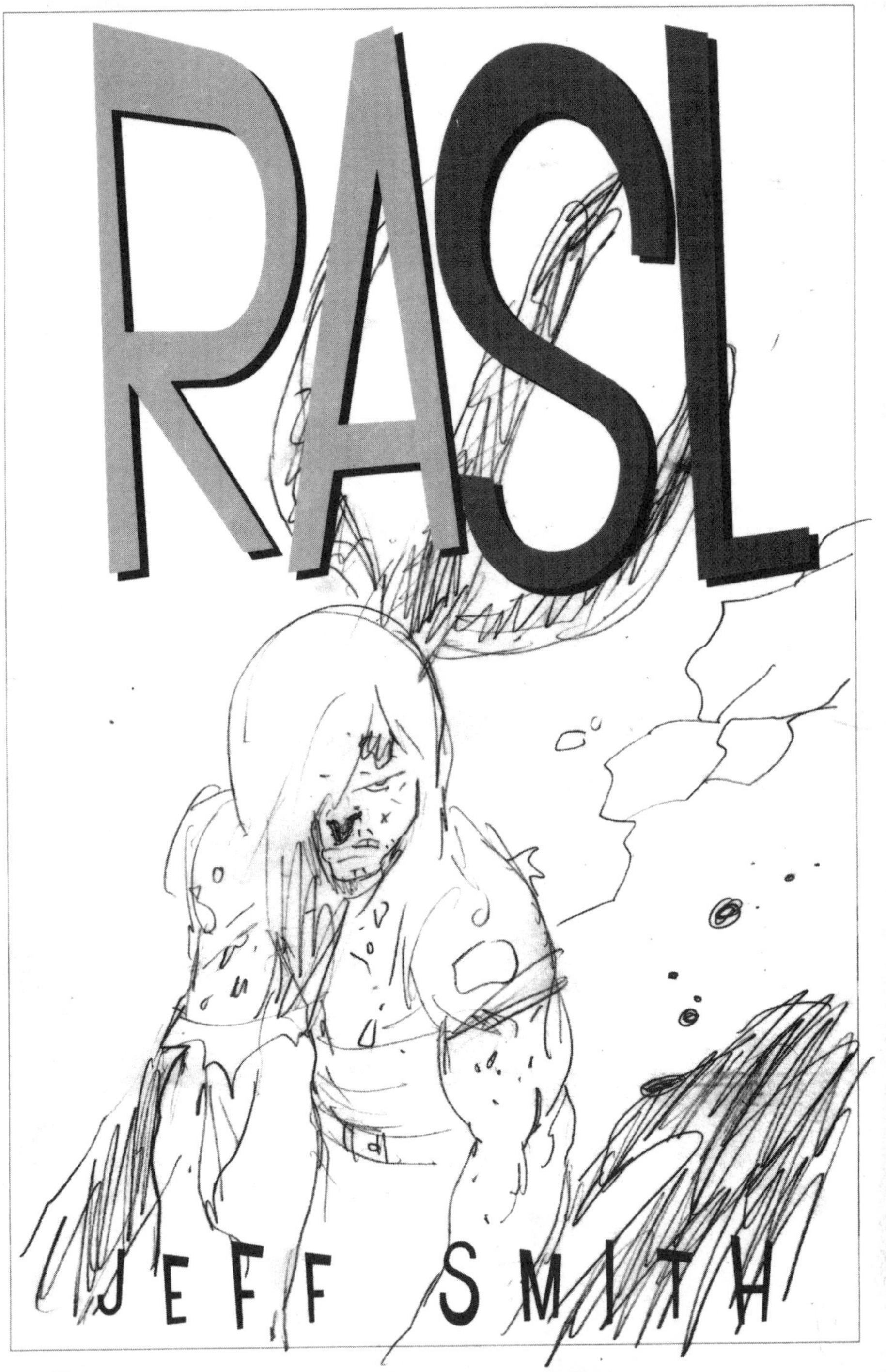
RASL
JEFF SMITH

**Above and facing page:**
Concept sketches for the alternate cover for RASL #1.

**Right:**
Rough pencils for alternate cover.

**Below:**
The forked shadow cast by this saguaro cactus inspired the drawing used for the alternate cover.

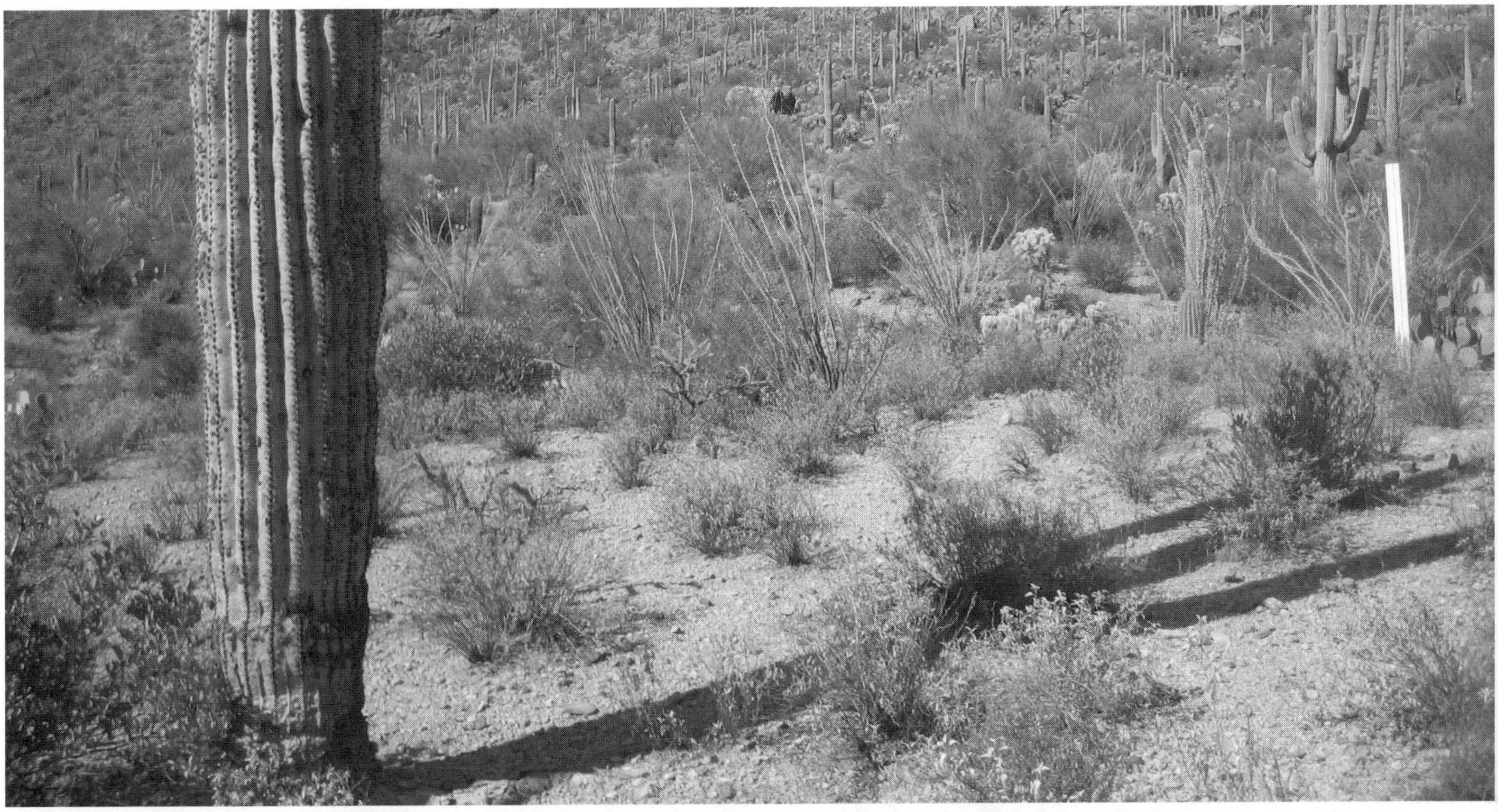

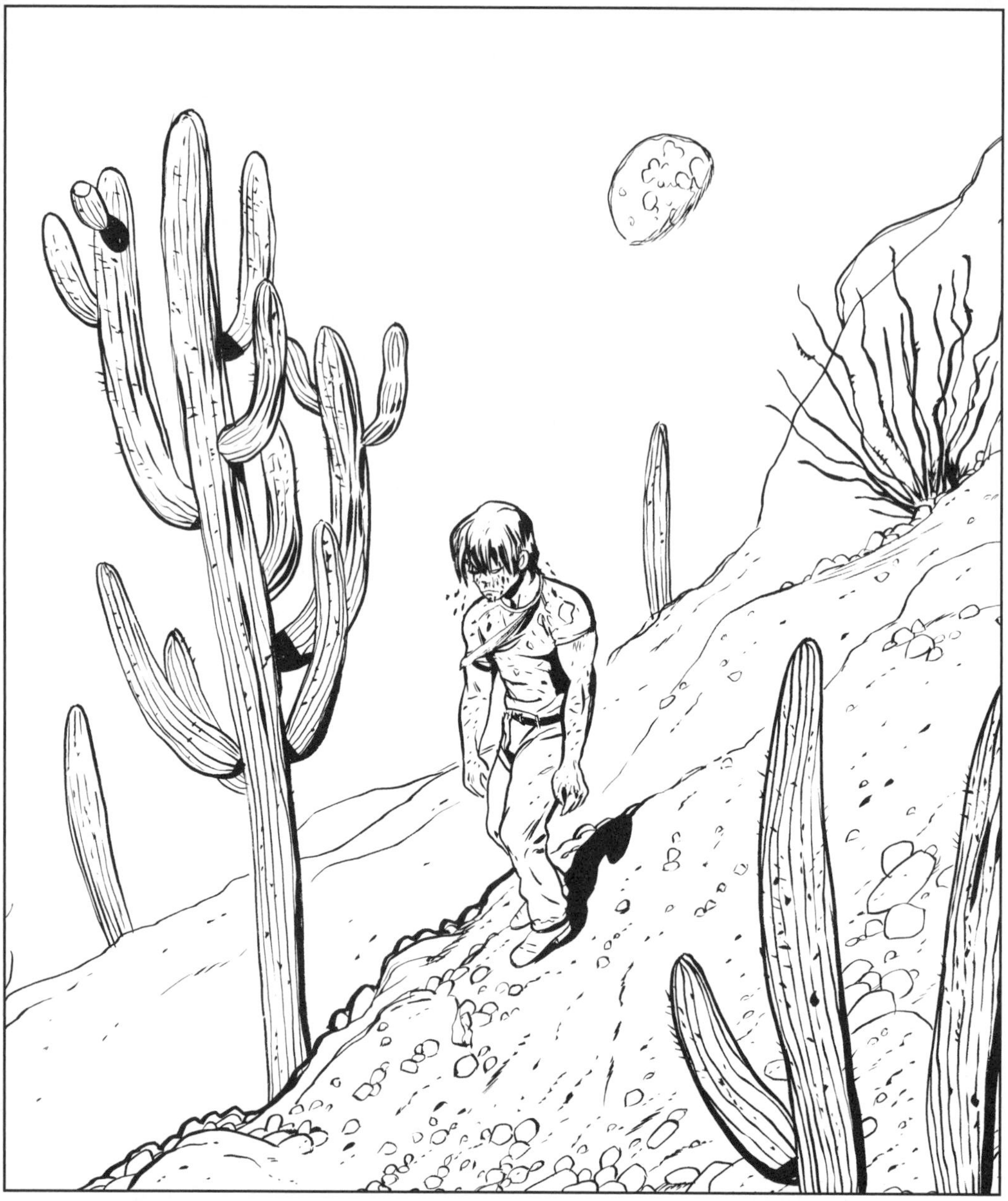
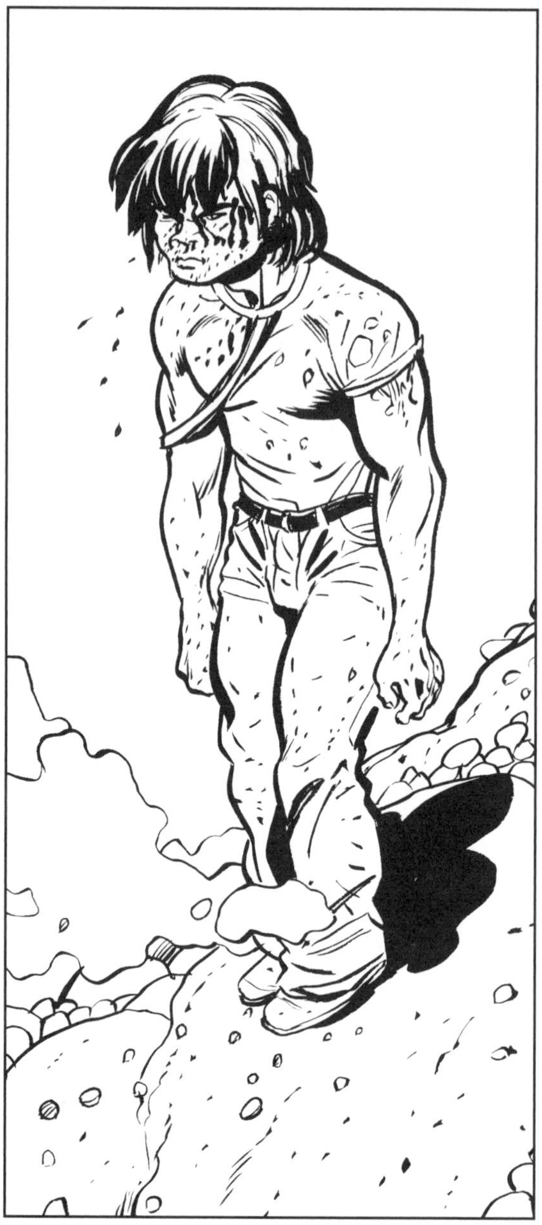
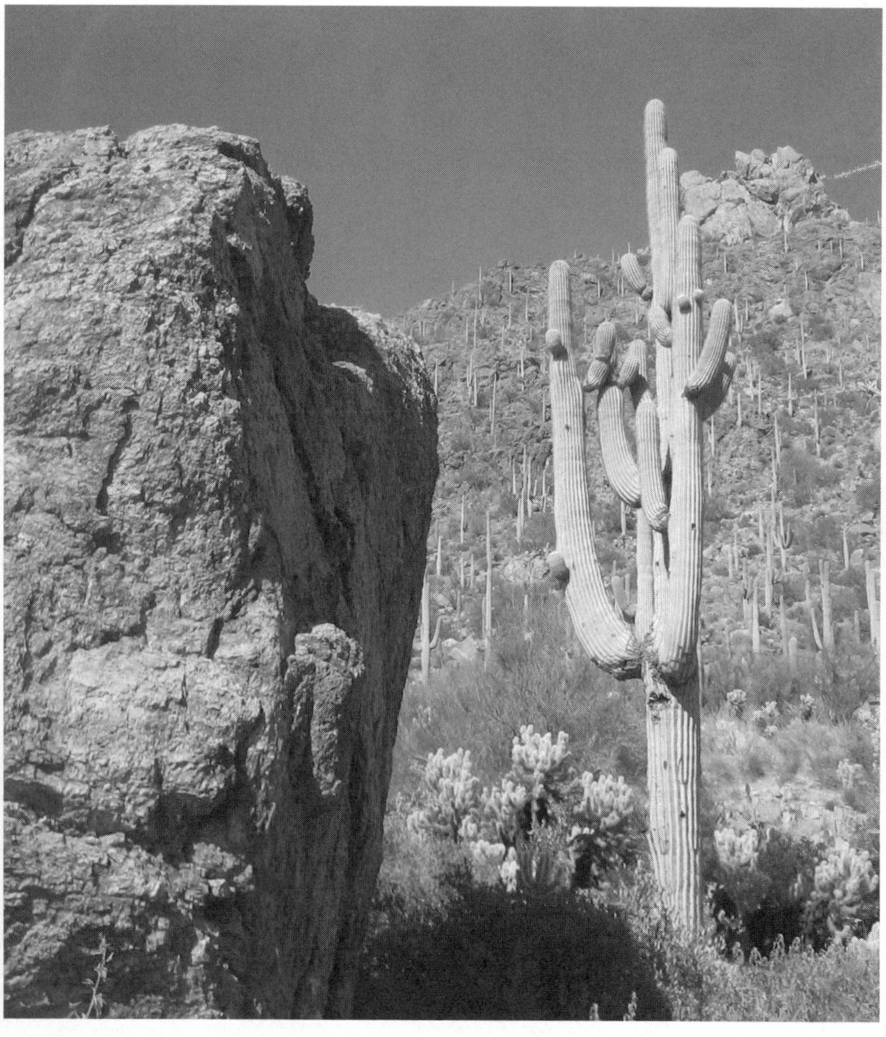
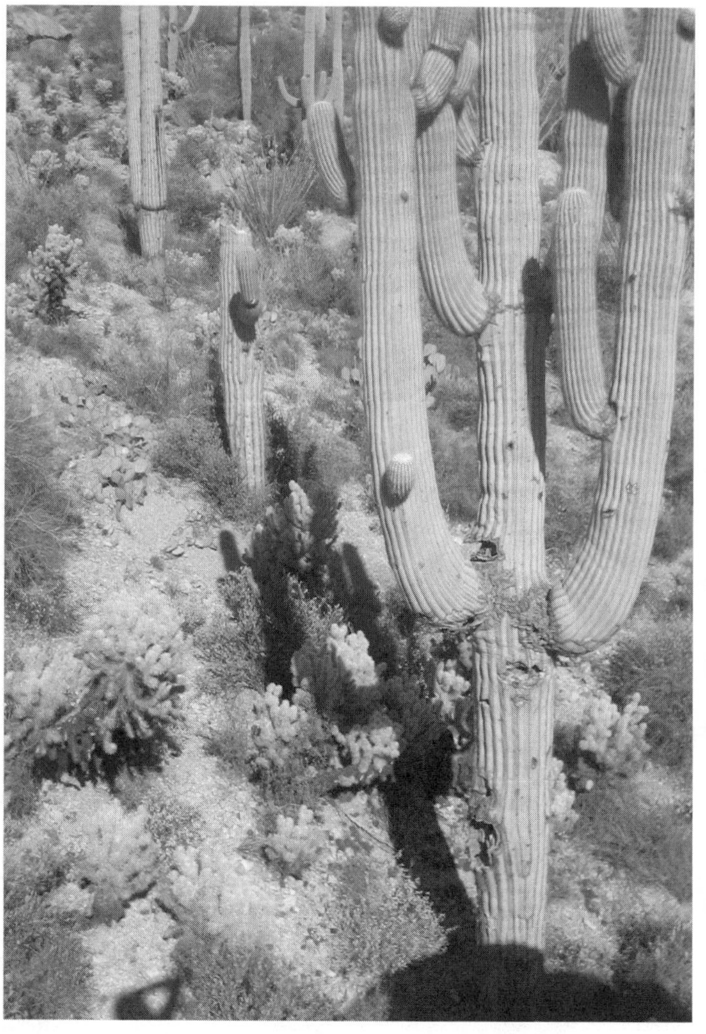

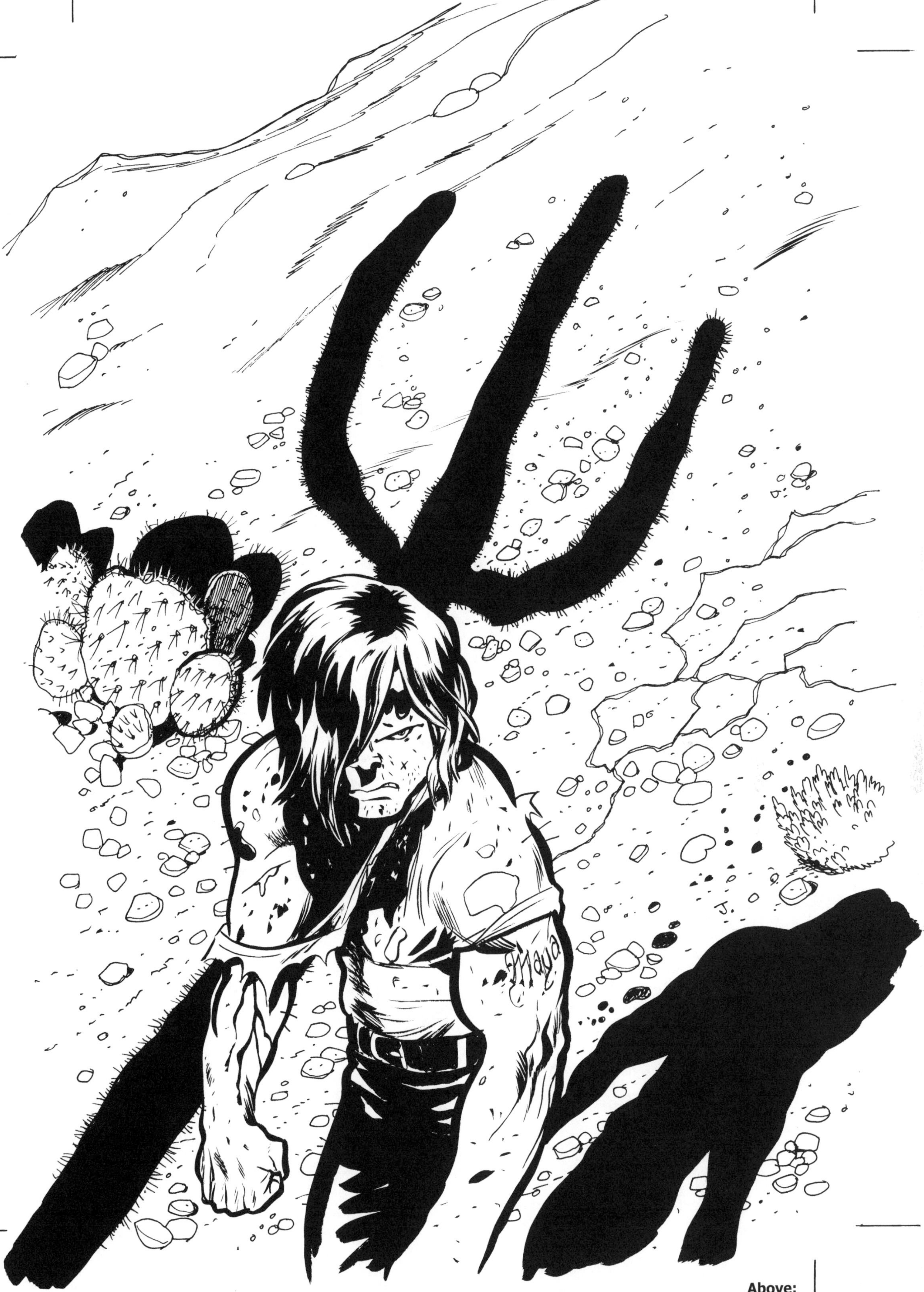
Maya

**Above:**
Finished inked artwork for RASL #1 alternate cover.

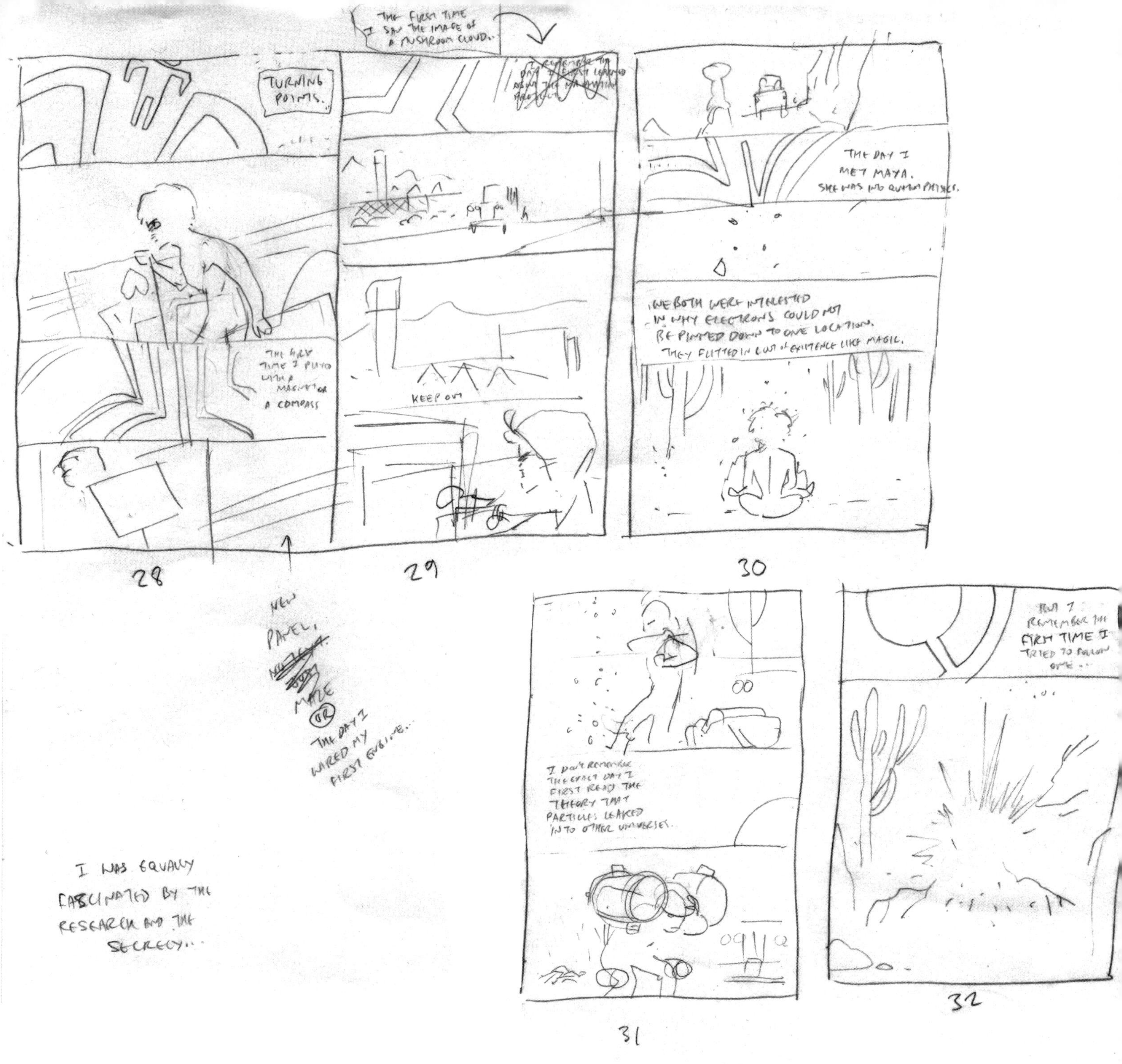
THE FIRST TIME I SAW THE IMAGE OF A MUSHROOM CLOUD...
TURNING POINTS...
THE FIRST TIME I PLAYED WITH A MAGNET OR A COMPASS
KEEP OUT
THE DAY I MET MAYA. SHE WAS INTO QUANTUM PHYSICS.
WE BOTH WERE INTERESTED IN WHY ELECTRONS COULD NOT BE PINNED DOWN TO ONE LOCATION. THEY FLITTED IN & OUT OF EXISTENCE LIKE MAGIC.
28
29
30
NEW PANEL, MAZE OR THE DAY I WIRED MY FIRST ENGINE...
I WAS EQUALLY FASCINATED BY THE RESEARCH AND THE SECRECY...
I DON'T REMEMBER THE EXACT DAY I FIRST READ THE THEORY THAT PARTICLES LEAKED INTO OTHER UNIVERSES.
BUT I REMEMBER THE FIRST TIME I TRIED TO FOLLOW ONE...
31
32

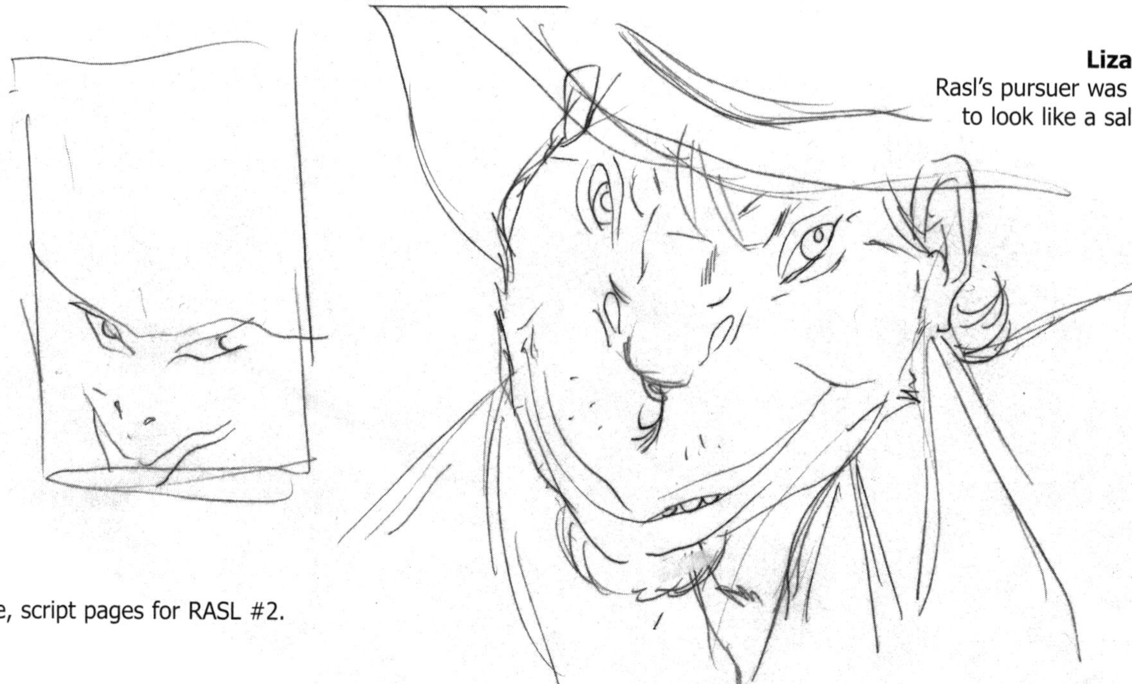

**Lizard Face:**
Rasl's pursuer was designed to look like a salamander.

**Above:**
Shown at actual size, script pages for RASL #2.

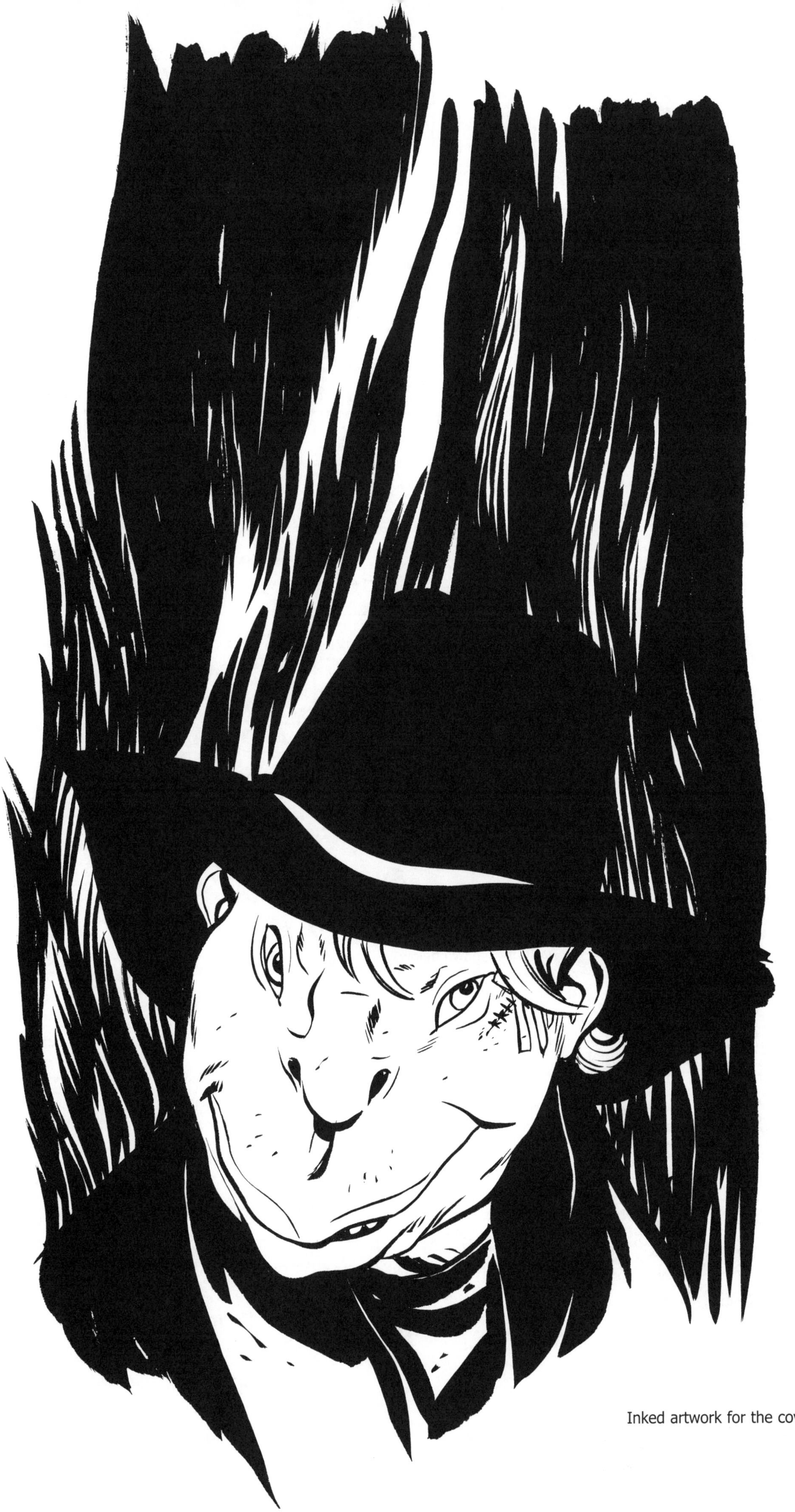

**Above:**
Inked artwork for the cover of RASL #2

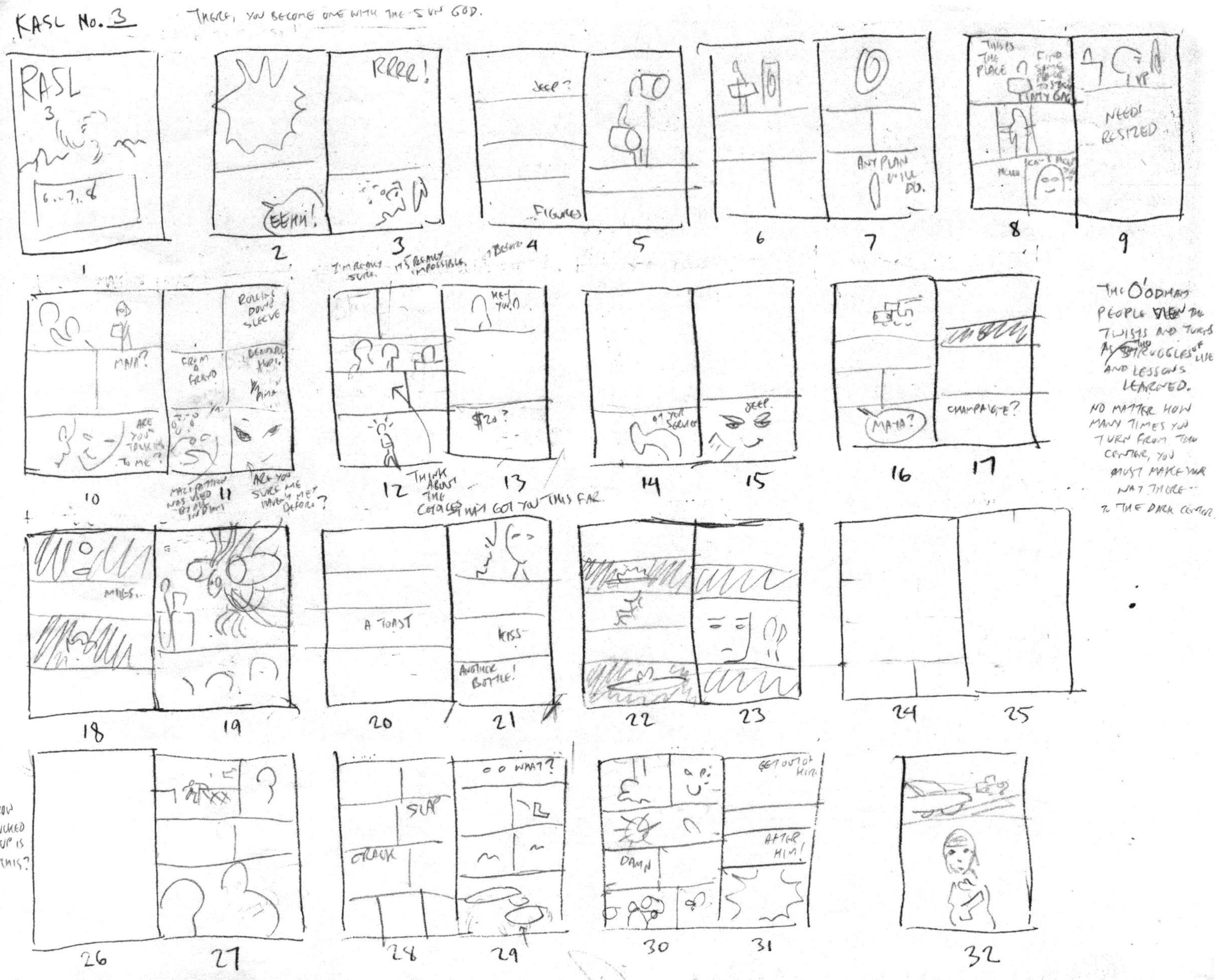
RASL No. 3
RASL
RRRR!
JEEP?
FIGURED
ANY PLAN WILL DO.
THIS IS THE PLACE
NEEDS RESIZED
ROLLING DOWN SLEEVE
MAYA?
FROM A FRIEND
ARE YOU TALKING TO ME?
ARE YOU SURE WE HAVEN'T MET BEFORE?
AT YOUR SERVICE
JEEP.
MAYA?
CHAMPAGNE?
THINK ABOUT THE CHOICES THAT GOT YOU THIS FAR.
A TOAST
KISS
ANOTHER BOTTLE!
SLAP
CRACK
SO WHAT?
DAMN
GET OUT OF HERE
AFTER HIM!
NO MATTER HOW MANY TIMES YOU TURN FROM THE CENTER, YOU MUST MAKE YOUR WAY THERE...
TO THE DARK CENTER.
HOW FUCKED UP IS THIS?

**This page:**
Thumbnails for the RASL #3 script. These small, fast drawings let me look at the overall story for pacing.
On the same page that the thumbnails are on I doodled this drawing of Rasl leaping into action. It later became the cover for RASL #4, shown below.

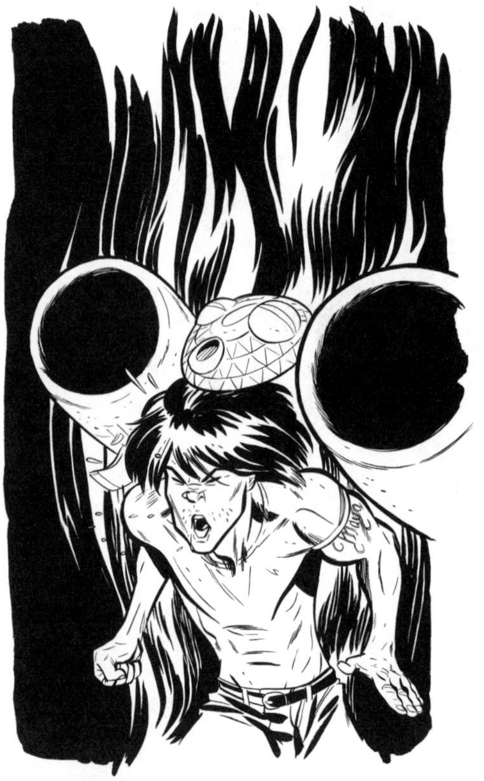

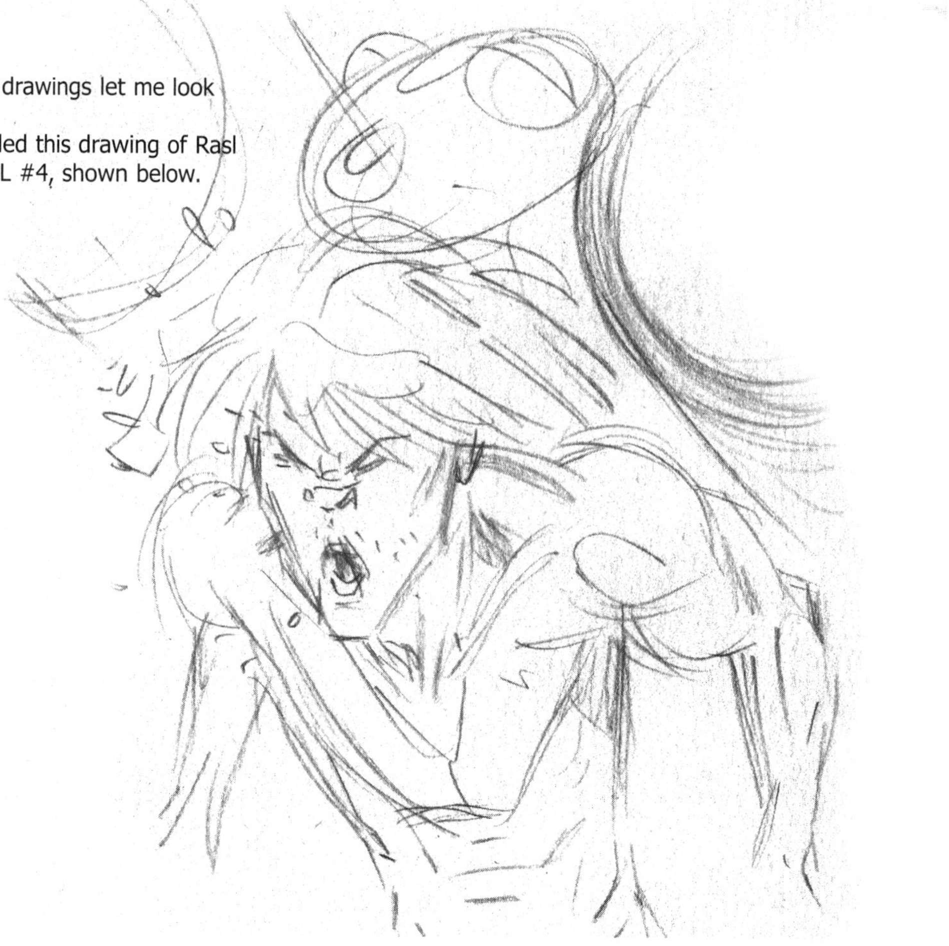

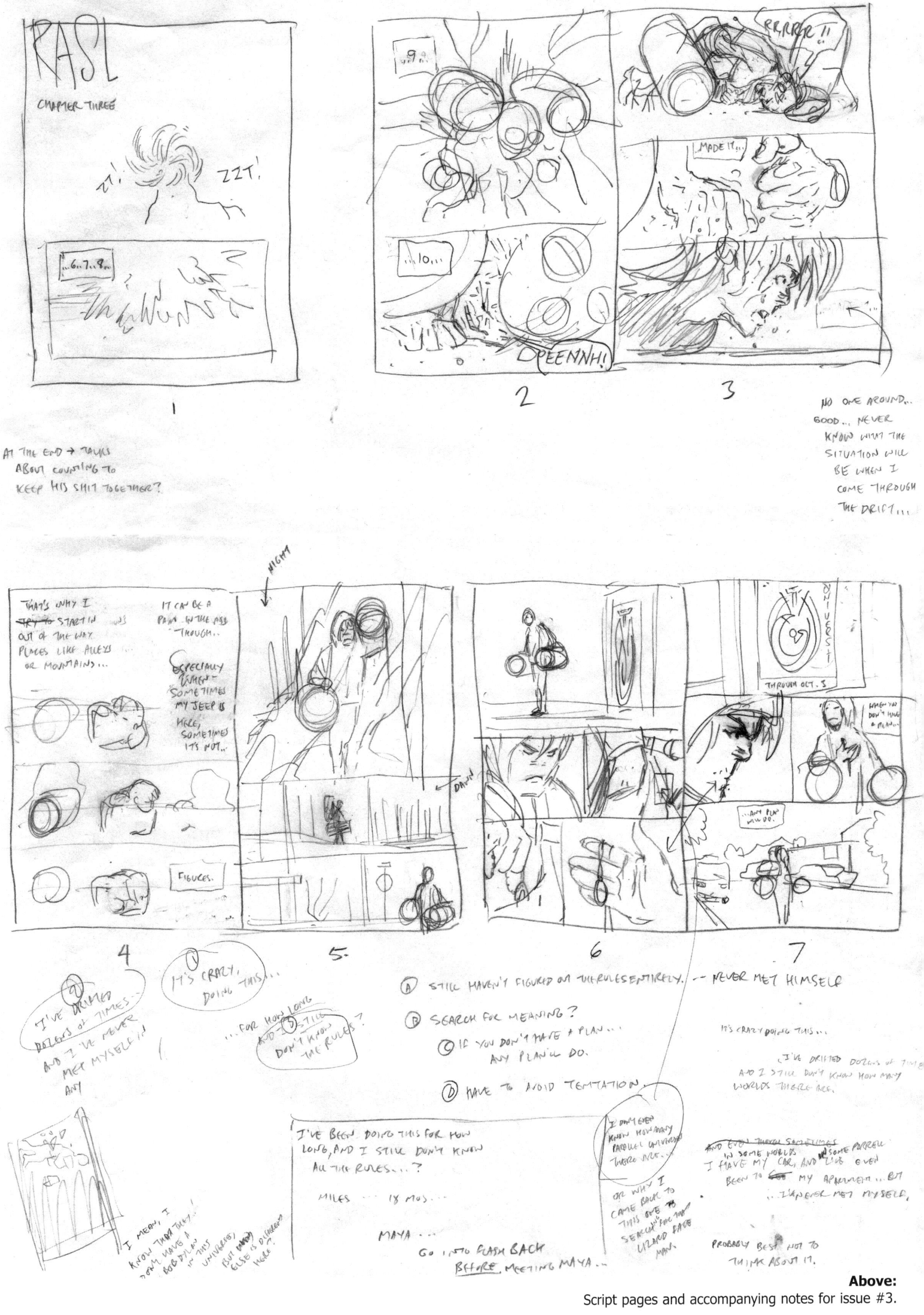

RASL
CHAPTER THREE
ZZT!
...6..7..8...
..9..
..10..
DPEENNH!
RRRRR!!
MADE IT...
1
2
3
NO ONE AROUND... GOOD... NEVER KNOW WHAT THE SITUATION WILL BE WHEN I COME THROUGH THE DRIFT...
AT THE END → TALKS ABOUT COUNTING TO KEEP HIS SHIT TOGETHER?
NIGHT
THAT'S WHY I START IN OUT OF THE WAY PLACES LIKE ALLEYS OR MOUNTAINS...
IT CAN BE A PAIN IN THE ASS THOUGH..
SOMETIMES MY JEEP IS HERE, SOMETIMES IT'S NOT...
FIGURES.
DAWN
THROUGH OCT. 5
...ANY PLAN WILL DO.
4
5.
6
7
I'VE DRIFTED DOZENS OF TIMES AND I'VE NEVER MET MYSELF
IT'S CRAZY, DOING THIS...
A STILL HAVEN'T FIGURED OUT THE RULES ENTIRELY. -- NEVER MET HIMSELF
B SEARCH FOR MEANING?
C IF YOU DON'T HAVE A PLAN... ANY PLAN'LL DO.
D HAVE TO AVOID TEMTATION.
IT'S CRAZY DOING THIS...
I'VE DRIFTED DOZENS OF TIMES AND I STILL DON'T KNOW HOW MANY WORLDS THERE ARE.
I'VE BEEN DOING THIS FOR HOW LONG, AND I STILL DON'T KNOW ALL THE RULES...?
MILES ... 18 MOS...
MAYA...
GO INTO FLASH BACK BEFORE MEETING MAYA...
I DON'T EVEN KNOW HOW MANY PARALLEL UNIVERSES THERE ARE...
OR WHY I CAME BACK TO THIS ONE TO SEARCH FOR THE LIZARD FACE MAN.
IN SOME WORLDS I HAVE MY CAR, AND I'VE EVEN BEEN TO MY APARTMENT... BUT I'VE NEVER MET MYSELF.
PROBABLY BEST NOT TO THINK ABOUT IT.
I MEAN, I KNOW THAT THEY DON'T HAVE A BOB DYLAN IN THIS UNIVERSE, BUT WHAT ELSE IS DIFFERENT HERE?


**Above:**
Script pages and accompanying notes for issue #3.

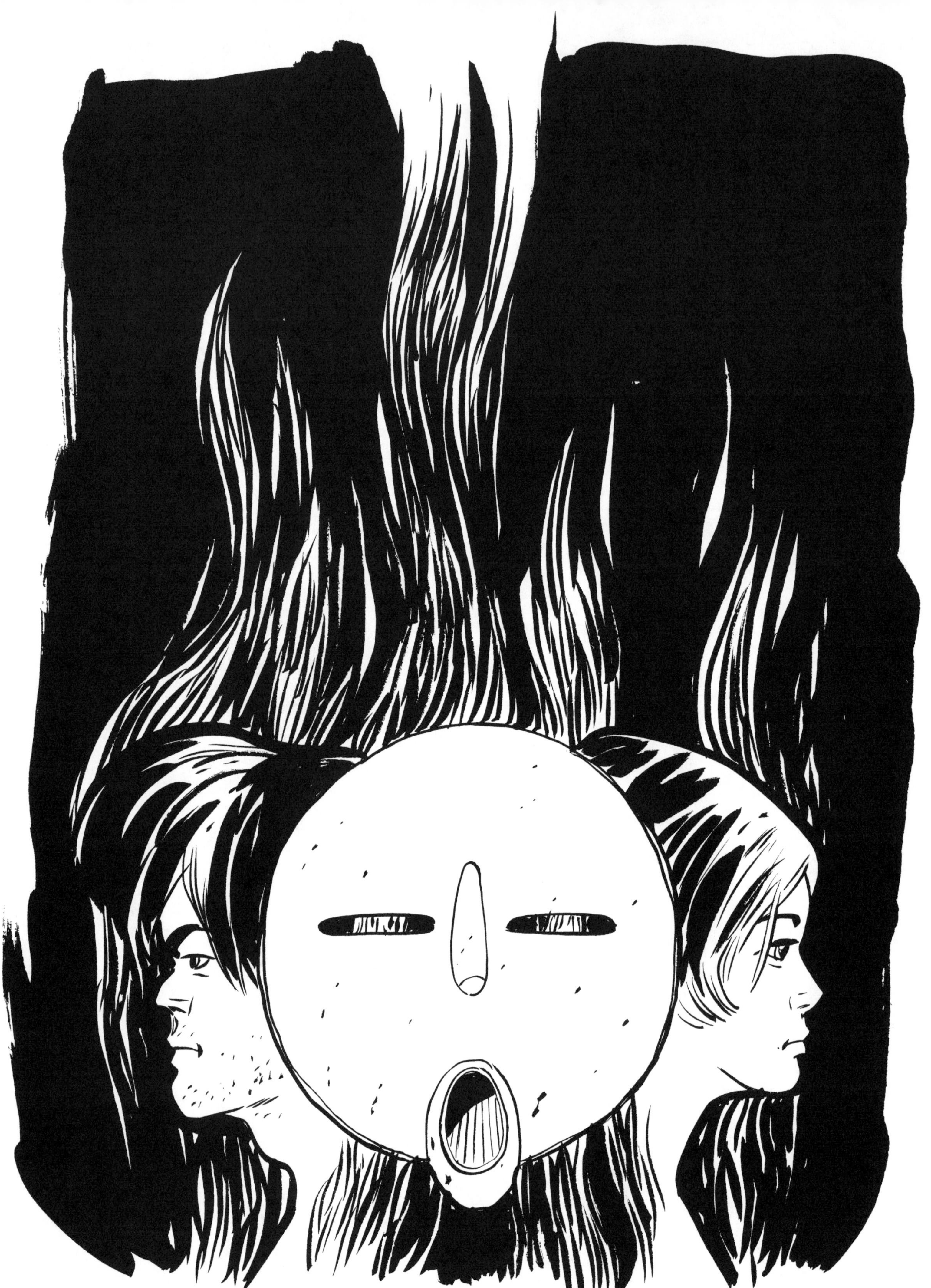

**Above:**
This was going to be the cover for #3, but it wasn't well received in our staff meeting, so it was discarded for a possible use later.

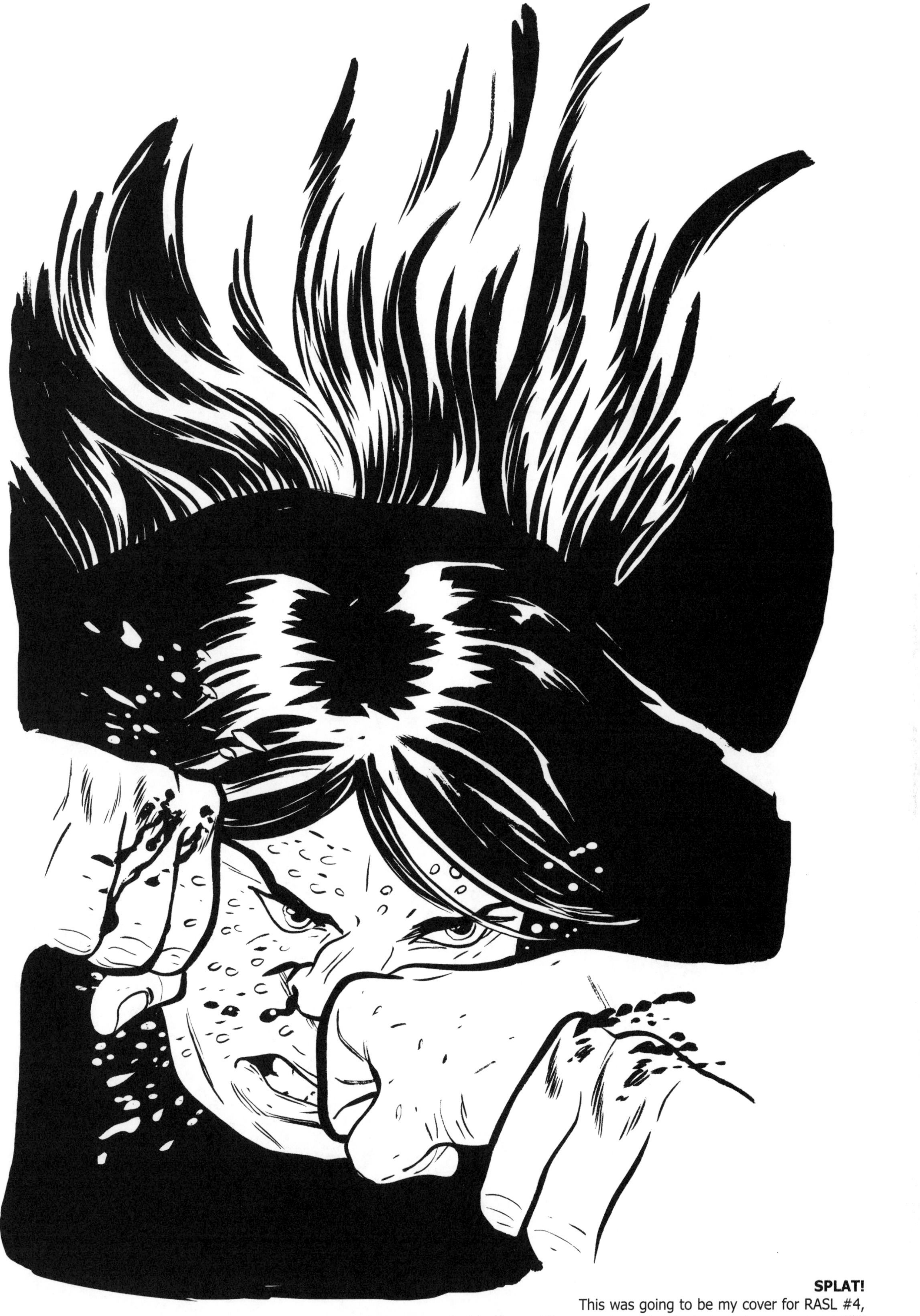

**SPLAT!**
This was going to be my cover for RASL #4,
but in the end it was replaced by the image shown on page 110
before finally becoming the cover for RASL 10.

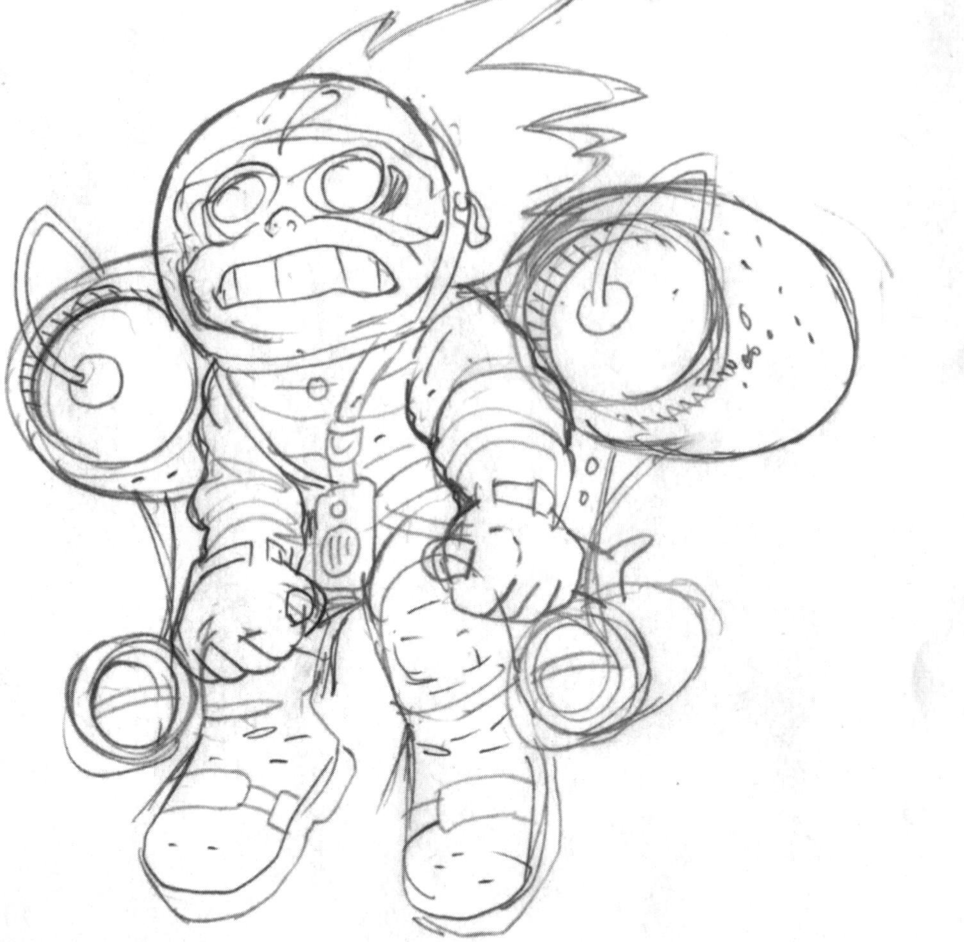

**Phoney Bone in Space:**
Early concept sketches for the character had a distinctly cartoony look. Later, as I began to write a more hardboiled story, the realistic version began to emerge.

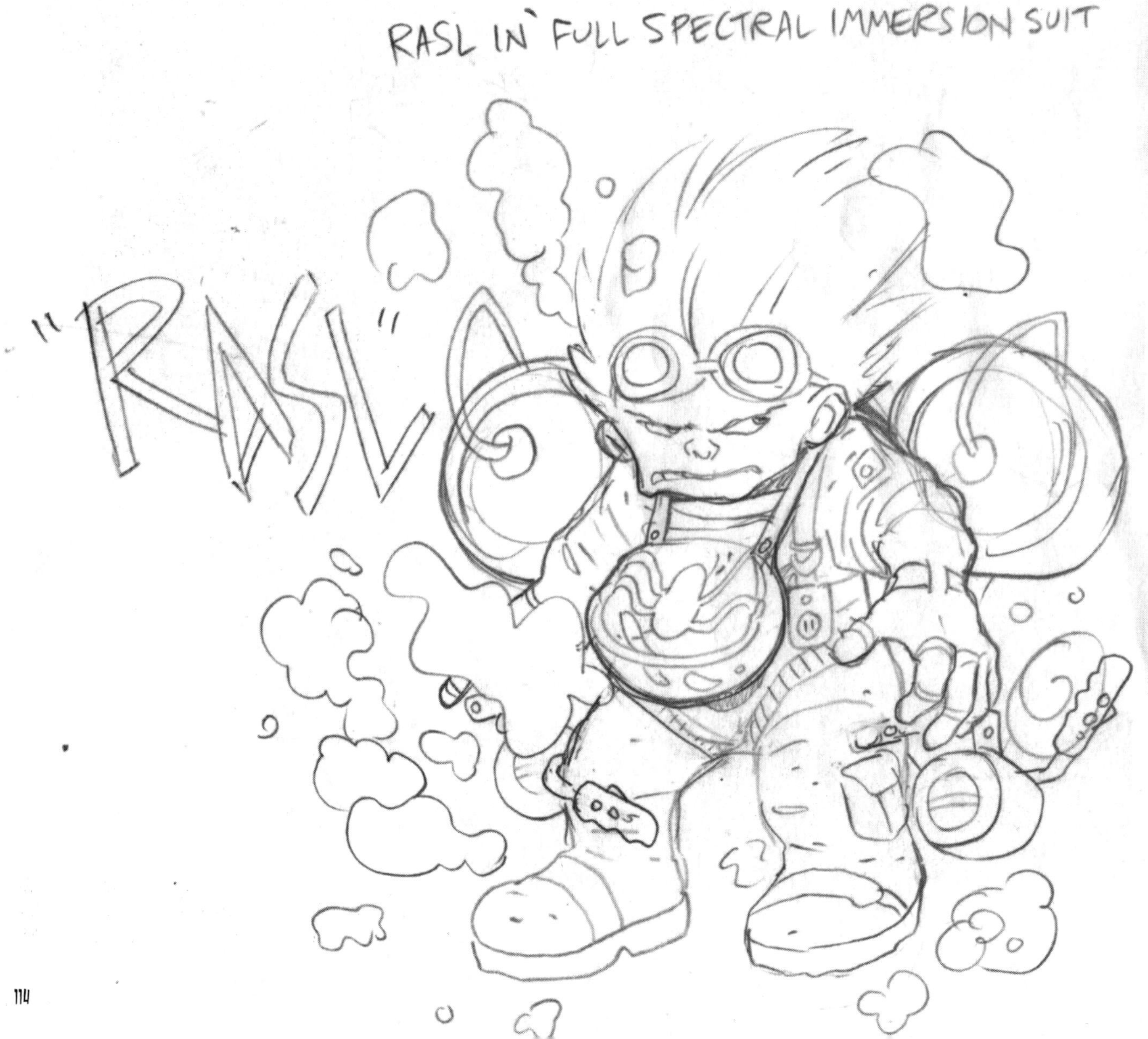
RASL IN 'FULL SPECTRAL IMMERSION SUIT'
"RASL"

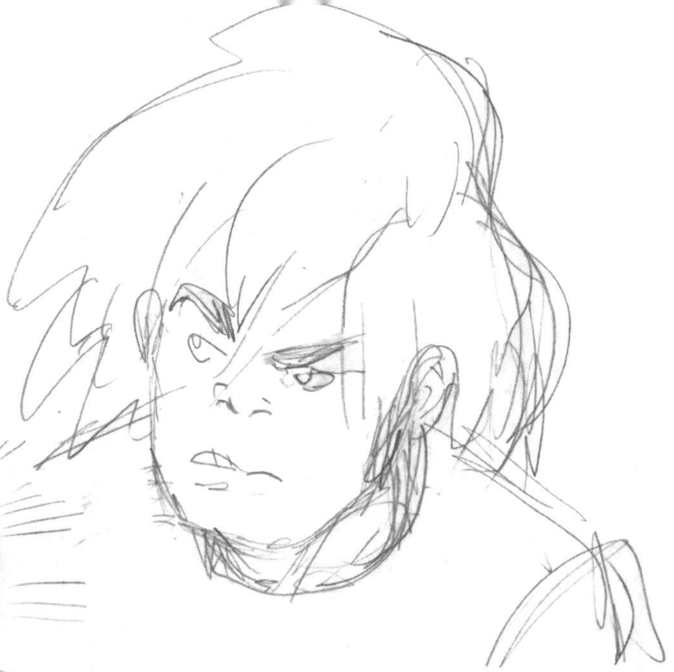

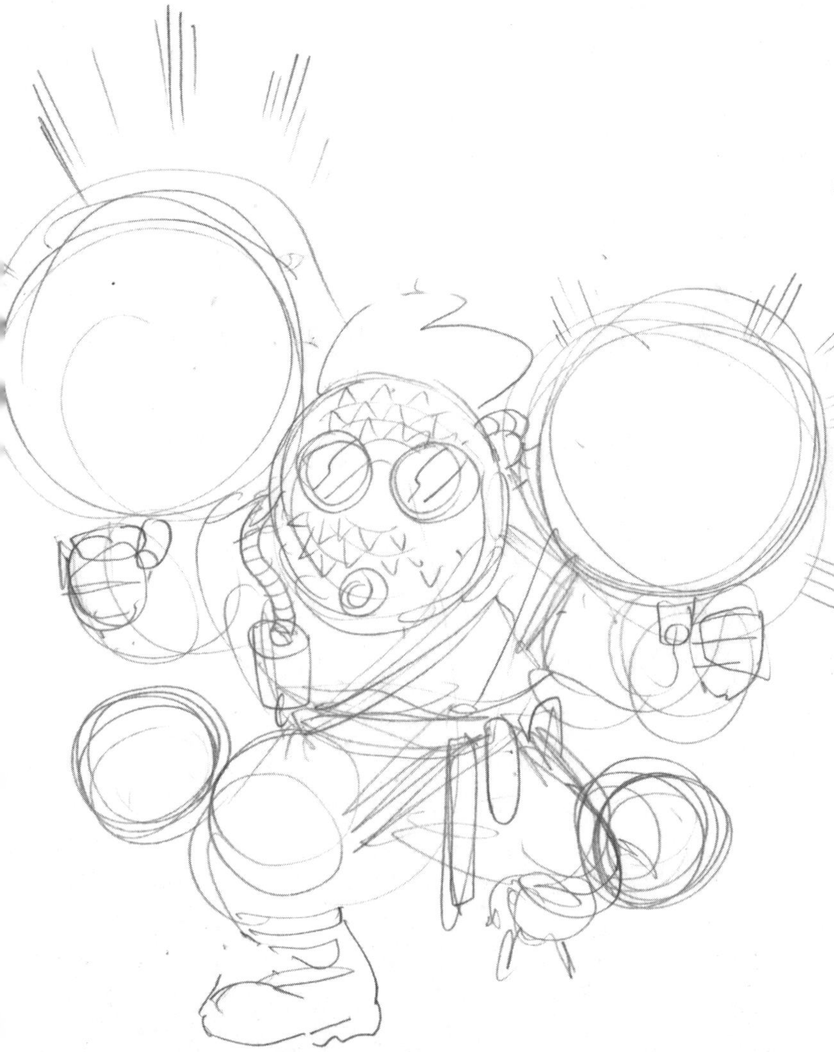

**Above:**
A version of Rasl during the transition from cartoony to more realistic.

**Left:**
Early concept sketch for RASL's costume.

**Below:**
Penciled panels before final inks are completed.

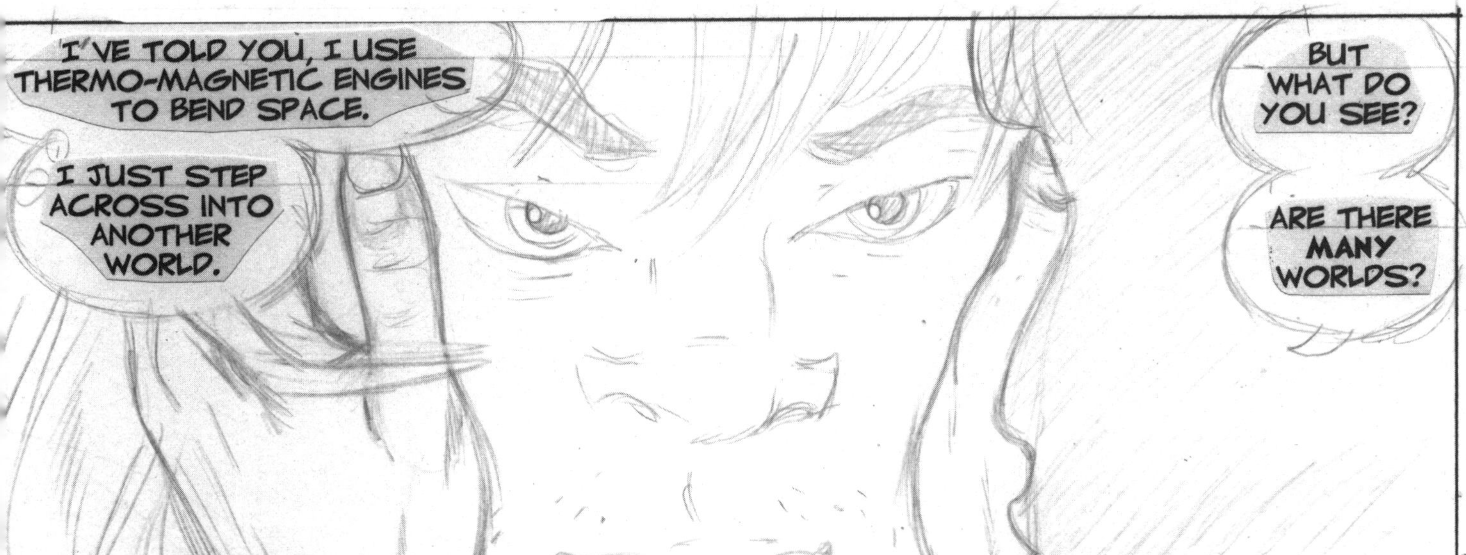
I'VE TOLD YOU, I USE THERMO-MAGNETIC ENGINES TO BEND SPACE.
I JUST STEP ACROSS INTO ANOTHER WORLD.
BUT WHAT DO YOU SEE?
ARE THERE MANY WORLDS?

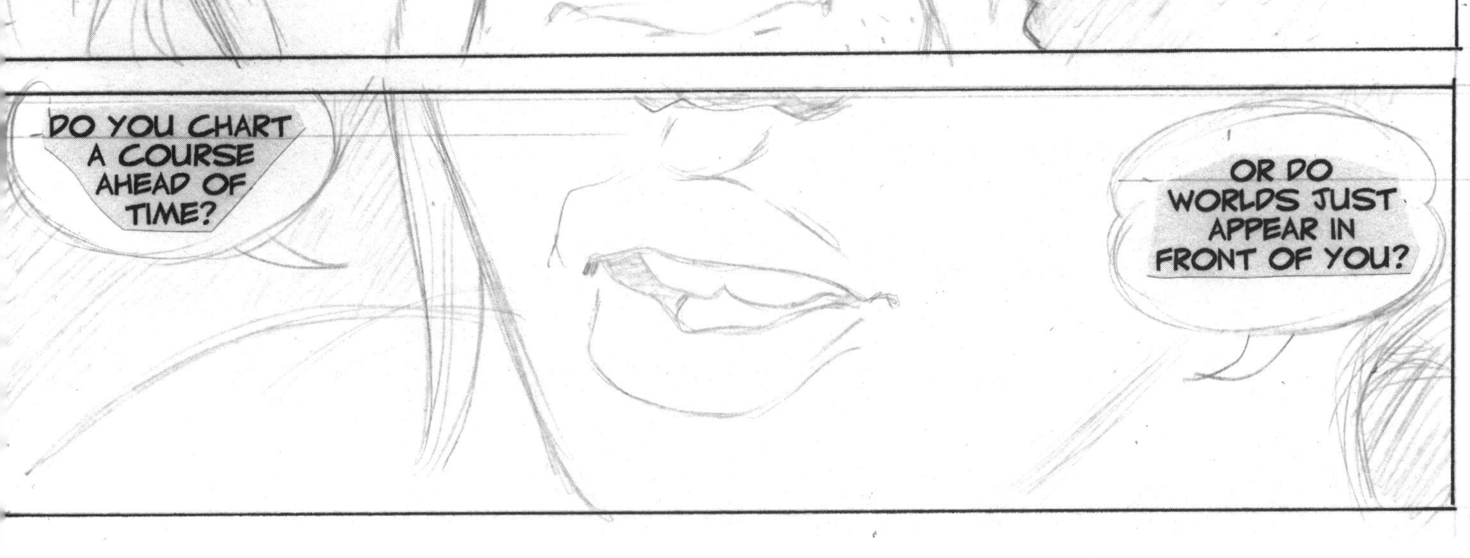
DO YOU CHART A COURSE AHEAD OF TIME?
OR DO WORLDS JUST APPEAR IN FRONT OF YOU?

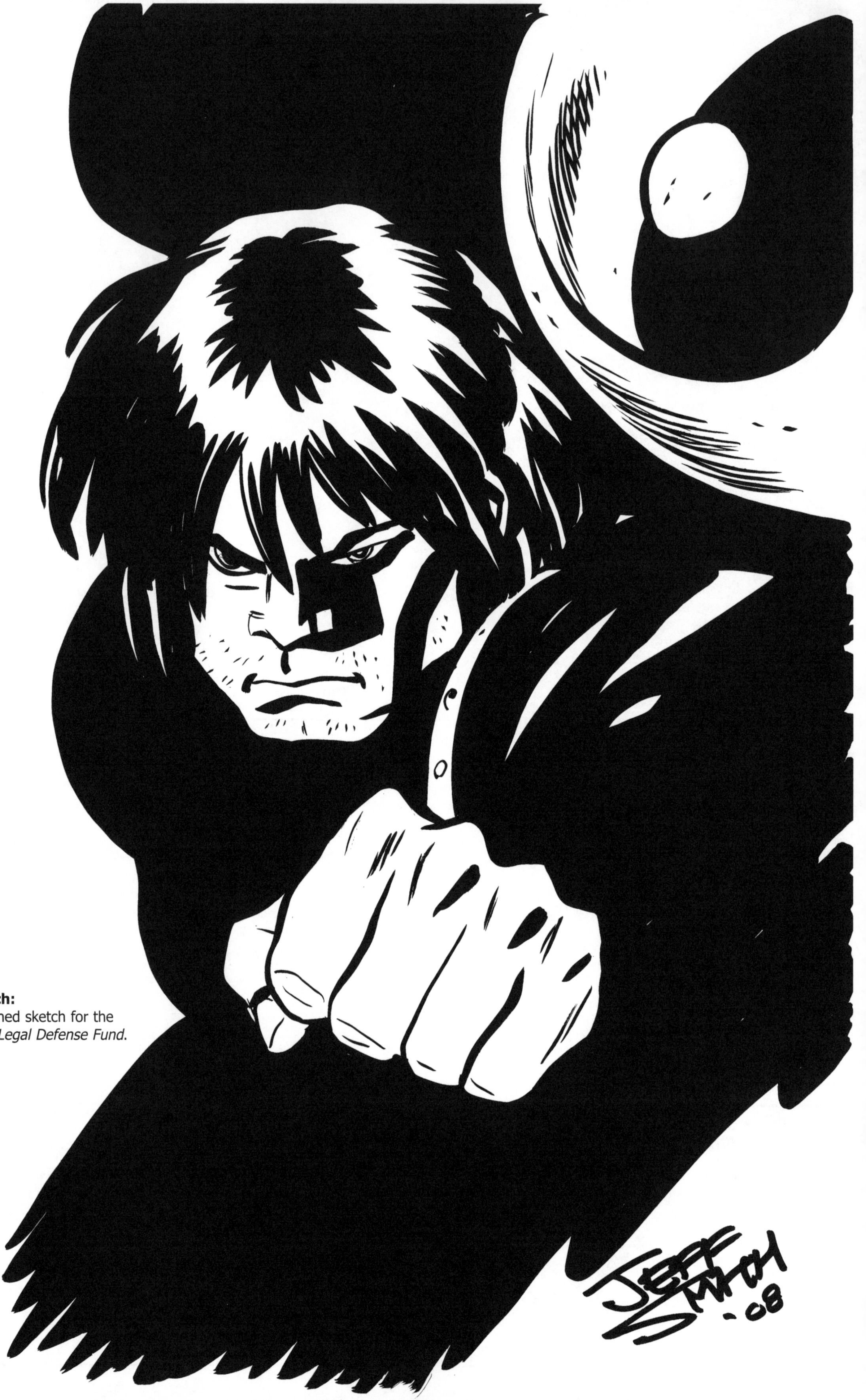
JEFF SMITH '08

**Quick sketch:**
A commissioned sketch for the *Comic Book Legal Defense Fund*.

# Tales of Tesla

## Behind the Scenes of RASL 2: The Fire of St. George

As I began writing the second volume of RASL, one of the main tasks was to tell the art thief's history and provide an anchor for the strange technology that allowed him to ply his trade in parallel universes. The key to both was Nikola Tesla, the mysterious and tragic 19th century experimenter and scientist.

The more I dug into popular conspiracy theories and fringe science, the more Tesla's name popped up; from the Philadelphia Experiment to the Tunguska Event, from Ronald Reagan's Star Wars missile shield to Alaska's H.A.A.R.P. (The High Frequency Active Auroral Research Program which is the basis for the fictional St. George Array), Tesla technology is everywhere.

It was the scientist's sad career, however, that started so brilliantly, only to end in penniless isolation that really lent itself to telling Rob's story up to this point. All of it is true, too, I swear. I had no idea the electric chair was invented to discredit Tesla!

In the following pages of this Special Oversized Edition, you'll find more pencil sketches and promotional art, photos of Tesla and his Colorado Springs laboratory, plus behind the scenes efforts to create images of the U.S. Navy Destroyer Escort the U.S.S. Eldridge and her sailors during the Philadelphia Experiment. Elsewhere in this book you'll find a brief bibliography of some of the books and films that inspired the science and philosophy of RASL.

As I look up from my laptop, the spooky girl is telling me that it's time to start the conclusion of RASL.

I better get to it.

*Jeff Smith*
*June, 2011*

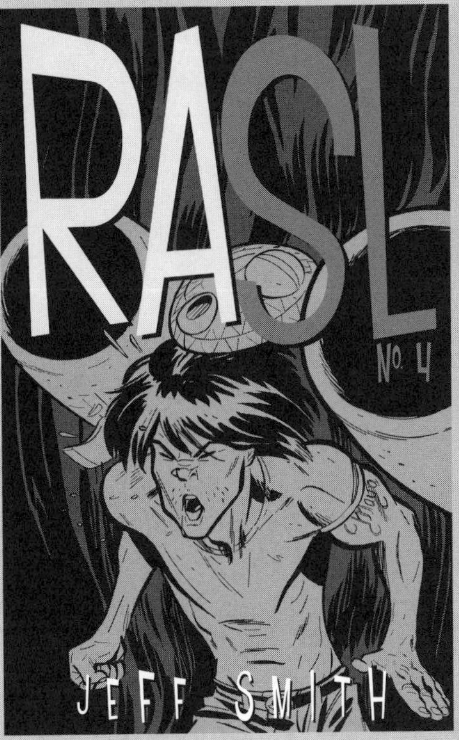
RASL
No. 4
JEFF SMITH

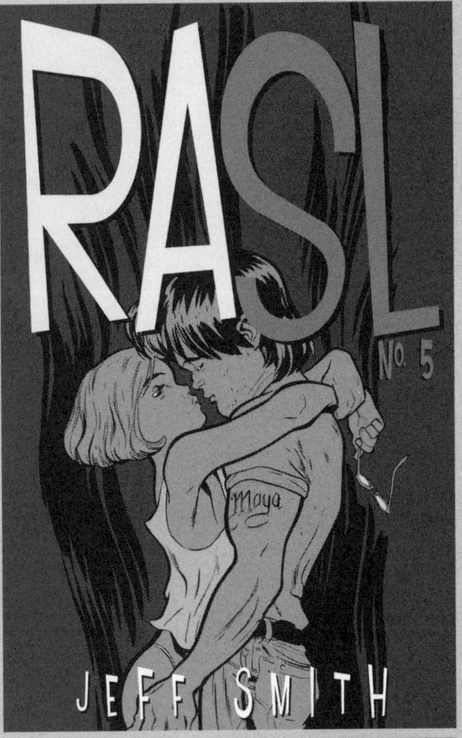
RASL
No. 5
Maya
JEFF SMITH

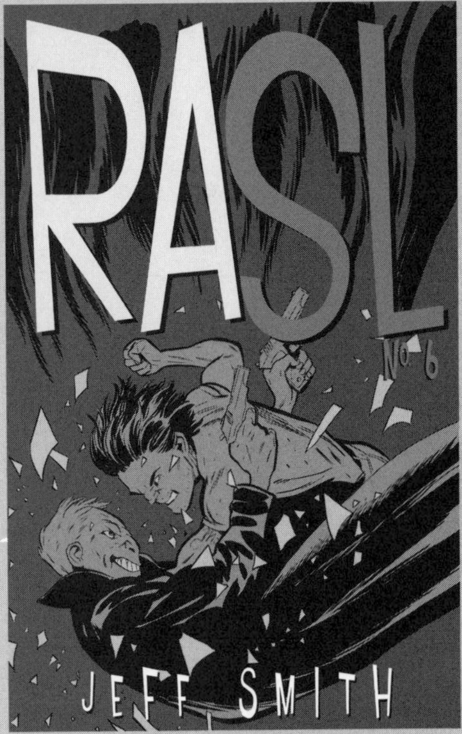
RASL
No. 6
JEFF SMITH

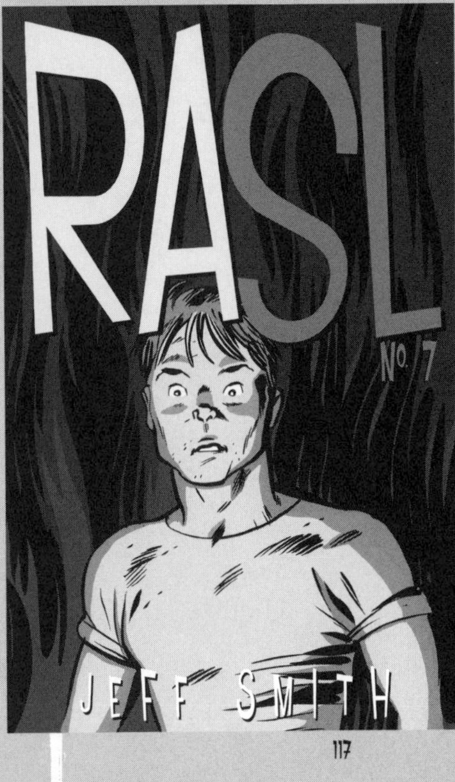
RASL
No. 7
JEFF SMITH

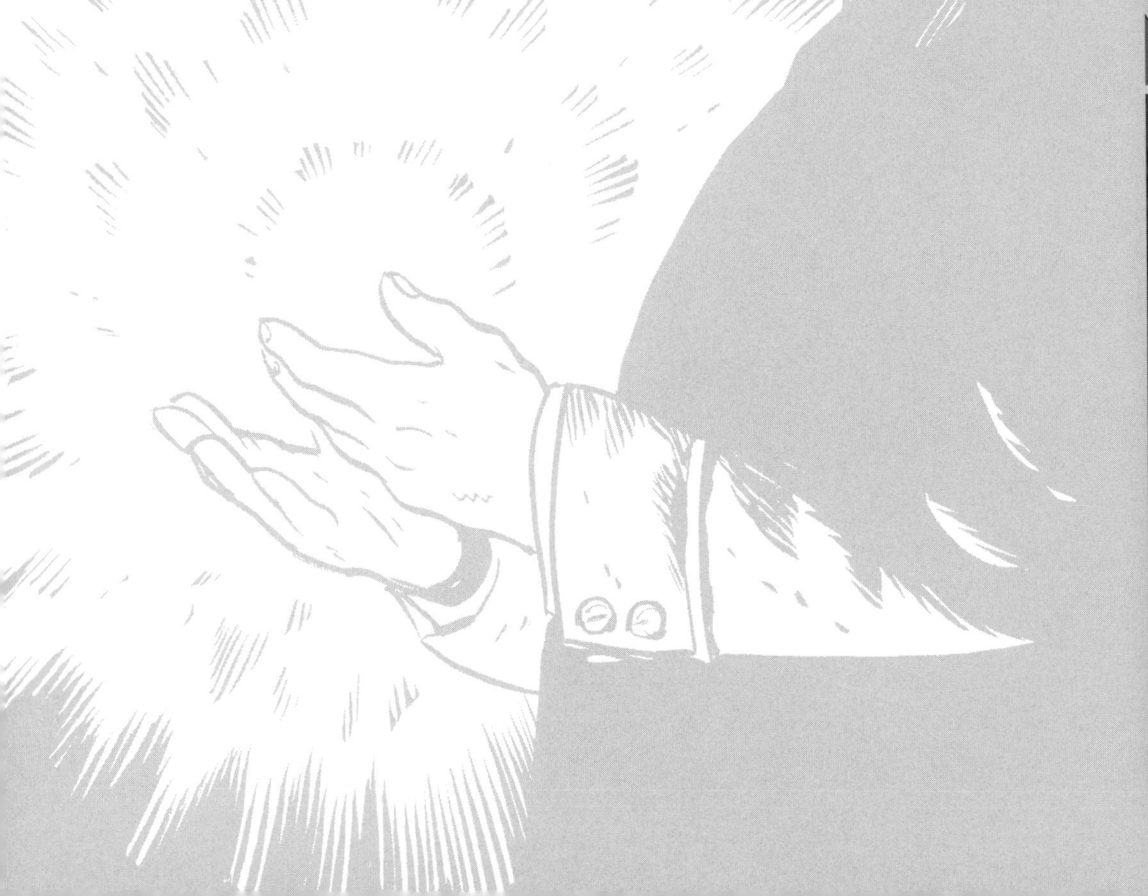

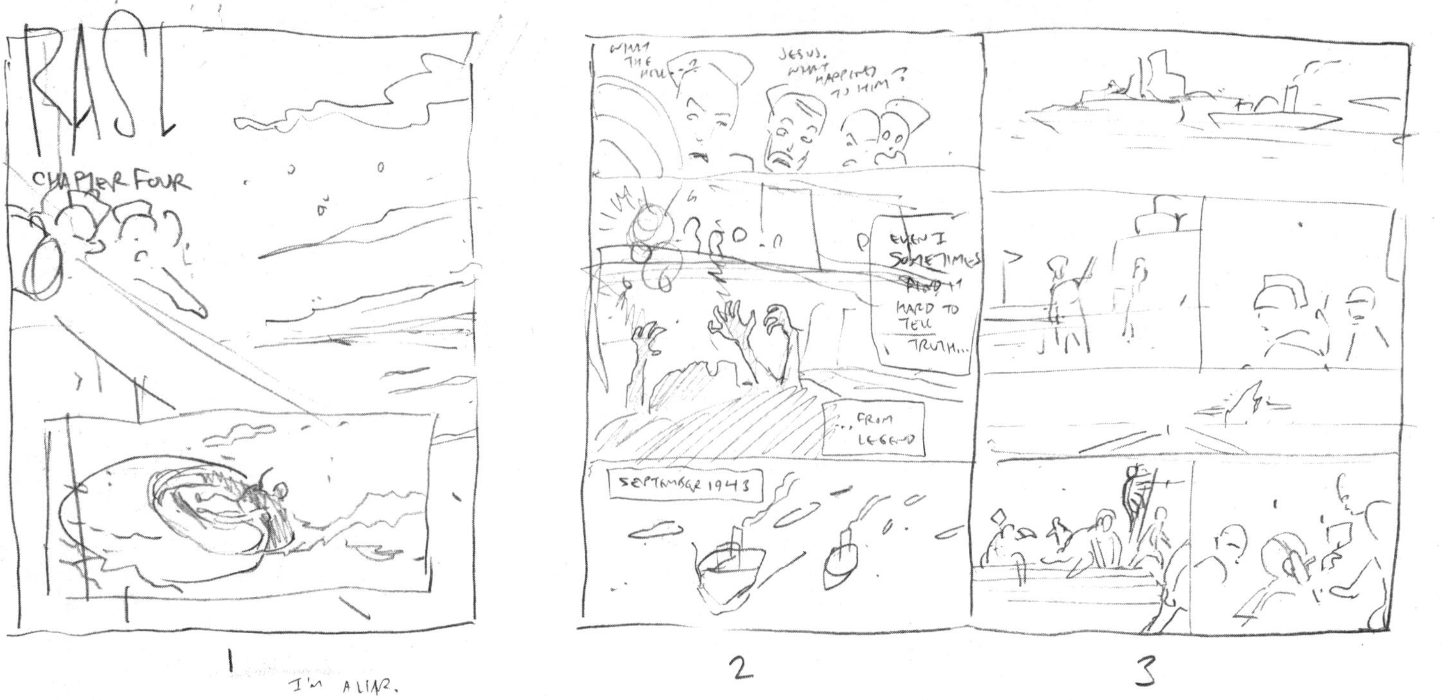
RASL
CHAPTER FOUR
WHAT THE HELL—?
JESUS, WHAT HAPPENED TO HIM?
EVEN I SOMETIMES FIND IT HARD TO TELL TRUTH...
...FROM LEGEND
SEPTEMBER 1943
1
2
3
THERE! GET THE LIGHT!
I'M A LIAR.
A LIAR IN A WORLD FILLED WITH LIARS.
MILITARY ESCORT PROVIDING PROTECTION FROM GERMAN SUBMARINES.
WHAT THE HELL'S
HE'S NOT MOVIN'!

**This page:** Shown at actual size, the script pages for the Philadelphia Experiment sequence from RASL #4.

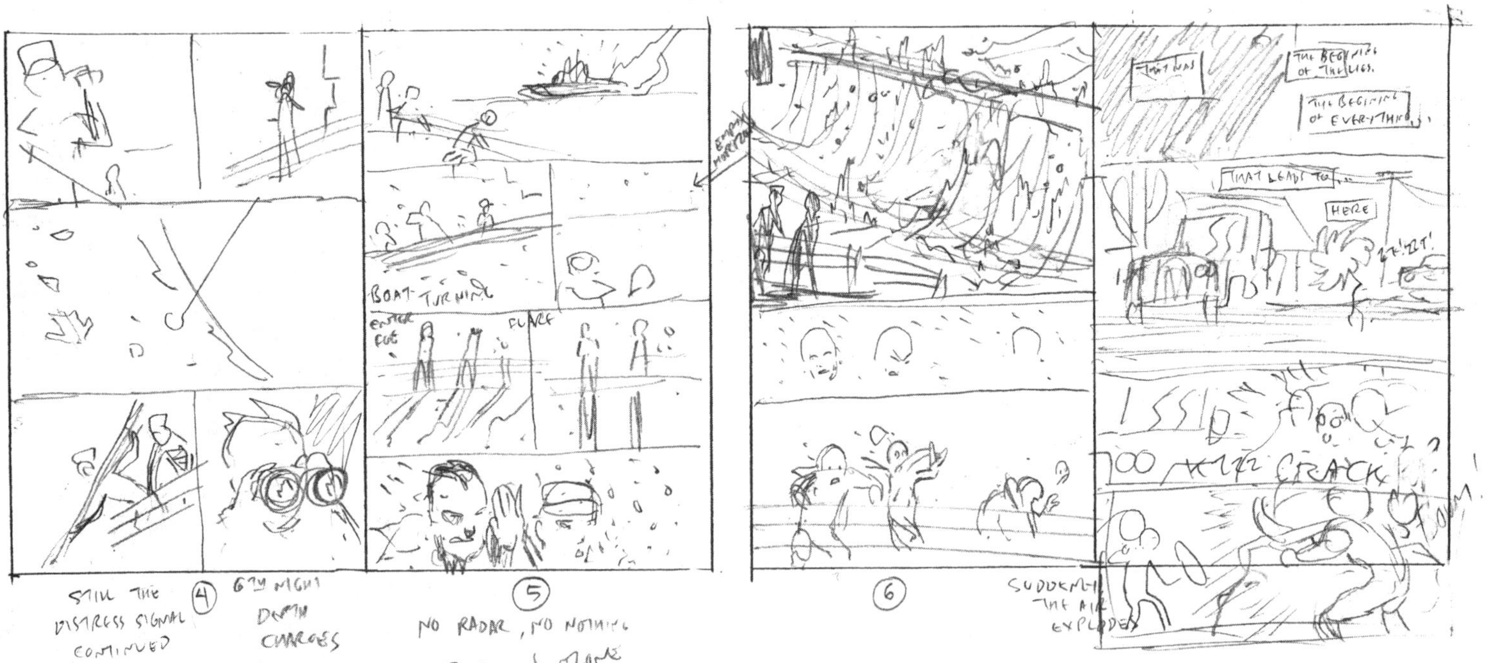
BOAT TURNING
ENTER FOG
FLARE
THAT WAS
THE BEGINNING OF THE LIES.
THE BEGINNING OF EVERYTHING.
THAT LEADS TO...
HERE
CRACK
4
5
6
STILL THE DISTRESS SIGNAL CONTINUED
6TH NIGHT DEPTH CHARGES
NO RADAR, NO NOTHING
SMELL OF OZONE
SUDDENLY THE AIR EXPLODES
FOR 6 DAYS THEY SEARCHED.
NO SHIPS. NO SUBS,
~~STILL THE DISTRESS~~

**Right:** I watched a lot of World War II movies to get the ships and uniforms right. Even the handheld spotlight is accurate.

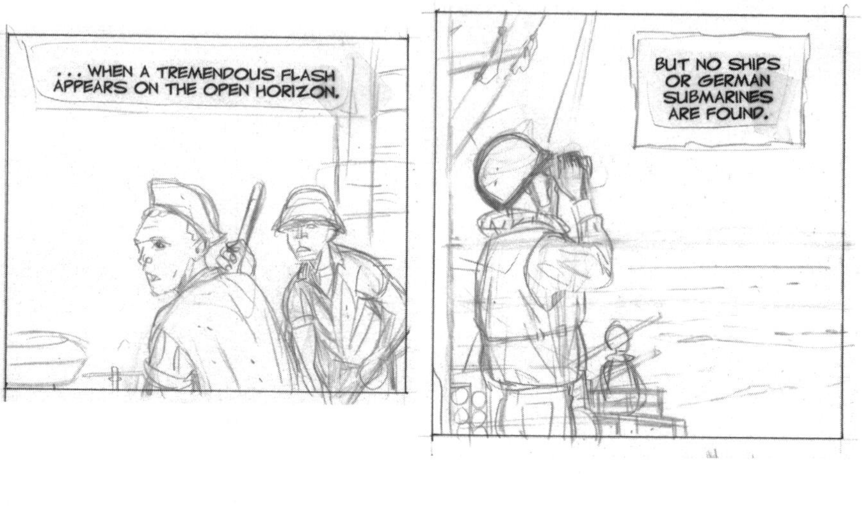
. . . WHEN A TREMENDOUS FLASH APPEARS ON THE OPEN HORIZON.
BUT NO SHIPS OR GERMAN SUBMARINES ARE FOUND.

RASL No. 4

**This page:** Pencils and inks from RASL #4. The real trick for this sequence, though, was finding a convincing way to depict the invisible ship. After reading several books on the topic, I was able to visualize a huge, displaced trench that would be spraying and boiling because of the high frequency electronic field.

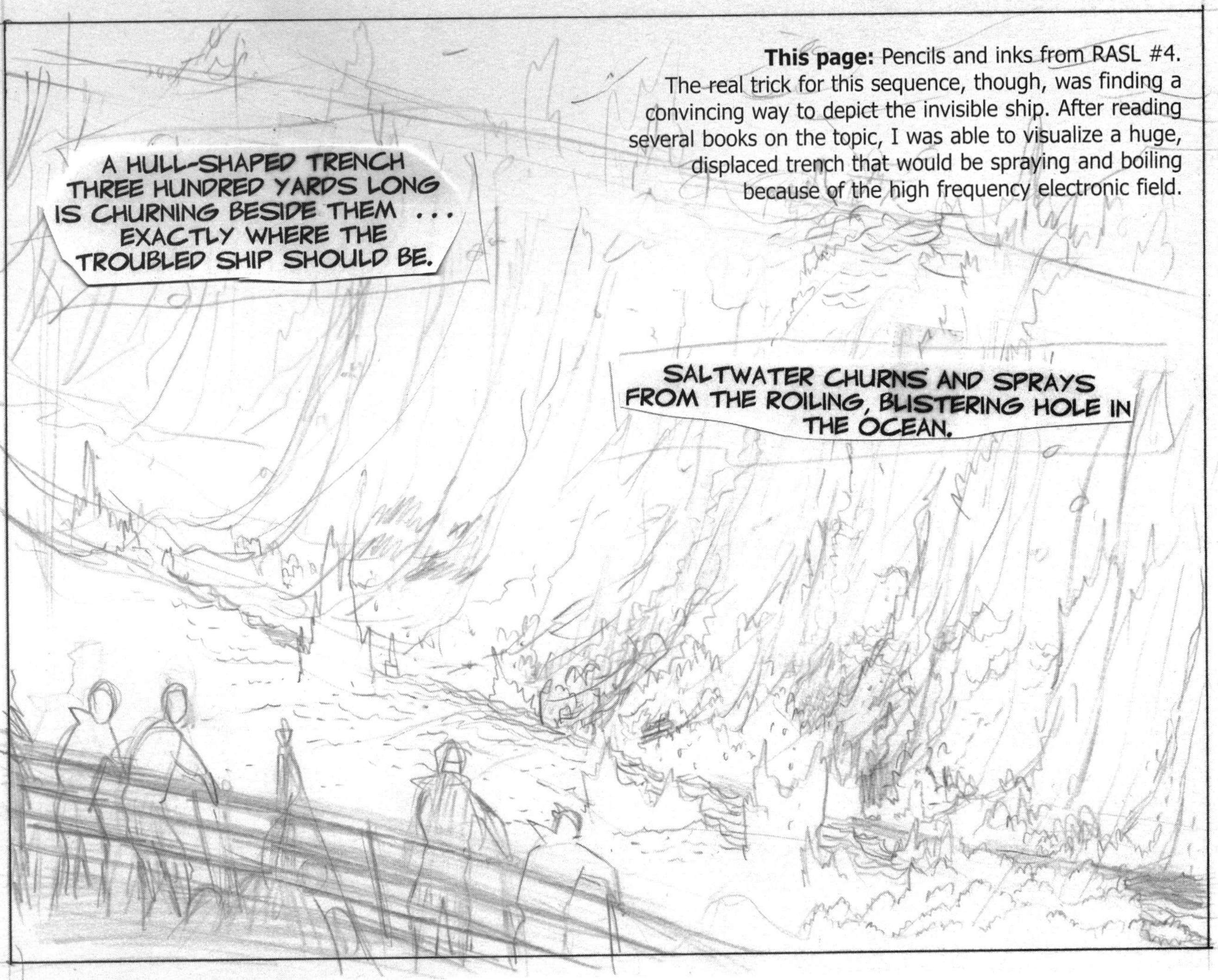
A HULL-SHAPED TRENCH THREE HUNDRED YARDS LONG IS CHURNING BESIDE THEM . . . EXACTLY WHERE THE TROUBLED SHIP SHOULD BE.
SALTWATER CHURNS AND SPRAYS FROM THE ROILING, BLISTERING HOLE IN THE OCEAN.

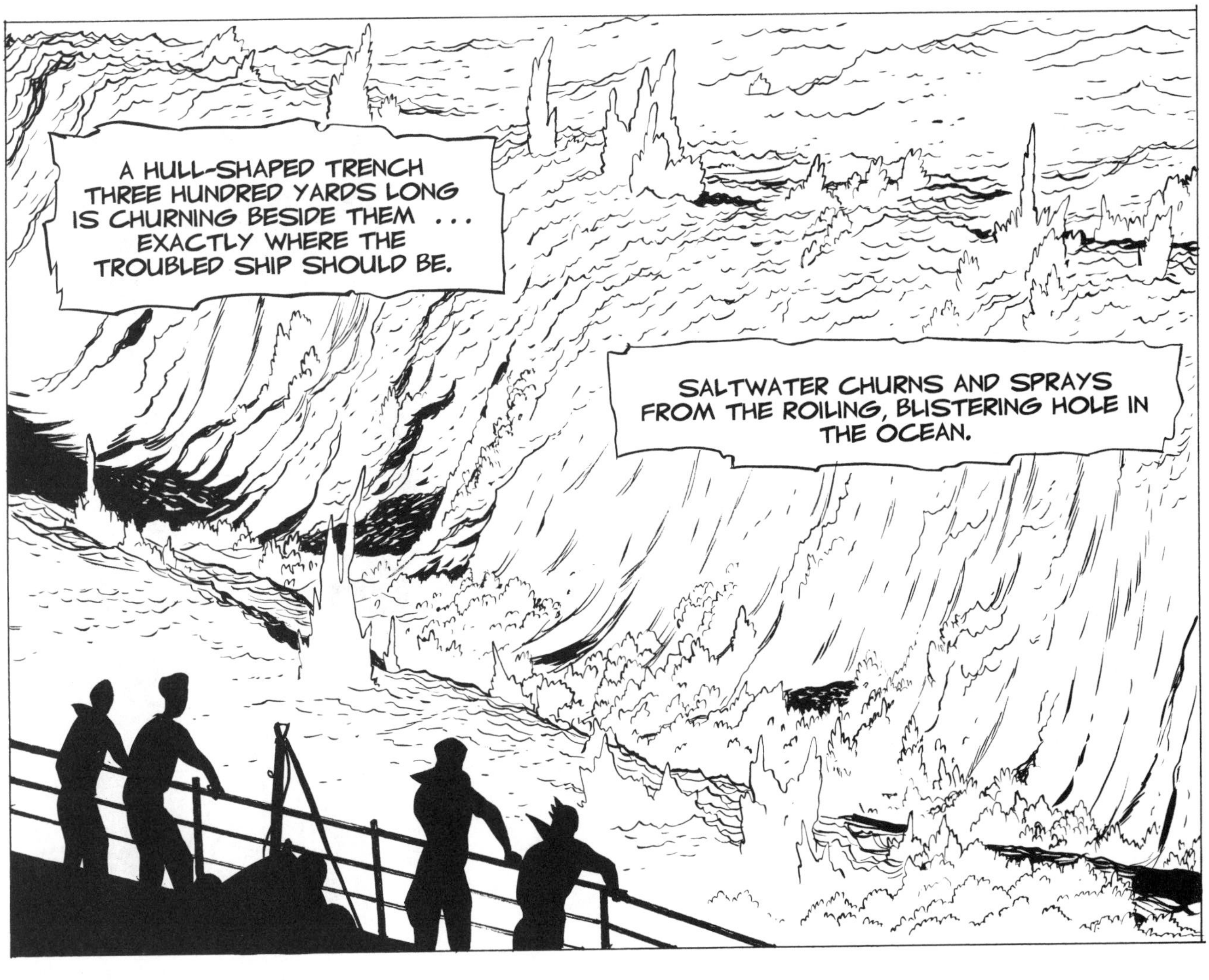
A HULL-SHAPED TRENCH THREE HUNDRED YARDS LONG IS CHURNING BESIDE THEM . . . EXACTLY WHERE THE TROUBLED SHIP SHOULD BE.
SALTWATER CHURNS AND SPRAYS FROM THE ROILING, BLISTERING HOLE IN THE OCEAN.

**Right and opposite:**
Script page & Penciled art for RASL #5, page 1. Like most male cartoonists, I love to draw sexy women, and RASL is full of them. Annie opens chapter 5.

**Below:**
Rob and Uma in an embrace for the cover of RASL #5.

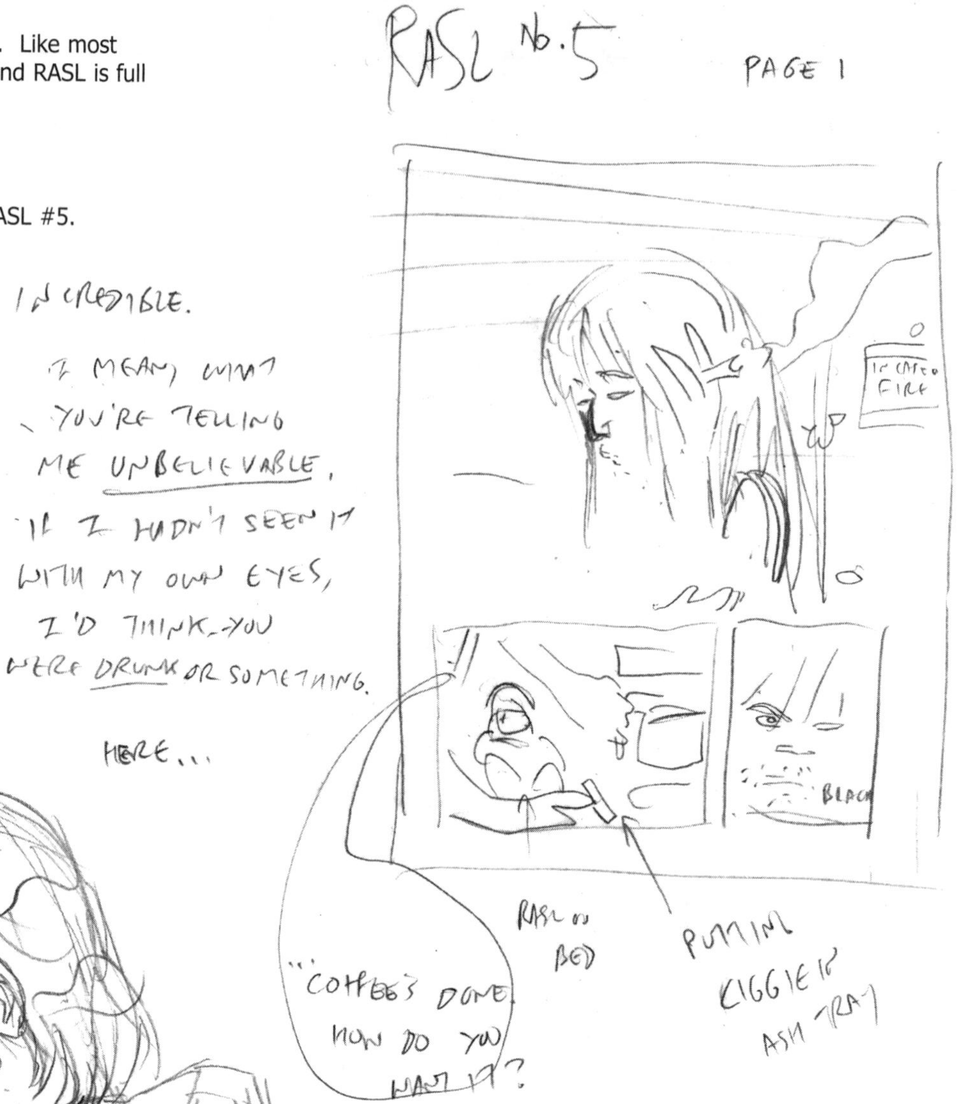
RASL No. 5
PAGE 1
INCREDIBLE.
I MEAN, WHAT YOU'RE TELLING ME UNBELIEVABLE.
IF I HADN'T SEEN IT WITH MY OWN EYES, I'D THINK YOU WERE DRUNK OR SOMETHING.
HERE...
"...COFFEE'S DONE. HOW DO YOU WANT IT?
RASL IN BED
PUTTING CIGGIE IN ASH TRAY
BLACK

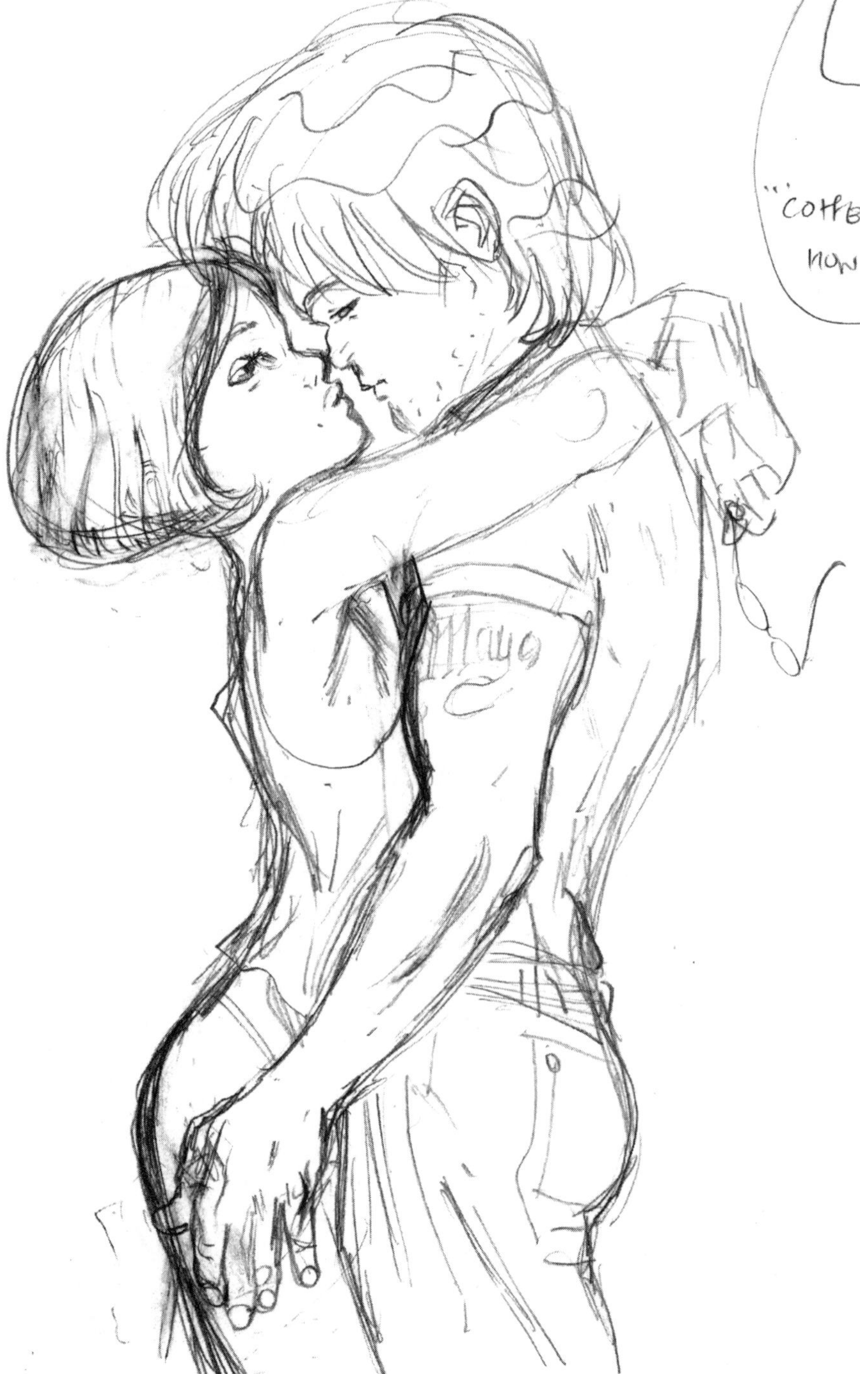

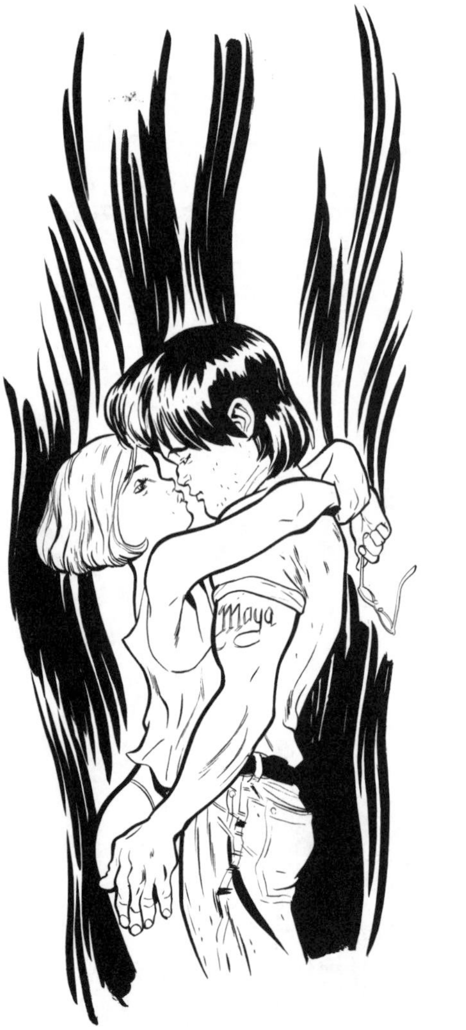

Inventor
Nikola Tesla

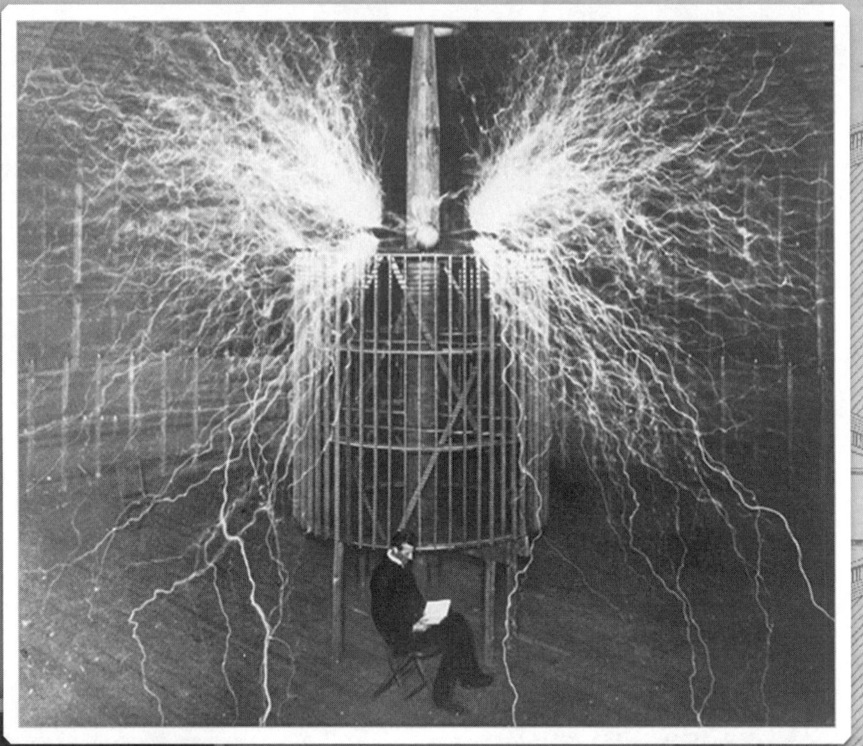

Fig. 2

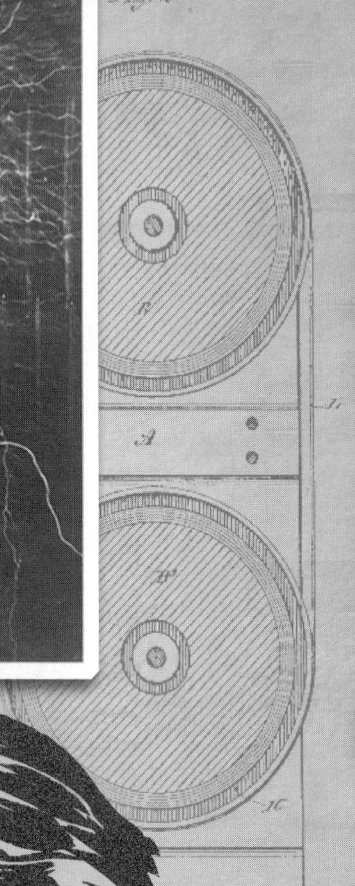

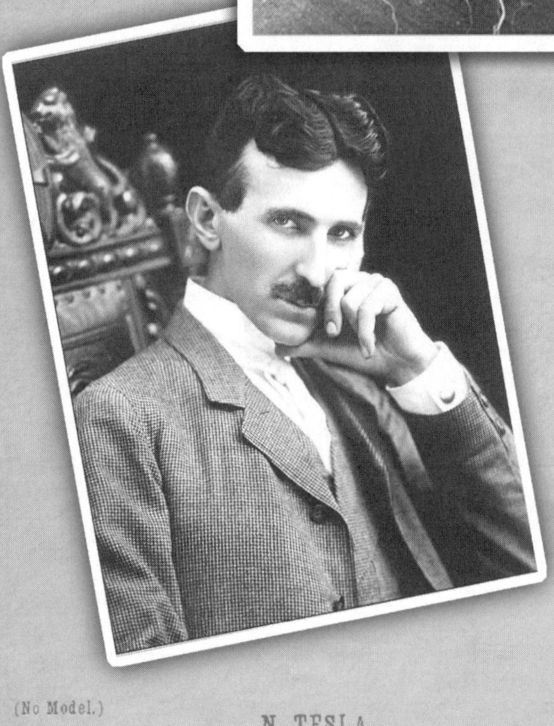

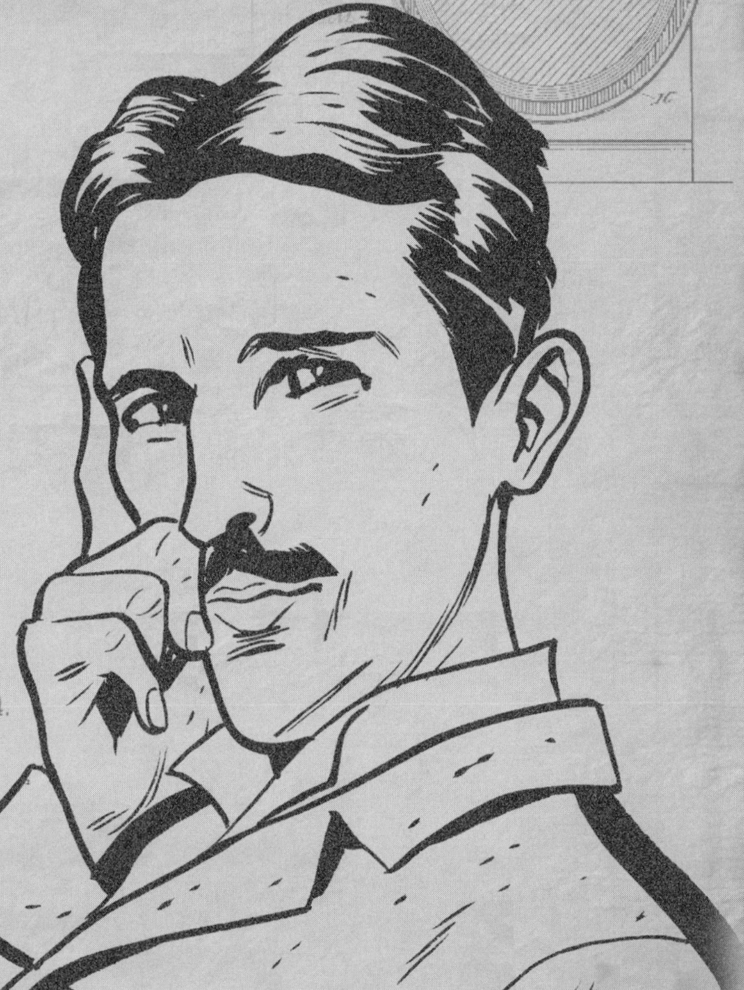

(No Model.)

N. TESLA.
COIL FOR ELECTRO MAGNETS.

No. 512,340. Patented Jan. 9, 1894.

Fig. 1

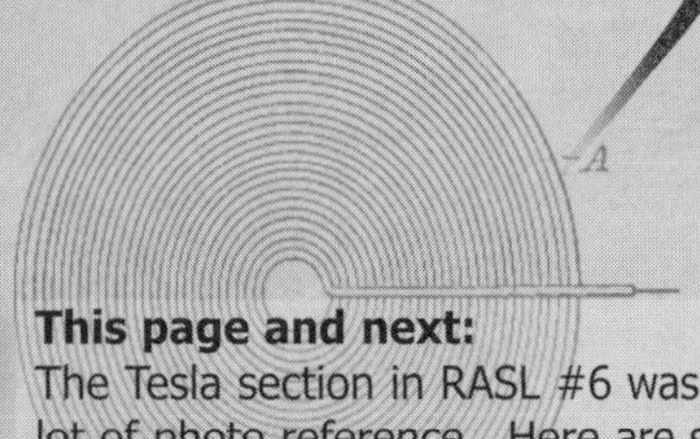

**This page and next:**
The Tesla section in RASL #6 was something different for me, and required a lot of photo reference. Here are some photos from the 1893 World's Fair, and Tesla in his Colorado Springs laboratory. The actual picture I used for the panel in the comic was too low-res to reprint, but the one at the top gives you the idea! Crazy, huh?

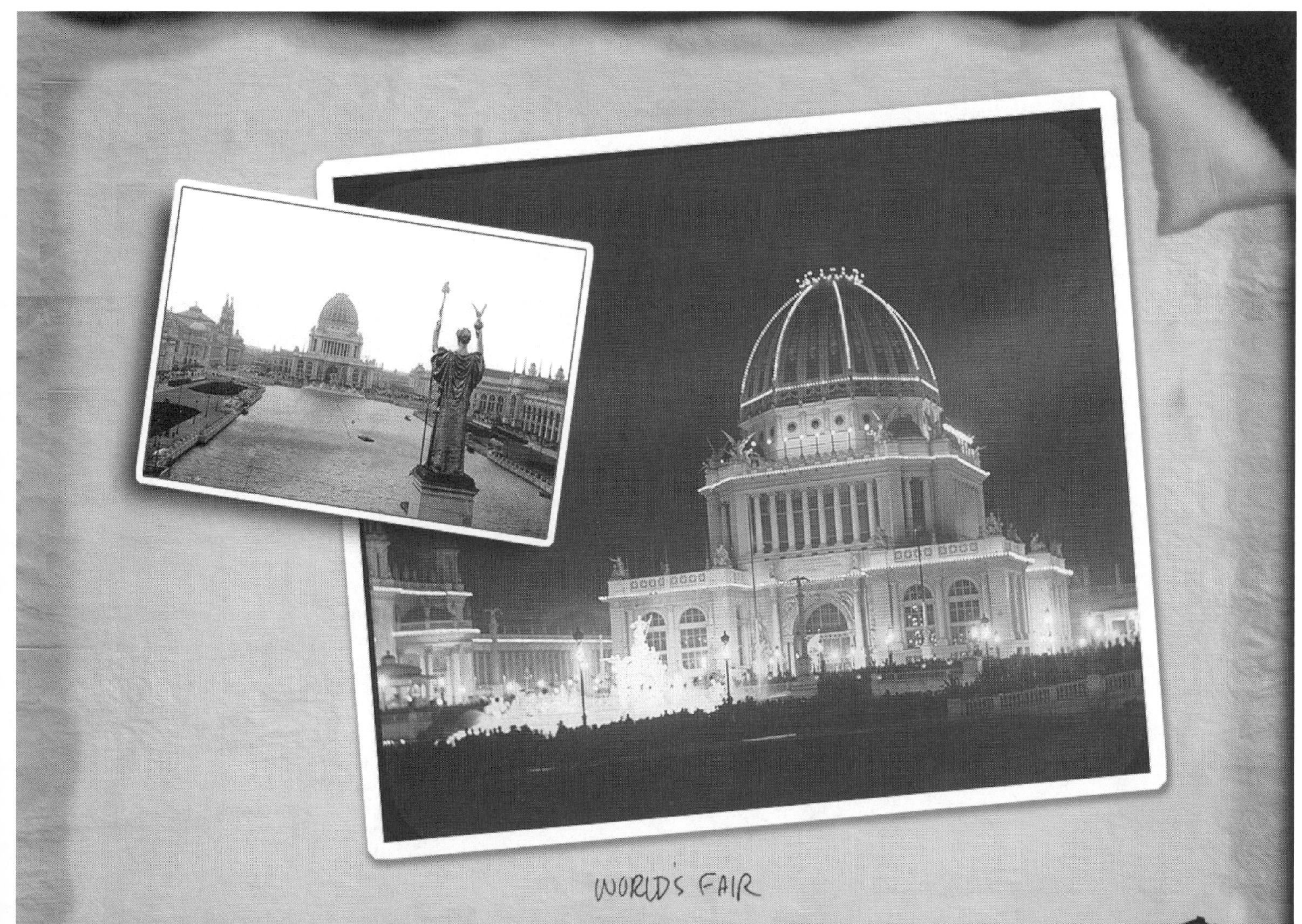

WORLD'S FAIR

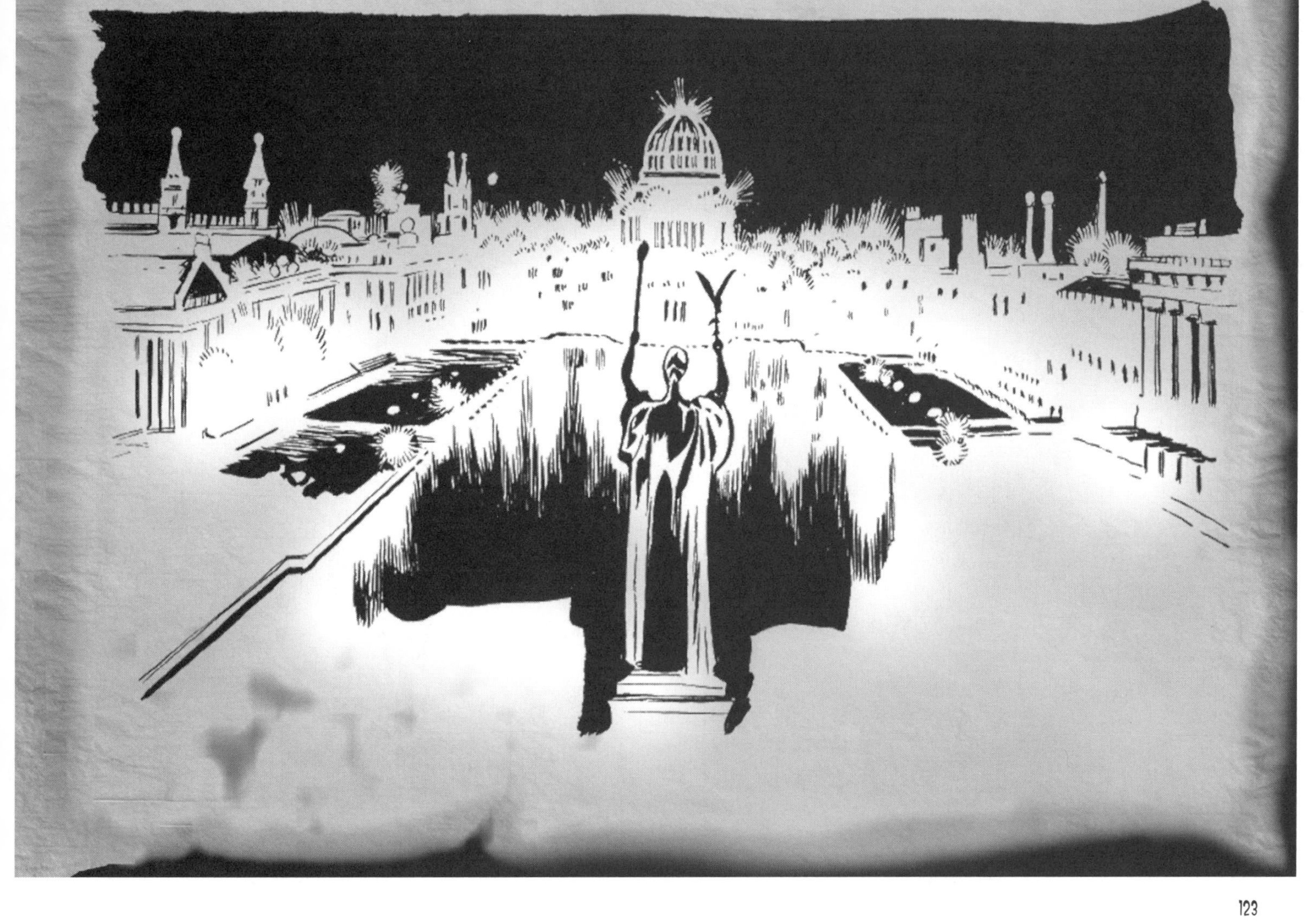

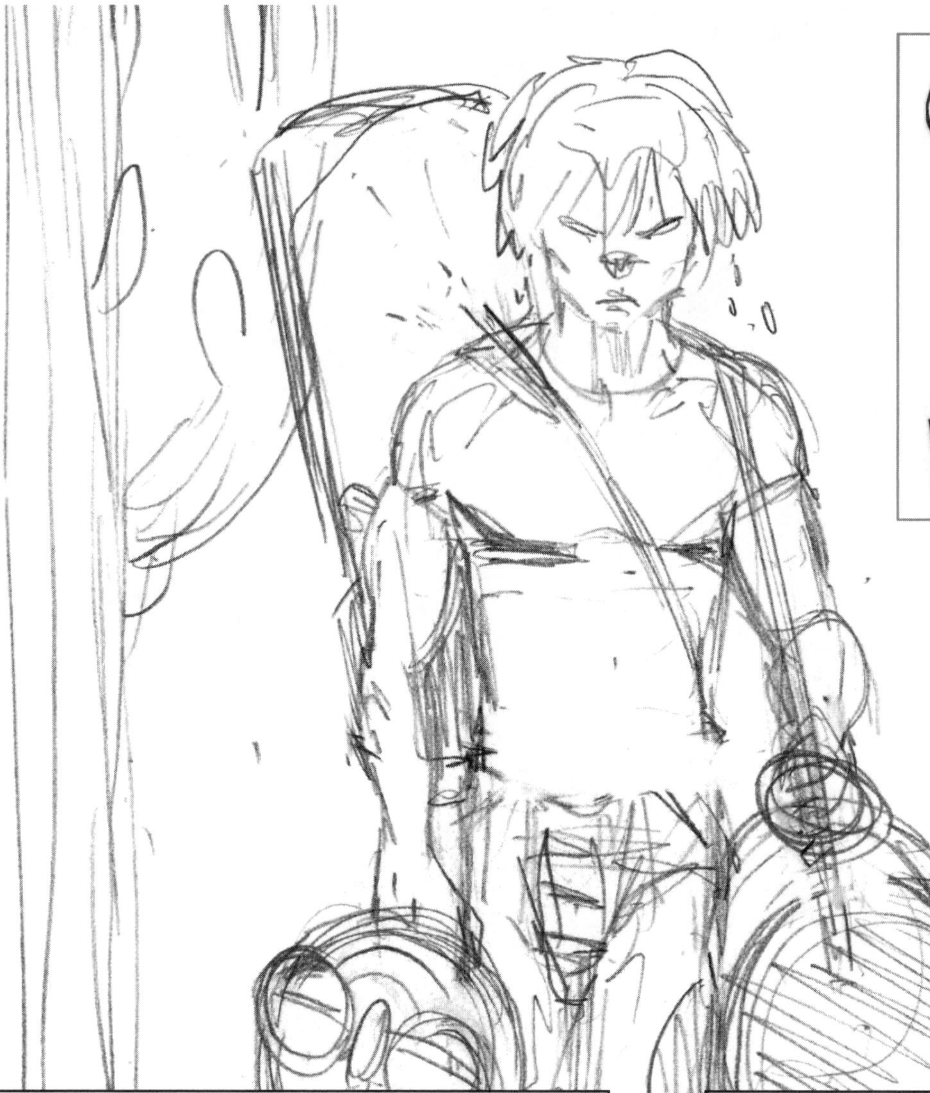

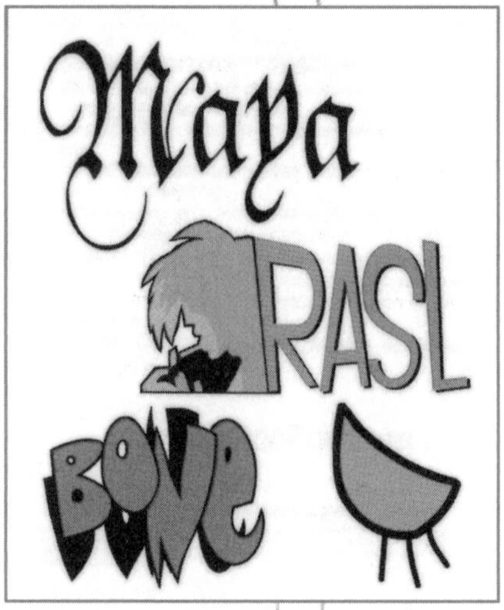

Maya
RASL
BONE

**Above:** A BONE and RASL temporary tattoo sheet that were used as give-aways for the 2009 season of comic book shows.

**This page:**
The pencils and final art for limited edition prints that Terry Moore and I made for Comic-Con International in San Diego 2009.

**Next page:**
Black and white version of Steve Hamaker's color modeling for the RASL Pocket Book One cover.

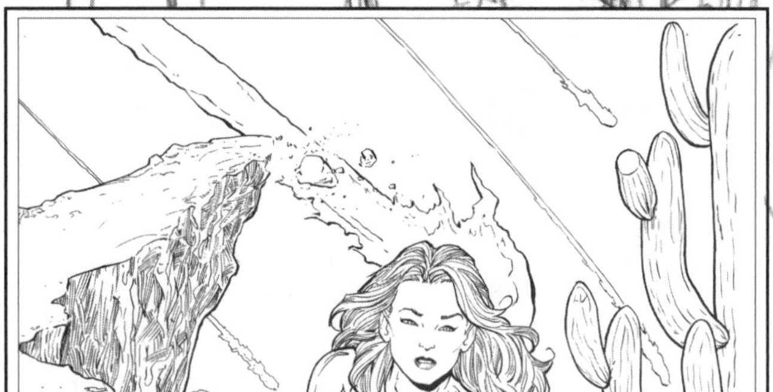

ECHO
BY TERRY MOORE
SAN DIEGO COMIC-CON 2009
/150


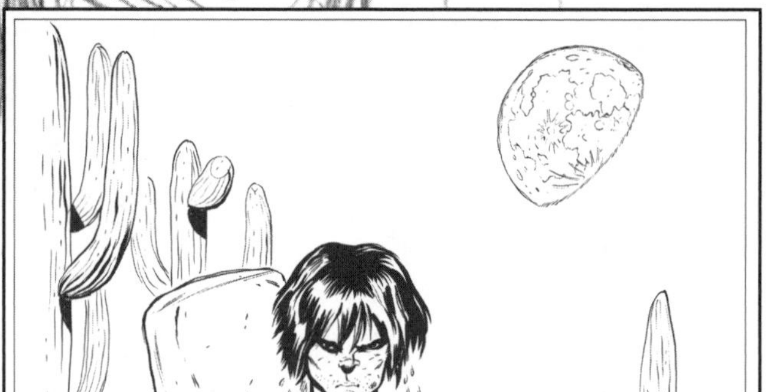

RASL
BY JEFF SMITH
SAN DIEGO COMIC-CON 2009
/150

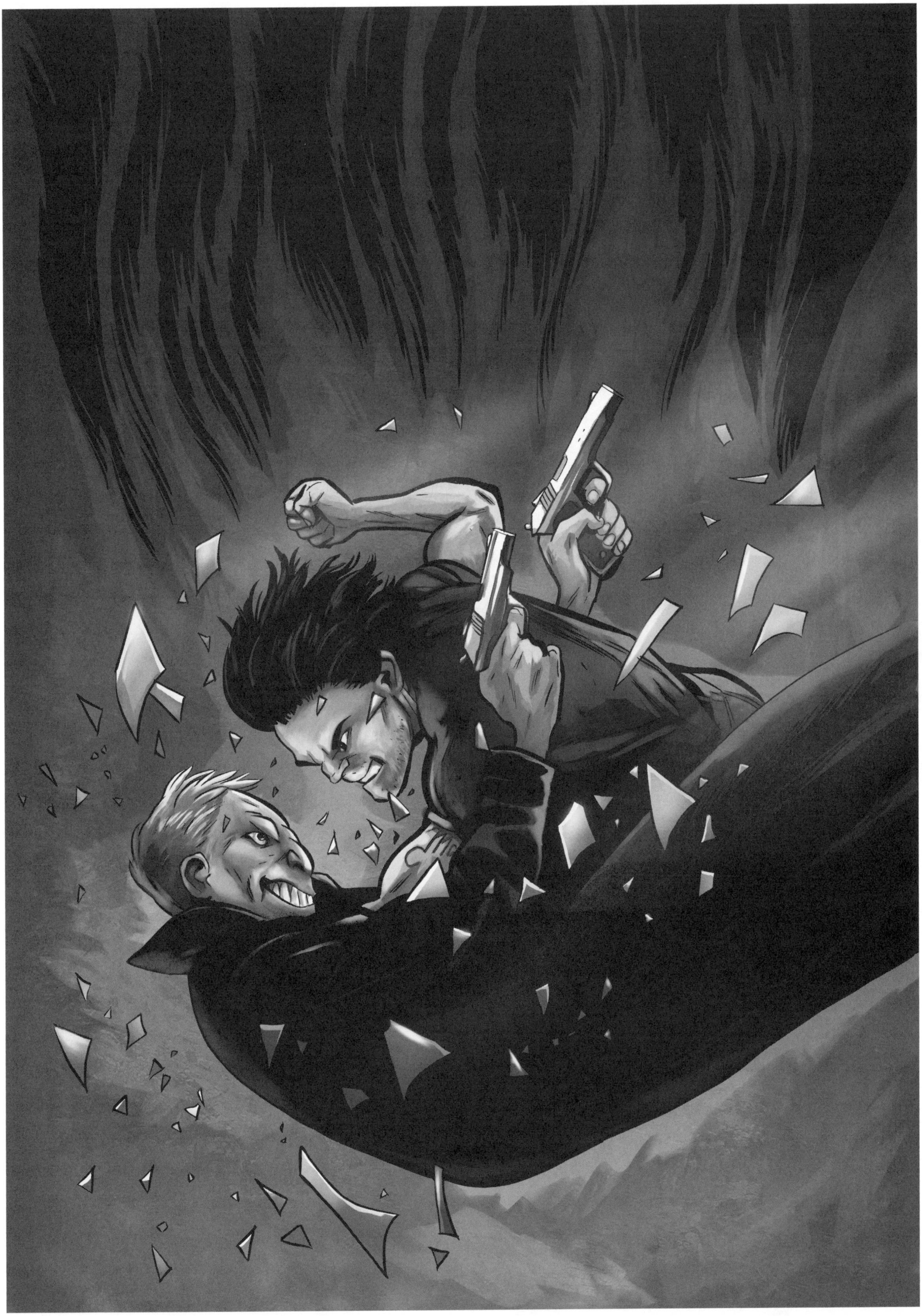

Special thanks to
Howard Fine, Jennifer Oliver,
Marty Fuller, Vijaya Iyer,
Kathleen Glosan, Steve Hamaker
and Tom Gaadt for sharing
their knowledge, advice
and patience.

A BRIEF BIBLIOGRAPHY

**Books:**

*Fabric of the Cosmos*
by Brian Greene
(Vintage)

*Parallel Worlds*
by Michio Kaku
(Anchor Books)

*Secrets of the Unified Field*
by Joseph P. Farrell
(Adventures Unlimited Press)

*Paths of Life*
edited by Sheridan & Parezo
(University of Arizona Press)

*The Philadelphia Experiment*
by Moore & Berlitz
(Fawcett)

**DVDs:**

*Tesla: Master of Lightning*
(PBS Home Videos)

*Nova: The Elegant Universe*
(WGBH Boston Video)

*Cosmos by Carl Sagan*
(Cosmos Studios)

*Holes in Heaven? H.A.A.R.P. and
Advances in Tesla Technology*
(NSI)

*Frankenstein*
directed by James Whale
(Universal Studio)

**Google:**

Key words: Tesla, H.A.A.R.P.,
Philadelphia Experiment, Tunguska.
Enter any combination of these words
and hold on to your hat!

## About the Author:

A co-founder of the 90's Self-Publishing Movement, and an early adopter of the graphic novel format, Jeff Smith is best known as the writer and artist of *BONE*, an award winning adventure about three cartoon cousins lost in a world of myth and ancient mysteries.  In 2009, Smith was the subject of a documentary called *The Cartoonist: Jeff Smith, BONE, and the Changing Face of Comics*.

Besides *BONE* and *RASL*, his other books include *Shazam: The Monster Society of Evil*, and *Little Mouse Gets Ready*!

boneville.com